MEIN

A Memoir

METH
A Memoir

By
Wayne Huffman

Former Meth Cook

Published by

MIDNIGHT EXPRESS BOOKS

METH
A Memoir

Cover art by: Cory & Crystal

Published by
MIDNIGHT EXPRESS BOOKS
POBox 69
Berryville AR 72616
(870) 210-3772
MEBooks1@yahoo.com

METH
A Memoir

By
Wayne Huffman

Former Meth Cook

Chapter 1

In the beginning, God created the heavens and the earth. Now, the earth was formless, and empty, darkness was over the surface of the deep, and the Spirit of God was hovering over the waters. And God said, "Let there be light." and there was light. God saw that the light was good, and he separated the light from the darkness.

Many thousands of years later, in the kitchen of my home, I created meth for my first time, and it too was pretty damn good. My coffee filter was full of dope and anhydrous hydrogen chloride gas hovered in the air. The Spirit of Akira Ogata was near. (Akira Ogata first created the crystal form of meth we know today as "ice".)

There is a reason I seem to put the creation of meth on a level with the creation of earth. The reason being, every meth cook I know, myself included, has at one time or another, either considered himself to "be" God, or, at the very least, had aspirations of becoming God.

When you are a meth cook, you are basically worshipped by those in the meth world who are not cooks. You are definitely put on a higher level, no pun intended, and treated as if you were a greater being. As a meth cook, your word is law in that world. I can, and have, taken over people's homes for my own use. I've dictated who could, and could not, enter those homes, and when.

People have committed criminal acts for me, both at my direction, and under their own initiative, because they felt their actions would please me enough to reward them. Their reward would not be in the form of loaves and fishes mind you, but in the form of a few grains of their personal God's creation. Meth. In my world, everything is done in the name of creating meth. The games we play and the battles we fight amongst ourselves are all for one goal that everyone shares. Creating more meth.

Meth addiction is more than just a simple drug addiction. Meth addiction is a lifestyle. A lifestyle where people have, and work towards, personal goals. Just like anyone who is climbing the corporate ladder, there is a system each person must go through in order to be accepted into the meth world. Without that acceptance, there can be no success. In many cases, such as mine, the meth lifestyle is a chosen lifestyle. This is a fact I don't expect you, the reader, to fully understand at this moment. I only ask you to keep this in mind as you continue to read this story, because this knowledge may make some of the unusual events you will soon be learning about easier to comprehend.

It is well known that meth addicts commonly engage in conduct that, to those on the outside looking in, may seem to defy logic, or in some cases, sanity. To those who are on the inside however, irrational behavior is often considered to be perfectly normal. It is the normal that we find suspicious. As a meth addict and cook, I know there are many aspects of our world that can only be understood by experiencing it firsthand.

While at times it will not seem so, it is not my intention to glamorize my past crimes, or life as a meth cook in general. My goal with this book is to guide you through the realm and inner circles of the meth world. This book is meant to be an autobiographical account of my connection, throughout my life, to the drug world, my drug use history which led to my life inside the world of meth, and my rise to the top of that world, as a cook.

I will take you inside my meth labs. You will learn, more than you ever could have imagined, about what is going on inside those barns, garages, motel rooms, and meth houses. You will learn what a "mobile meth lab" really is and how dangerous the occasional late night traveling vehicle really can be. Look inside a world where we use and trade our women, not as bargaining chips, but as pawns in a twisted game of humiliation. A world where friends poison friends and pregnant women are given massive doses of meth to try to induce miscarriages.

When talking about the world of meth, fact really is stranger than fiction. As bad as the actual truth is, the public has still been presented with an image of meth that isn't entirely accurate. Would it surprise you to learn that meth labs rarely blow up, despite what law enforcement and the news media would have you believe? This is true and I will explain this, and more, as you read.

While my story is being told in the raw, simplistic way of an insider, I do not want to give the impression that I am downplaying the dangers of using and/or manufacturing meth. I no longer promote the use of meth. and I will not defend meth use because, meth destroys. If, during your reading, it seems as if I am glorifying the meth lifestyle, keep in mind that

I am only telling the story as I lived it, and at the time, I loved the life I was living.

One of the things I hope to be able to do is dispel some of the myths about meth. I believe ignorance can be as dangerous as any meth lab has ever been. If a person reacts the wrong way in a dangerous situation, they can put themselves, and others, in even more peril than necessary. Just as likely, reacting incorrectly in a non-dangerous situation can end up creating needless hazards.

This book is not a "how to" book. While there are a few books out there that will teach you how to become a meth cook, this is not intended to be one of them. This is not a history book, and it will not be tracing the history of meth since its invention in Japan, in the late 1800's. It will not follow the path taken in order for meth to make its way to America. In fact, I will only refer to the history of meth as it is relevant to my story.

This book does not contain statistics or scientific data. There are studies out there that document and analyze, not only the effects of meth on individual users, but on entire communities as well. While all of that information is both important, and relevant, this book will not address those issues either.

Like it or not, virtually everyone in America is affected by meth in one way or another. It is because of meth that there are limits on the amount of cold medicine you are legally permitted to purchase and possess. That law, since its creation, has done little to slow meth production, especially when the law hasn't been enforced equally in all areas of the United States, and only serves to inconvenience those people needing the medicines for legitimate reasons.

As a meth cook, I preyed upon the misfortunes, wants, needs, and ignorance of people to help keep myself supplied with everything I needed to stay in business. Homes, guns, cash, and more were put at my disposal when I needed them. Some people wanted my money, while others wanted my drugs. Several people wanted my knowledge, and a few even wanted me dead.

Today, I am not proud of a lot of the things I have done, both while I was involved with meth, and before. By the end of this book, I hope to not only answer some of the questions most people didn't even know they had about meth, but to also be able to answer a question I seem to be asked a lot these days. "Do I regret ever being involved with meth?"

Let's find out...

Chapter 2

Drugs have never seemed unusual to me. I guess this is because, for as long as I can remember, I have always been exposed to drugs and drug use in some form.

I can remember, as a child, watching friends of my mother's using a driver's license and an old record album cover to separate the seeds from their marijuana. At the time I thought this to be a real cool trick, and I would use it myself many years later.

My earliest memory of actually seeing someone use drugs was when I was about seven years old. I walked into the living room of our house to find my mother and some other woman, a friend I'll assume, sitting on the couch sharing a cigarette.

Back then, I knew what cigarettes were and I knew my mother smoked. What I thought was weird about this scene was that I had never known my mother to share any single cigarette like she was doing.

I also remember that this cigarette did not smell like mom's usual brand and it was odd that they were holding the cigarette with their fingertips. Mom had always held hers between her fingers before.

While I do not remember exactly what it was that I asked about the situation, I do remember what I was told. The friend explained to me that they had acquired a bag of weeds from California. These weeds, she said, were growing out of control and had to be killed before they had the chance to spread all across the country. The only way to kill these troublesome weeds? Smoking them.

Maybe I had a contact high, or maybe I was just a stupid kid, but I believed every word of that explanation. After all, who would make a story that fantastic up? Oh yeah! A pothead!

Growing up with my younger brother and sister, we traveled a lot. Our mother and father were divorced, and mom had custody of us. It seemed like we were forever on the move.

When we started the school year somewhere, it was a pretty safe bet we would not be finishing it at the same institution. Where, or with whom, we would be living, was always in question. And dinner? That was anybody's guess.

We grew up poor to say the least. Things came hard for us and we learned fast not to expect anything from anyone, at least, not without a price.

I guess mom was restless and impulsive, and that must be where I got it from, because I am the same way. Sure, mom could have thought things through a little better. Planned a little more. But, if she had, my life would probably not have been as interesting as it had been.

Mom kept it together for the most part. If we were really stuck for food and a place to stay, she would go to the hospital and fake a nervous breakdown. Then, us kids could stay in the waiting room and the nurses would feed us, while mom "got better". Usually mom would "get better" after social services got us an apartment in the projects somewhere, and some emergency food stamps.

Mom had other ways of making sure we had a place to stay. Sometimes, she would leave us with a "friend" while she went MIA for a few days. When she showed back up, we always had a place to go.

One particular incident stands out in my mind. Mom had left us kids with someone we didn't know, and hauled ass. After about a week, the woman we were staying with loaded us up into her car, and went looking for our mother.

We arrived at a trailer and the woman knocked on the door. When mom came to the door, the woman pointed back at the car and said, "Did you forget something?"

The guy mom was staying with had no idea she had three kids stashed someplace. Once we arrived, he welcomed us in, and he was a really nice guy. Of course, it wasn't long before mom decided that there were greener pastures elsewhere, and off we went.

Several years later, mom would reunite with this guy, Elwood. and today, they have been married to each other for over twenty years. I guess mom either found whatever it was she was looking for all of those years, or she got tired of looking. Either way, I hope they have many more happy years together.

During some of our travels, we found ourselves living in Gray Mountain, Arizona. I was eleven years old at the time.

Gray Mountain was a very small town located about fifty miles from Flagstaff. The town basically consisted of two motels, a convenience store, a trailer park, a Dairy Queen, and several small houses. There was also a trading post, which was kind of western store, with a restaurant and a liquor store in it. Everything in town belong to one guy. It was his town.

We lived at the trailer park in an old school bus mom had bought somewhere. The bus had been converted into an RV of sorts by removing the seats and putting in a couple of small beds, and a dresser. There was also a small propane heater for wintertime.

The bus had no electricity, so we used kerosene lamps at night for light. Water came from jugs we filled from a hose in the back of the convenience store. Laundry was washed in five gallon buckets, and "baths" consisted of pouring a jug of water over your head, soaping up, and then another jug to rinse.

Bathing was done at the front of the bus. You had to stand on the steps so the water would run down them, and out the door, instead of running back into the living area.

We also had a portable toilet at the front of the bus. As the oldest of the siblings, it was my job to drag the toilet out into the desert and dig a hole to dump the waste into. I had to do this every couple of days, and I would usually wait until late at night before doing it, to avoid being seen by anyone.

There was a school bus that would shuttle the town kids to and from school in Flagstaff. The school bus driver lived directly behind us in the trailer park. She would always park the school bus along the side of our bus. I can only assume she did this to block the view out of her front window. I couldn't blame her.

Living beside a school bus, in a school bus, was always an issue for me. It was embarrassing enough to be the poor kid in town. Being asked, "Hey, why don't you just drive your house to school?" made it even worse. God how I hated every one of those little bastards.

I did have one friend in Gray Mountain. A Navajo Indian kid. His name was Benson and he, along with his younger brother and sister, lived in a tiny one room house with his grandmother.

When we were not in school, Benson and I would spend our days roaming throughout the desert catching lizards and scorpions. If one of us came across a little money, we would buy some pellets and BBs for the old Crossman pellet rifle I had. Then we would spend our time roaming through the desert, shooting lizards and scorpions.

It was with Benson that I would get high for the first time. I don't remember where we learned it, but we started "huffing" gasoline, and Coleman camp fuel. Huffing was done by pouring a small amount of gas or camp fuel into a soda bottle. Then, you'd inhale the fumes through your mouth. This would give you a little bit of a buzz that lasted several seconds. Huffing several times in a row would give you crazy visual and auditory hallucinations.

It wasn't long before everyone in town knew Benson and I were getting high off gas. Anytime somebody saw us we would be carrying empty soda bottles wrapped up in old rags.

If we couldn't find any gas or camp fuel we could steal, we would run over to the convenience store and get a few drops out of the gas pump hose before the clerk would run out and chase us off.

The only place safe from our thievery was my bus. I wasn't taking a single drop out of that tank, in case mom had ever planned to fire that big white beast up, (thankfully, our bus was painted white, and not yellow. Thank God for small miracles..) and get us the hell out of town.

Late one night, the trading post caught fire and burned to the ground. I didn't know what started the blaze, but I'll be willing to bet you know who got blamed for it. Benson nor I were even anywhere near the place when it happened. Well, Benson's grandmother's house was right behind the trading post, so I guess you could say he was near it... nevertheless I was in bed, asleep. Although the two of us were suspected, nothing was ever proven, so it was left alone.

After the fire, mom was without a job. That meant there was no money for rent, kerosene for the lamps, or food for any of us.

One day, just for fun, Benson and I talked my younger brother, who was about six at the time, into stealing us a beer from the convenience store. He got away with it, so we sent him back in a couple more times to steal other things. On his last trip in, he tried to steal us some hamburgers, but he got caught.

With me already being under suspicion for burning down the trading post, and now Kevin getting caught shoplifting, we were basically kicked out of town. We packed a few belongings and, abandoning our bus, caught a Greyhound to Mississippi, our mother's home state.

Chapter 3

By the time I was thirteen, we were living in Starkville, Mississippi. Mom had hooked up with some dude from there through a singles ad she placed in the newspaper, or a magazine, and he moved us there. I'll call the dude "Junior" because I think that really was his name.

Junior was pretty cool. He taught me to drive his Chevy pick-up truck with 3-speed on the column. He also made sure I had cigarette money every day. Mom didn't want him supporting my smoking habit of almost a whole pack a day, but where else was I going to get money?

We lived in a nice trailer park called, "The Pines." This place even had a community swimming pool. It was great, and I stayed in the pool as much as I could.

A few trailers up from ours was a guy who had a beautiful 1965 Mustang Fastback. It was drop-dead gorgeous, red, and according to the owner, completely original.

Early one morning, as I walked past the old Mustang on my way to catch the bus to school, I noticed something on the roof of the car. I stepped up closer to see what it was, and to my surprise, it was a wallet! The car was wet with morning dew, and the wallet was as well, thus indicating to me that it had been there all night.

Naturally, I grabbed the wallet and ran like hell. When I got to school, I went straight into the bathroom to see if there was any cash in it. I was not disappointed. In fact, there was about three hundred bucks in it. I pocketed the money and dropped the wallet in a trash can on my way out of the bathroom. I. Was. Rich.

On the bus ride home, I was sitting with this black kid I knew who lived in the apartment complex that was behind the trailer park. I showed him the cash, and lied, saying I had earned it from a part time job.

This kid's dad sold weed, and the kid asked me if I wanted to buy some joints. He said he could steal some from his dad and, thinking this would be a fantastic financial investment for a thirteen year old, I agreed.

I ended up giving him forty dollars for fifty joints. I sold most of the joints at two bucks a piece, and made a decent little profit. Naturally, I also ended up smoking several of them as well.

I never reinvested in more weed because I ended up spending all of the money while I was high. That was the point where I became an almost full time casual drug user.

I liked getting high. I didn't care if it was weed, alcohol, or whatever. I just genuinely enjoyed being high. It wasn't at all because it "made me forget about my hard life," or any of that other bullshit that people use as an excuse. I just liked the feeling.

Speed eventually would become my drug of choice. Back then it was pink hearts, .357's, and white crosses. Things of that nature. I had heard of the harder stuff; coke, crank, crystal, but I hadn't tried any of it.

Another person I knew who lived in the apartments behind the trailer park was named Sharon. Sharon was a friend of Junior's, or a friend of one of Junior's friends, or something like that. In all honesty I don't recall exactly how I met Sharon, but I spent a lot of nights at her house.

Sharon had several children. Some were hers, and some were adopted. She liked having me around and I liked being there. I think part of the reason I liked being there was because the two oldest girls would supply me with beer.

One day, Sharon announced that she would soon be moving to New Mexico, where she was from. I was pretty upset about it and she knew it. Before she left, Sharon offered to take me in as a foster child, and let me move to New Mexico with them. She knew quite a lot about my unstable life.

Unfortunately, mom wouldn't let me go, so I was forced to say good bye to her, and my friends. Before they left, Sharon gave me a picture of her and the other kids in front of their home in New Mexico. The home she was returning to. It was a large house with a beautiful mountain behind it. I think I could have been happy there.

When I was fourteen, I came home from school one day to find out that we were moving to Arkansas. This really sucked because I had made several friends where we were currently at. I liked my school, and where we lived, and pretty much everything else. Hell, I was more than even content, I was happy.

Unfortunately, we had to pack and move. Mom wasn't leaving Junior, all of us moved. We ended up living with some people Junior knew in Wynne, Arkansas.

I don't remember how long it took, but soon after the move, I pretty much lost my mind. I was tired of always being uprooted, always moving, and never having a steady home. I was tired of making friends and leaving them all behind. I was tired of never feeling any sense of security. I was tired of worrying, "Will we have somewhere to go when we leave here? Will we get anything to eat today?".

As adults, we don't always realize that children have worries and they know when their parents are having hard times. The way I grew up, I had shit to worry about that most people couldn't even imagine.

I remember a time as a kid when someone "borrowed" me to run a scam. The guy who borrowed me had a broken fan belt from a car. We would walk around grocery store parking lots asking for money to "buy a new fan belt" so we could fix the car and get home. My job was to wait for the sucker(s) that fell for this to start handing over loose change, then I'd say "Daddy, I'm so hungry..." This was followed by a stern, "I don't have any money for food right now.." by the guy. The result? A few extra dollars for hamburgers.

My worry during this scam wasn't that someone would figure out that this was actually a scam. Though that did happen once when we ran into the same guy at a second store. My worry was that someone would want proof that this dude was really my dad. I've got no idea why I was worried about this, but I was. Chalk it up to being a kid I guess.

Picture this and tell me that it's normal for most kids, if you dare. One way mom would feed us from time to time would be to beg from restaurants. She would march into McDonalds and ask to see the manager. When the manager came out, she'd explain that we were hungry and she had no money for food. Granted, it worked. We got fed, but this is still one of the most humiliating things I can think of to do to a child. My biggest worry during this scam? That the manager would think I'm too old to eat for free, so I really would go hungry. Though now, I don't think I was. I was about nine at the time.

So anyway, when I say I was tired of worrying, I mean it. All I could think of during this time was how I could have gone to New Mexico and have been happy. Well, since Mom wouldn't let me go, there was only one thing I could do. Go anyway.

I threw a couple of changes of clothes in a bag and headed towards the interstate. I knew Sharon was in Alameda, New Mexico, and so that's where I headed. Fairly sound reasoning for a fourteen year old, right? I walked to a rest area so I could look at a map to figure out my route. With all the traveling I had done in my life, I could read a map very well. Once I had my trip planned out, I started hitching. This was back in the early 80's, when it was still safe to do this sort of thing. I also knew to ask truckers at rest areas and truck stops for rides because they'll get on the CB radio to get you a connecting ride from where they'd drop you off.

I made really good time getting to Alameda. Once I was there, it was just a matter of finding Sharon's house. It was at this point in my plans that I ran into two very important problems. The first being, I didn't know Sharon's actual address. I could have looked it up in a phone book, except for the second problem. I didn't know her last name either.

Okay, no big deal, right? I still had the picture of Sharon's house. It was in front of a mountain. Except that there are mountains everywhere in Alameda. It was then that I accepted the fact that my plan had fallen completely apart, and I was seriously screwed.

Suddenly, I found myself standing on a sidewalk with no place to go, and no money to get there. I must have even had the look of 'screwed' tattooed on my face, because it was at this moment, that something strange happened to save my ass.

I was walking down a sidewalk, thinking that I should start hitching back to Arkansas. (What other choice did I have?) This is when I heard someone ask me, "Are you lost?"

I turned to see a mini-van driven by a young woman in what appeared to be her mid-twenties had stopped in the street. I just stared at her for a few seconds, dumbfounded, then said "Yes." I figured, Fuck it; what did I have to lose?

I don't remember the girl's name, but she told me to get in the van. I got in. As we rode to her house, she asked where it was I was trying to get to, and I told her the same story I just told you.

Once I finished telling her just exactly how I got to New Mexico, she simply smiled and said that I was welcome to stay with her at her house until I figured out my next move. I had told her that I didn't want to go back to my mom's if I didn't have to.

The girl's husband came home from work that evening, and she explained the situation to him. This dude didn't seem upset about any of it, thankfully. The girl did explain that she and her husband were deeply involved in their local church so maybe that explains some of it.

I spent the next few days there, mowing the grass and straightening their garage in order to earn my keep. The fact that these people didn't even act like I was intruding was kinda freaking me out a little bit. I was starting to go a little crazy, and wanted to get the hell out of there.

One night, at supper, I mentioned to them that my dad would most likely let me stay with him if I could contact him. They got on the phone to try to get a phone number for him, but had no luck. I knew my dad lived in Oil City, Pennsylvania, but there was no number listed under his name.

We talked a little while about other ways to find him, and before long, we ended up with some luck. I somehow remembered my grandfather's name and we were able to contact my dad through him.

When I talked to my dad, he said that my mom had already called him. He told me that he was expecting my call, and that he would send me a plane ticket to come to Pennsylvania the next morning.

The ticket was waiting for me at the airport the next morning as promised, and I got a ride to the airport from the people I was staying with. We said our goodbyes and I got on the plane. In my duffel bag with my clothes was a really cool bong I had found while cleaning the garage. I felt a little bad for stealing it, but, as I said, it was really cool. Besides, it wasn't as if they needed it anymore. They were Christians.

Chapter 4

I was met at the airport in Pittsburg by my dad and step-mom, Butch. I don't really know why she went by that name. I guess she was just weird like that. I also had a step-brother whom everyone called "Goober." He was born in Georgia, and got the nick-name at birth. Unfortunately for him, the nick-name stuck.

A few days after arriving in Pennsylvania, my dad said it was time to call my mother. I really, really didn't want to talk to her, but my dad thought it would be better if I was the one that told her I'd rather stay with him.

I got on the phone with my mom, and she tried to get me to come back. I told her I wanted to stay where I was, and that was my final decision. I wanted a stable home.

Dad went to a court hearing and took me with him. I had to tell the judge that I wanted to live with my father, which I did. The judge granted my dad custody of me and we left. The whole thing was rather anti-climatic. It only took a few minutes.

Now that my dad was my legal guardian, he enrolled me back in school. I was in the ninth grade and the school year had just started, so at the very least, I wouldn't be too far behind.

I got enrolled to the same school as Goober; Oil City High School. Since Goober was four years older than I was, but had been held back a year in grade school, he was a senior, while I was a freshman.

Despite our age difference, Goober and I got along great. Around school, I was known as the "little brother" by Goober's friends, most of whom were seniors as well.

The "little brother" title had a benefit. I got to hang out with the seniors. This gave me a little bit of status with the rest of the lower classmen. I was looked upon with awe by my freshman friends when one of the seniors would take the time to stop by my locker to see how I was doing.

Okay, maybe I wasn't looked upon with "awe", but I at least felt like I should have been.

Along with the benefit of being Goober's little brother, there were also drawbacks. The first of these was that Goober and his friends were known as the troublemakers of the school. This, of course, meant I was labeled a troublemaker as well.

I'm not going to try to say that I was unjustly considered to be a troublemaker however, because I did get into a lot of shit. Little brother or not, I was still a freshman, and was expected to earn my place in the pack, just like everybody else. Usually, this was accomplished by me having to pick a fight with someone who had offended one of the older guys who would get into too much trouble if he handled it himself. Unfortunately for me, these guys were easily offended, and I got into a lot of fights.

I skipped school a lot, and would end up in detention for my trouble. Skipping detention always got me a two day out-of-school suspension. I never did realize exactly why, if you didn't go to school, your punishment would eventually be, not going to school, but I guess that's neither here nor there at this point.

Dad gave us two dollars every morning for our lunch at school. I always used my two dollars to buy a joint to smoke before school started. This would be my daily routine you see, which usually led me into the "trouble" that I would "make".

After I was in Pennsylvania for about six months, Butch, my step-mom, found out that I was smoking weed. This got me sent to a psychologist once a week for about two months. I never knew what the point was to all of that.

Goober never did drugs back then, but he did drink beer whenever he could. I would drink when I didn't have any weed, or pretty much anytime I was offered any sort of alcohol.

One night, while I was at a school dance, a friend of mine showed up with two large bottles of schnapps. One was apple flavored, and one was cinnamon.

We drank both bottles between the two of us, and before long we were both puking our guts out. I've never been so sick in my entire life. I managed to get home just minutes before my dad got home from work. By the time he walked through the door, I was out cold.

Sometime later that night, my dad woke me up by yelling up the stairs to tell me to get up, and come to the living room. I thought I was busted. I got there, and he handed me the phone. It was my uncle. Apparently, my cousin Gail had ran away from home and he was wondering if I knew where she was or not. I told him I had no idea, and then promptly went back to bed.

While in Pennsylvania, most of my drug activity was weed and alcohol, but I did do acid one time. The only time I was able to come across any speed, was when I found a bottle of Fastins, (A.K.A Blue and Clears) in our bathroom at home. The Fastins were prescribed to Butch for low blood pressure. I stole them and spent the next three days speeding my ass off. It felt awesome!

After graduation, Goober moved out of the house. He stayed with different friends for a while, but most of them were leaving to go to the military. It wasn't long before he didn't have anywhere left to go at all.

Goober had no job, no car, and no money. He also had no intention of moving back in with us. He was grown, and didn't want to live by anyone's rules but his own. That's what he told me anyway.

Goober wanted to leave town. He had no idea where he wanted to go, but he wanted out of Oil City, and out of Pennsylvania altogether. My mom was still in Arkansas, and Goober started talking to me about how cool it would be for us to go there. I called my mom, and she told us to come on down.

We scraped together what cash we could get our hands on and got a ride to the Greyhound station in Franklin, PA. Unfortunately, we only had enough money to get us two tickets as far as Louisville, KY. From there, we'd have to hitchhike the rest of the way to Arkansas.

Once we got to Louisville, we walked straight to the interstate to start hitching. Within two minutes, a car stopped. A cop car. Apparently, it is illegal to hitchhike in the state of Kentucky.

The cop started asking questions and, upon learning that I was a minor, took me into custody. Goober was told to get off the interstate, and left to fend for himself.

Goober ended up contacting Dave, one of his friends from high school, who moved out to Kansas right away after graduation. Dave sent Goober money for a bus ticket, and Goober went to Kansas. The cops called my parents, then put me on a bus to my mom in Arkansas.

I was fifteen, about to turn sixteen, and back to a life of uncertainty. Again. This sucked.

Chapter 5

The next several years would be eventful, to say the least. Goober would end up getting married, then divorced, while in Kansas. Dave moved to California. After Goober's divorce, Goober pretty much just mooched off of other friends he had made. He wasn't much into working and supporting himself.

I quit school soon after getting to Arkansas. I would eventually go to prison for a string of burglaries and thefts, but at least I was able to acquire my GED while I was locked up. After being released, I moved to Mountain View, Ark. Mom had moved there, and it was the only place I had to go.

I ended up meeting a girl in Mountain View whom I got pregnant. Before the baby was born, I violated my parole, and had a choice to either leave the state, or go back to prison. She didn't want to leave, and I didn't want to go to prison, so I ended up leaving alone.

I went to Kansas where Goober and I joined forces once again. We lived in Wichita for a little while before stealing Goober's girlfriend's car and heading to Mississippi where my mom, brother, and sister were moving too. Even though I didn't like moving, it seems to me at least, that everyone I knew, and myself, were pretty good at it.

After a few weeks in Mississippi, Goober decided to join the United States Army. This idea lasted about a month into his basic training before he went AWOL. He made his way to San Francisco to hide out with Dave, from Kansas.

Goober kept in contact with me, and once he got kinda settled, he invited me out. Dave was all for it, so I packed a bag, and went to California.

Now California was a lot of fun. Dave had a '71 Buick with a bad master cylinder. This left us cruising around San Francisco with no brakes. I honestly don't believe any of us had a driver's license, and I know for a fact there wasn't any insurance on the car, so all in all, I have no idea how we avoided getting arrested or killing ourselves.

None of us worked. We were all living with a girl Dave had been friends with since he first arrived in the area.

Dave, who happened to be a pretty good drummer, was trying to "make it" as a singer with a heavy metal band. He wasn't as good a singer as he was a drummer, but we never told him this. We would spend all our weekdays in the malls and on the streets trying to sell tickets to whatever show his band would be playing at that weekend.

The way the clubs worked was, the band paid the club to be allowed to play. In return, the club gave the band a stack of tickets. It was up to the band to sell enough tickets to make their money back, and some profit to live off of. Selling these tickets, however, was harder than door to door vacuum cleaner sales. Something I now know a little about.

On the nights Dave's band would play, Goober and I would carry the equipment in for them. Playing "roadie" got us in for free, and it got us into the band room. The band room of course, is where the guys in the bands got ready for their shows before they played and partied their asses off after they played.

It was in the band room that I ended up developing my first cocaine habit. The guys in the bands might have been starving and basically homeless, but there was rarely a shortage of drugs. It was also because of being in one of these band rooms that I encountered meth for the first time, and it was completely by accident that I did.

Dave and I both smoked cigarettes. Since we didn't work, we didn't always have money to support this particular habit, not to mention any other ones we had. This meant we would always pocket any unprotected cigarette packs that'd be laying about the band rooms.

One night after a show, one of the guys in another band was raising hell because someone stole his smokes. He was making a pretty big deal out of it, so Goober, Dave and I decided it'd be best if we left before someone started patting people down and found all of the cigarettes we had stolen. Although Goober didn't smoke, he still would steal cigs for Dave and me.

When we got back to the house, we dumped all the cigarette packs we nabbed out on the coffee table. That's when Goober happened to notice a small baggie of white powder. "That's why dude was pissed, his dope was in the pack!" he mentioned upon noticing it.

Thinking it was coke, Goober handed it to me. I looked at it, but it didn't look right. I showed Dave, and he determined it was crank. "Cool!" I thought to myself. I hadn't tried that yet.

Goober was still drug-free, but we talked him into doing the crank with us. We cut it into three lines, and snorted it. I loved the high I got off of it, and was suddenly a huge fan of Methamphetamine.

Things stayed pretty good until we lost our place to stay one morning. We were having a party the night before, and Goober fucked the girl we were staying with while she was drunk. The next morning, she flipped out and told all of us to get the fuck out. There was a reason that this psycho bitch was off-limits, and this was it.

Wayne Huffman

Chapter 6

Dave was getting discouraged in San Francisco anyway, so after we packed our shit we decided to head to LA. Dave felt as if he'd have a better chance of success there.

We ended up blowing the motor in the Buick just north of LA on Highway 101. We had enough money for one motel room for a week in the town of Buellton, so we checked in.

During that week, Dave decided to give up on his Rock 'n Roll dreams. His parents were now living in Houston, so he called them for money to come home on. We went with him to the bus station, to see him off as he left for supposedly greener pastures.

While we waited for the bus, Goober noticed a "Help Wanted" sign in the window of the bus station/video store/UPS pickup/Western Union. This town was apparently so small, that this one store offered all of these wonderful conveniences under one roof.

By the time Dave left, Goober had a job as a clerk in the video store. I was hired on as a clerk at yet another video store owned by the same person. My store did nothing but rent videos and VCR's, and was only a couple of miles from the motel we were staying at, so I could easily walk to work. Goober's store was just around the corner from the motel.

The good news for us was that we had jobs. The bad news for us was that we were completely broke, and our week at the motel was almost up. We sold the Buick to a service station for parts, so we had a few dollars left for food until we got paid in two weeks.

We only trained for one day, and then we were set loose to run the stores ourselves. If we had a problem, we just called the owner who told us how to solve it. No sweat. We made sure we didn't have many problems. In fact, the only problems might have been us.

After our first day alone at the stores, we got back to the motel room and started to talk about what we were going to do for dinner. I suggested we go to the store to buy chips, soda, and sandwich makings. This was pretty high living considering our meager available funds from the sale of the Buick. Goober looked at me kind of funny, and I smiled as I pulled a small wad of bills out of my pocket. He started laughing his ass off as he pulled an even larger wad of bills out of *his* pocket. Apparently, we had both been on the same wavelength all day. Now that we had both figured out ways of skimming money, things were going to be a lot easier for us.

What we were doing was simple. At my store, I simply took the paper out of the printer. When a customer came in and wanted a few movies, I'd write them a hand written receipt and pocket the money. Half of all late fees went in my pocket as well. Absolutely none of these transactions went into the computer.

Goober had more opportunities to skim money at his store because of the Greyhound. Greyhound wasn't computerized at this location in those days, and so the tickets were handwritten.

When someone came in to buy a bus ticket, Goober, the clerk, removed a ticket packet from a box. The ticket packets were numbered, so he would take one from the middle of the box, instead of the front, like he was supposed to do. He would write the ticket, then tear off the carbon copy. The copy and money went into a drawer. When the customer left, Goober would take the money out and pocket it. The carbon got wadded up and thrown into the ceiling rafters. Those carbons are probably still there today.

We were stealing several hundred dollars a day between the two of us. We had plenty of money for my cocaine, Goober's alcohol, and our motel and food. Life was great and so, we did what we always do when life was great, started partying heavily again. My cocaine was being supplied to me by the video store owner's daughter. Ironically, or maybe coincidentally, she had recently been fired by her father for doing the exact same thing we were doing, robbing him blind. Although we never told her, I'm sure she knew what we were up to.

We knew everything was about to fall apart when the owner came in and made a remark about how the Greyhound sales were down. The next day, Goober and I pocketed every single cent we brought in. After work, I met Goober at his store, and he had two tickets written up for us to go to North Carolina. We were out of town before the sun set. I'm not sure exactly why Goober decided on North Carolina, but three days after leaving California, we were stepping off the bus in Charlotte.

We worked when we could at day labor places, and stayed in motels for several months. I kicked my coke habit for a while, but got back on it after meeting a girl who was strung out pretty bad. Since she had no problem supplying me with free drugs, I had no problem *using* free drugs. In order to make money, we created a scam where the girl would pose as a prostitute. She would get picked up and bring the guy back to a motel we had rented. When the guy, walked in, Goober and I would beat the hell out of him and rob him.

This shit went on for weeks, and one day, Goober and I decided we had to get away from this bitch before we all went to jail or got shot. We left without telling her where we were going, and started to hitchhike back to Mississippi.

We got a ride from a small family who were also going to Mississippi to look for work around the Gulf Coast area. They were as broke as we were and running low on gas. Goober and I stole a couple of gas cans out of some garages to help get us a little further down the road. After dark, we were able to siphon enough gas from cars in a hospital parking lot to get us most of the way to our destination.

We started running low on gas again in Evergreen, Alabama, so we stopped at a church to see if they would help. They called the local cops to tell them they were sending us there for a gas voucher.

We got to the cop shop, and the cop who came out to talk to us asked us for identification; all of us. We got the voucher and we were on our way; except Goober. When they ran his ID, he had a federal warrant for desertion from the Army. I guess we were so busy, we kind of forgot about that. He went to jail.

Goober would end up getting out of trouble from the military on a technicality. I left Mississippi and went to Kansas after Goober was released from military prison and decided to head there himself. I was off drugs completely by then, but I ended up in trouble for forging checks.

I ended up leaving Kansas, alone, and went back to Charlotte, because I knew I could get work there. I knew also that I needed to straighten up and settle down somewhere. That was my plan, and for almost twenty years, it worked out fairly well.

Chapter 7

Not long after arriving back in Charlotte, I met Karen. Karen was thirteen years older than I was, but you couldn't tell it by me. She definitely didn't look, or act, her age at all.

I moved in with Karen, and a couple of months later, we moved to Johnson City, Tennessee where she was from. One afternoon while riding around, we decided to go get married over in Elizabethton, Tenn. Because of where we lived, it was closer to go to the courthouse there instead of the one in Johnson City.

We went to the courthouse and got the marriage license but there was nobody there to perform the ceremony. We drove to Weaver's Store in Stony Creek to find Judge Weaver. He was there, mopping the floor, but kindly stopped long enough to marry us. Afterward, we thanked him by buying a couple of moon pies and some Pepsi. After all, what's a wedding without cake and champagne, right?

The marriage was doomed from the beginning. Mostly because Karen caught me with another woman a week after we were married. This would become a regular occurrence for the both of us, so after seven years, we came to the realization that we were better at being friends more than anything else, so we decided divorce would be the best option. Karen has always been a great friend to me ever since.

During my marriage to Karen, we constantly moved back and forth, to and from Johnson City, and Charlotte. There was no real rhyme or reason for this. We just did it.

After receiving a large insurance settlement from a car accident, Karen and I teamed up with her brother to buy a bar. One of our regular customers was an ex-marine who would become a police officer, and later a DEA agent. He was also the brother of a friend of mine, and my brother-in-law's girlfriend, Kelly.

Ironically, this would be the same DEA agent who would lock me up for fifteen years on federal charges almost twenty years later; funny how life turns out sometimes.

While separated from Karen a few years after we closed the bar, I met the woman who would later become my second wife. I'll call her, "Elvira."

Elvira was sexy and she knew it. She wore short, bright colored dresses, and spiked high heels. She certainly had the legs for it. Elvira also had beautiful, thick, long, dark, wavy hair. She tended to wear bright red lipstick, with bright red nail polish to match, on inch-long fingernails.

When Elvira stepped out of her showroom-condition '66 Mustang, she could stop traffic. She was HOT.

She was also a drunk, a pot-head, a pill popper, a coke junkie, and a whore. Elvira had a husband and two beautiful girls, Chris and Dee, but that didn't stop her from screwing anyone she took a liking to. One of those people happened to be me.

I started seeing Elvira and after about a year, her husband found out about our affair and beat her ass. That was the end of that marriage and, before too long, I ended up married to her.

To give her credit, Elvira was a good mother to her girls, who I would raise like my own, and to our son Damian, that we had together. She even gave up most of her drug habits. She just couldn't get being a whore out of her system, and that's what killed our marriage after seven years. I believe I'm noticing a pattern; seven doesn't seem to be a lucky number for me when it comes to marriages.

After Elvira and I divorced, I started to drink regularly, but it wasn't really much of a problem. I worked the night shift, 11PM until 7AM, and I would drink a 6-pack after work every day. On the weekends, I would go to the club, where my best friend Shane worked as a bouncer, and would get drunk.

Out of boredom, I let a buddy of mine from work talk me into joining a local gym. I was living in Elizabethton and the gym was only a few blocks from my house.

Every morning after work we would go workout together. It was a great way to kill time, and I enjoyed it.

Eventually, I was able to obtain and acquire a steady supply of anabolic steroids. Once I got on the juice, I really loved lifting weights.

Working out was a good substitute for drinking, and so, I got addicted to the steroids, and the gym. I stopped going to the club, so Shane started coming by my house to hang out just about every day.

I had beautiful hardwood floors in my house. For the hell of it, I took some cans of Liquid Gold furniture polish one day and shined my floors with it. I might as well have just poured oil on the floors.

That afternoon, after polishing the floors, Shane came running in through the front door. His feet went straight up into the air and he landed on the dining room floor, right on his ass. It was hilarious!

Shane was a good dude, but he was strange. He couldn't tell the truth to save his life, and I think he honestly believed most of his own bullshit stories. He was convinced he had a relative involved in every major world event from the Mayflower to the World Trade Center.

Shane's ex-wife Trina had a mixed baby, half white, half black, and he thought the kid was actually his own. He said the kid had some kind of rare pigment disorder. Trina being married to a black guy at the time did nothing to change his mind either.

Something about Shane that used to freak me out was that he was in love with his own mother, circa early 1970's. He had a photo of her that he used to carry with him everywhere he went.

In the photo, she was a young, pretty hippie wearing a t-shirt and tight bell bottom jeans. Her hair was long and straight, parted in the middle and falling over her shoulders. Shane would sit and stare at that picture, and talk about how beautiful she was. It was really creepy.

For all Shane's faults, and he had a lot of them, he was a good friend. I knew I could trust him, and no matter what, I knew he had my back if I needed him.

Shane could do one thing right. He could pick up beautiful women. He was never able to keep one for very long, but he had no trouble getting them, short term. Shane's trouble with keeping a girl was usually due to them figuring out pretty fast that he was full of shit.

Lying wasn't the only thing that drove women away from Shane. A lot of girls, even some that knew him well, thought he was gay. Sometimes I even had to wonder if he was fighting some sort of buried homosexual feelings. He definitely had some strange ways.

Sometimes, when getting to know a woman for the first time, Shane would start talking about how good he cooks, how good he cleans house, and what soap operas he liked to watch. If he was going for a sympathy approach, he would tell a story about how he was molested as a kid. Not really the kind of shit you want to tell a girl you just met.

I tried pointing these mistakes out to him, and also tried explaining that he was never going to keep a girl like that, but he was sure women found his sensitive, victimized game irresistible. Personally, I think he made a better stalker than a Romeo sometimes.

The biggest problem Shane had with trying to have a relationship, was his living arrangements. Shane had two sons, and custody of them, because his ex, Trina, isn't worth a damn as a mother. The three of them, Shane and his boys, lived with Shane's mother, because Shane simply does not like to work.

The only job Shane has ever held for any length of time was his part-time bouncer job at The Nashville Sound club in Johnson City. That job paid just enough to cover the bar tab he'd run up on his days off.

When Shane would hook up with a girl and would "fall in love," (which was at least once a month) he would say, "I need to get a job, so I can get my own place." The job rarely happened, and when it would, he would quit or get fired due to some great injustice. There would be some long story that always sounded similar to the last one.

I felt bad for the guy most of the time, because he was my friend. As I said, I would try to point out what he was doing wrong before he had a chance to screw up, but in the end, the girl always left.

In October of 2003, Shane's flaws and bad luck with women actually worked to my advantage. Well, I might have manipulated the situation a little bit so that everything that happened benefited me, but it was definitely his hopelessly incessant, simple-minded, moronic bullshit that made it possible for me to screw him over in the first place. Therefore, I don't feel bad about it. If you saw Lisa back then, you would understand.

Chapter 8

Shane met Lisa for the first time at The Nashville Sound on a Thursday night. Thursdays were ladies nights and Shane made sure he always worked on those nights.

At the time Shane met Lisa, I was working as a machine operator at Exide Technologies, a car battery manufacturer, in Bristol, Tennessee. Since I was working the graveyard shift, I rarely went to "The Sound" on Thursdays. I never had to worry about missing anything though, because Shane would be at my house by the time I got home from the gym to fill me in on everything that went on during the night. His story would always end with him having crazy sex with some girl who had never been to the club before, and oddly enough, would never return for Shane to point her out to me to prove she existed at all.

Whenever Shane would meet a new girl, (a real one..) he couldn't wait to tell me all about her. I mean, he was worse than a kid at Christmas. She was always "the one". But, when he first met Lisa, he never said a word about her to me. Maybe my feelings should be hurt.

The first I ever heard of Lisa was on a Saturday night a week after Shane had met her. This was the first night she had been back to The Sound since their first meeting, and as soon as Shane saw her again, he decided he was going to ask her out. He had just one problem, and he would need my help solving it.

I was on my way to Johnson City thinking I would go see a movie and get something to eat. As I drove down 1-26, my cell phone rang. I checked the caller ID, and saw that it was Shane. I started to ignore the call, because I was looking for a quiet night, but I answered it anyway. Shane asked if I could come to The Sound as soon as possible. It was important, he'd said.

I figured Shane had gotten himself into some shit, or was about to, and needed someone to watch his back. This had happened a time or two before, so that was what I was expecting when I got there. Either that or he would be wanting to borrow some money that he'd never repay.

Shane met me in the parking lot, and when I asked what was up, he just started walking towards the club and said, "Follow me." We walked in, and I walked to one of the bars to get a beer, so I would have a bottle for a weapon, if I needed it. This also gave my eyes some time to adjust to the light, so I wouldn't get jumped from behind. I was fully prepared for a bar fight, if one were to ensue.

It was a little after 9 p.m. and the live band was just starting to play. They were the Sharkadelics from over in Asheville, North Carolina and were a great band that was very popular at The Sound. The place was already crowded, and Shane stood by the railing of the raised platform we were standing on where the bar was located. There were three bars in the club, and they were all raised above the floor level, so you could sit at a table and see across the entire place.

Finally, Shane pointed and asked, "Do you see that group of girls right there?" I did. "Do you see the tiny little girl with brown hair?" I saw her. "I need you to find out what her name is for me." I wanted to hit him with my beer bottle.

This was my friend. Call me and ask me to drop what I'm doing to come to the club. No explanation, just come. Which I did, out of friendship, and the goodness of my heart, and this asshole asks me to ask some girl what her name is..? What the fuck was this, high school? What else would he ask me to do, pass her a note?

We walked over and Lisa excused herself from the group and joined us. Shane asked her if she wanted a drink, which she did, then he walked off to get it. I introduced myself, and she did as well. Mission accomplished. I could leave now, but once I got a good look at Lisa, I knew I wouldn't be going anywhere until closing time.

Lisa really was tiny, about 4 foot 11, and around ninety pounds. She had long light brown hair and hazel eyes. I could see that, although small, she had a nice body; hourglass figure, with a great ass. Something I really liked about her was that her nails were long enough to be sexy without being obnoxious. I have a thing for long fingernails.

The three of us hung out together all that night. We walked around the dance floor when the band was taking a break. When the band was playing, we were standing by the stage and dancing. Well, Lisa was dancing, and Shane was doing something similar to having an epileptic seizure. I just drank beer.

Lisa was a lot of fun and full of energy. She was very flirtatious, but I didn't take any of it seriously since she and Shane were making plans to go out. I had a good time simply watching Lisa have a good time; this was a girl I could get used to being around, at least, that was my impression of her by the end of the night.

Right before The Sound had last call I decided it was time for me to head home. Shane asked Lisa for her phone number, and since he didn't own a cell phone, he asked if I'd put the number into my phone. I didn't mind, and to be honest, I kind of liked the idea of having Lisa's number.

I handed the phone to Lisa and she punched in her number, and then decided to call her own phone to be sure that it worked. When her phone rang, she held it up for me to see. "And now I have your number," she said with an angelic smile. Then she added, "in case I need to call you to get a hold of Shane." Damn! My heart sank at those words.

I left the club and headed towards home. When I got to Elizabethton, I stopped at a Taco Bell for something to eat. While I waited for my order, I picked up my phone, and noticed that there were several missed calls from Lisa's number. I must have had the stereo turned up too loud to hear the phone ring.

I called Lisa's number back to see what she, or more likely Shane, wanted. When Lisa answered, she said that Shane had wrecked his car and needed me to come back to the club to help him. I said I was on my way, and hung up.

On my way back to the club, I found myself getting kind of excited at the thought of seeing Lisa again. I knew I wanted her for myself, and knew I was going to have to figure out a way to get her before Shane did something stupid enough to run her off.

I got back to The Sound, and saw that Shane's little Celica was trashed. The entire passenger's side was smashed in and he had two flat tires. He had gotten it back into the parking lot, so it was good until morning when we would come back with some tires.

When I asked what happened, Shane said he was taking Lisa for coffee before she drove home. Lisa was already drunk when I got to the club, and we had been drinking for hours since then. Shane said that as he was pulling out of the parking lot, he decided to show Lisa "What my car could do," as he put it.

He revved the engine and popped the clutch. As the bald tires spun and he pulled onto the road, Shane reached down to blast the radio through his one good door speaker. That's about when he side-swiped the telephone pole. This was one of those stupid things I did not need Shane doing.

Lisa left in her own car, and I took Shane home. As we drove toward Shane's mother's house, he told me more about Lisa. He seemed to be able to remember an awful lot about her for someone who couldn't remember her name earlier; idiot.

The most surprising thing Shane told me about Lisa was that she had four kids, and that two of them, Tina and Faye, "The Twins," were fifteen years old. Lisa didn't look a day older than twenty-one herself, but she was actually thirty-one at the time. Lisa's other kids were Joy, who was about to turn nine, and Levi, who was about eighteen months.

Lisa currently did not have custody of any of her kids because of a little legal trouble she was having. Apparently, she had several counts of contributing to the delinquency of a minor for letting the twins have a party at home with several of their friends. A neighbor noticed a couple of drunk teens outside, and called the cops.

Lisa had temporarily lost custody of all the kids, and they, with the exception of Joy, were living with Lisa's parents in Hampton, Tennessee. Joy was with Lisa's oldest sister, Katy, who lived right down the road from their parents, with her husband, Rupert.

Lisa had also been charged with trying to run over a Unicoi County sheriff's deputy. The cop was blocking the road with his car in a blind curve, when Lisa came down the road a little too fast, and almost ran into him, as he stood in the road behind his car. The charge would eventually be dropped down to "failure to control a vehicle." Lisa was given a ten dollar fine. It was too funny to watch the cop get mad and storm out of the courtroom.

The day after Shane wrecked his car, Lisa called me to see if he was okay, and to see if we had gotten his car moved, which we had. We talked for a little while, and then Lisa said that she was on her way to Shane's house to see him. I told her I was going over there myself, and that I would see her there.

I wasn't really planning on going to Shane's, until Lisa said that she was going. There was no way in hell I was going to leave her alone with Shane if I could help it.

Going to Shane's house to cock-block, became an every day event that entire week. Lisa would call me to see if Shane was home, (I usually knew if he was), and to let me know she was on her way to see him. Just in case he stopped by my place before she got to his house, she said.

I would immediately drive over to Shane's house and when Lisa got there, we would all hang out together. Lisa and I got along great. We were always talking shit to one another, and the jokes would regularly turn to a sexual nature. This always embarrassed Shane, because for all his supposed wild, sexual conquests, he was shy when it came to talking about kinky sex.

Shane never seemed to think of Lisa and my joking around as anything more than a couple of friends cutting up together. Not everything I said to Lisa was a joke, and I was pretty sure she knew it. I never could tell if she was ever being serious with me, so I took everything she said as a joke.

Since I was working the 11pm to 7am shift, I wasn't getting much sleep that week, due to spending so much time at Shane's keeping Lisa's attention diverted. So, when Lisa said she was about to leave town for a week with the twins, I was happy. I could catch up on some much needed sleep.

I decided that I was going to try to hook up with Lisa when she got back. Since I didn't just want to take her from Shane, I decided to try to get him to think it was his idea for me and Lisa to get together. This was a pretty brilliant plan, in my eyes.

I started working on Shane's insecurities. I told him that he should realize, before he got too involved with Lisa, that she was probably looking for a whole lot more than he could provide. He didn't even have a real job, so how could he afford to take her out?

Between his two kids, and her four kids, that's six kids he would have to try to support. I told him that, since Lisa had lost her apartment and job after her arrests, she would need a place for her and her kids to live. There definitely wasn't room for all of them in Shane's mother's little trailer.

I strongly suggested to him that he get out of the situation before he got too attached to Lisa. Shane agreed that I was right, but he said he was in love with her. Of course he was. He fell in love with anyone who hung around for more than three days.

Okay, time for me to change tactics. I told Shane that I hoped things worked out for him, but, if things did go to hell, would he consider suggesting to Lisa that she would be doing good to hook up with me? The dumbass actually called her and told her to hook up with me if things didn't work out between them. He said he wanted to tell her now, in case she didn't believe him at the time of the breakup.

Lisa was due to return from her trip on Halloween day. I had four days of vacation time left for the year, so I put in to take them, starting on Halloween night. I was going to spend every minute of these days off trying to steal Lisa away from Shane. Little did I know then, that Shane was about to hand her to me on a silver platter.

Chapter 9

Lisa called me early, around 8am, the morning of Halloween day and left a voice mail saying she was back, and on her way to Shane's house. Maybe I should mention at this point, that I have never been around Lisa when she wasn't high, or drunk. She seemed to always be on something, and when I woke up and got the voicemail she had left me, she sounded completely wasted.

I got dressed and drove over to Shane's. Lisa was already there, passed out on the couch. Shane said she came in drunk, and laid down to sleep, without so much as saying even "hello" to him.

I sat down in a chair across the coffee table from Shane, who was sitting at the end of the couch away from where Lisa was laying. We talked for a while, and finally, Lisa woke up. She went to the bathroom, then when she was done, walked outside to her car. When we heard the car door close, we figured she was leaving, but she came back in with a beer in her hand.

Lisa drank her beer, without saying a word to us, then laid back down. When she did, Shane took a pillow and playfully hit her with it, and told her to wake up. Lisa jumped to her feet and quickly assumed the form of Satan himself, as she went fucking psycho.

She started screaming at Shane and throwing shit, ("shit" as in her beer bottle, the ash tray, books, etc.) at him. She was telling him she wasn't just going to sit there and let someone beat on her. It was insane. Lisa stormed out the door and told Shane never to call her again. It was over. I had thought, "Great. Now I'll never see her again, either."

I told Shane to forget about it, and we jumped in my truck to go to the beer store. It wasn't even noon yet, but it seemed like a good time to go ahead and start partying. After all, it was Halloween.

Shane actually had one legitimate talent, he was good at tattooing. One day, when he was really hard up for money, I bought all of his tattooing equipment from him for a hundred and fifty dollars, with an agreement that he could use the equipment to make money. In return, I get any work I wanted done for free.

Once we got our beer, we headed back to my house. We spent the day drinking and burning CD's off the internet. We were getting pretty buzzed when I suggested Shane should give me a tattoo. He actually does his best work drunk.

We got everything set up and he started working on my tat at around 5pm. Soon after he started, my phone rang. "Hey, what are you doing?" It was Lisa! I told her I was getting a tattoo, and she asked if she could come over and watch. I told her she could, then I gave her directions to my house. She had never been to my place before.

When Lisa got there, she acted as if nothing had happened earlier with the demonic screaming and all, and as a matter of fact, was laughing and joking with the both of us. She got up and roamed around the house, checking everything out a few times and commenting on what a nice house I had.

My house was three bedrooms with one and a half baths, living room, dining room, kitchen, and breakfast room. All of the floors, except the kitchen, were wood. The kitchen had white tile and the ceilings throughout were nine foot high. There were also nine ceiling fans scattered about and a set of French doors separating the living room from the dining room; all in all, very nice digs.

The house had a full, unfinished basement. That is where the laundry room was. I had new countertops and custom made birch cabinets in the kitchen. The front yard was small, but I had a large back yard, and there was a huge deck the width of the entire house in the back. My dog; a long-haired, black, German Sheppard named Pica, lived in the big backyard.

When Shane finished the tattoo, he ended up falling asleep. Lisa and I kept drinking and started snorting Lortabs we had crushed up on my coffee table. We were both pretty relaxed. She launched into a conversation about her kids, and I told her about my son, Damian, who came to stay with me from time to time.

Around midnight, Shane woke up and said he needed to go home. Since he had ridden to my house with me, he didn't have his car, so he needed a ride. Jokingly, I looked at Lisa and asked, "Do you want me to take him while you wait here, or do you want to take him and come back?" She laughed, got up and said she would take him.

After Shane and Lisa left, I turned out the living room lights to watch a movie that was just coming on. After about 10 minutes, my phone rang. It was Lisa again. She asked if I still felt like having company, or was I going to bed. I said I was just watching a movie, and she was welcome to come watch it with me, if she wanted. We sat on the couch and talked for hours with no lights on, except the TV. Around 4am, Lisa got up, sat in my lap, and started kissing me. We headed towards the bedroom, fucked for a couple of hours, and went to sleep.

About 7am, I could hear the sliding glass door that led out onto my deck open. I knew it was Shane, because I had shown him how to open that door when it was locked, in case he ever needed to get inside when I wasn't home.

I sat up and started putting my jeans on. Lisa woke up and asked me where I was going. "Nowhere," I said, "Shane's here." Lisa sat up quickly and asked, "Why the fuck is he here? Is he in the house?" The knock at the bedroom door answered her question.

I turned the door knob as I walked by on my way to the bathroom in my bedroom to take a piss. "Come on in," I invited as the door opened. Lisa looked like she was about to freak out.

Shane stepped in and just stood there for a second before he looked at Lisa and said, "I figured you were on your way back over here when you dropped me off last night."

"It's none of your business where I go," Lisa pointed out to him, "we aren't together" meaning her and Shane.

I walked back into the bedroom and told Shane to go wait in the living room while Lisa gets dressed. I told Lisa to take a shower, while I went to handle the situation with Shane.

I went into the living room and Shane looked really upset. He said he had a feeling he would find Lisa at my house, so he got up early and drove over. I told him simply, "If you didn't want to find her here, you shouldn't have come looking."

He started to whine about me knowing how he felt about her and how he was really going to try to make it work with her. I pointed out the fact that he told me he was cool with me getting with Lisa, if it didn't work out between them, which, apparently, it wasn't since Lisa had told him it was over between them. I also reminded him that he had told Lisa he *wanted* her to hook up with me if it wasn't working with them, so, my bases were covered.

Shane didn't like it, but he had to agree that I was right. When Lisa walked into the living room a few minutes later, being the friend that he is, Shane walked up to her, gave her a hug, and said, "Be good to my best friend, and we can all be friends. I just want my buddy to be happy." Then he left. I think he was crying like a little bitch.

Lisa and I spent every second of my vacation time together. I got to meet Tina and Faye on the second night, when they called Lisa to ask her if she would go buy them some beer and liquor. I met Joy and Levi when we went to Lisa's parents' house to drop off Joy's lunch money for the school week.

The night I was to return to work, I asked Lisa what she was going to do. She said that she wasn't sure, so I suggested that she just stay at my house. She said she wasn't sure if she should stay there while I wasn't there but I told her I would feel better knowing she had somewhere to stay. She finally agreed.

The next night, Tina and Faye stayed at my house with Lisa. As I was leaving for work that night, Lisa kissed me goodbye and said, "I love you." The twins heard her and both of them had a funny look on their faces as I left. I was thinking that, although we seemed to get along good, maybe the girls didn't think I was good enough for their mom.

On November 6th, seven days after Lisa basically moved in with me, six days after Shane caught us in bed together, and only three weeks since I first met Lisa, we got married.

I don't know how it happened. One minute, we were having breakfast at IHOP, and the next, we were at Wal-Mart buying a couple of wedding rings. Shane called me as Lisa and I were leaving Wal-Mart and I told him what we were doing. He said he wanted to go with us and he would meet us at my house.

I don't know where he got the money, but when Shane got to my house, he had a half gallon of SKYY vodka, my personal favorite. "A wedding gift," he said. We drank quite a bit of it, then went to the courthouse to get married. After that was done, we went back to my house to finish off the bottle.

Lisa was pretty wasted and started crying about not having her kids. Shane took that as a sign that it was time for him to go, and he left. I had to put up with the crying drunk lady I barely knew and had just wed, all by myself. Lisa kept saying that all she needed was me and Faye in her life and she could be happy. I remember thinking, "You have more kids than just Faye, right? What about needing the rest of them in your life?" I would find out later that the answer to those questions was both twisted and heart-breaking on several different levels

Chapter 10

Lisa settled right into her domestic role and was an awesome wife. I came home from work and the gym in the morning to a freshly cooked breakfast and a spotless house. Lisa would stay up at night to clean house so she could sleep during the day with me, both literally and figuratively. In the evening, I would wake up to dinner cooking.

Lisa finally went to court for the contributing charges, and they were dismissed. All of the kids had said they were having the party without her knowledge and that she had just come home and caught them moments before the police arrived.

Lisa's parents fought her for custody of the twins, mostly because they had raised the girls for most of their lives, and won. Lisa was able to obtain custody of Joy and Levi again, however. Levi came to live with us right away, but Joy stayed with Lisa's sister until the school year ended.

Joy and the twins would stay with us on the weekends. Tina didn't technically stay with us, because she would take off with her twenty year old boyfriend Bernie, for the entire weekend.

I got along great with the twins, and they started telling me a lot of disturbing things about Lisa. One night, Tina made the statement, "As far as I know, mom hasn't cheated on you, yet." Lisa and I had only been married for a month at this time.

The twins also told me that they were really surprised Lisa had married me. According to them, anytime someone started getting close to Lisa, she would dump them. She was not into commitment. I guess this explained the funny looks they had given me when they witnessed Lisa telling me she loved me.

The twins also said that Lisa had admitted to them once that, by the time Lisa was seventeen, she had had sex with over two hundred different men.

The most disturbing thing the girls told me about Lisa was that she hated Tina. The story they had given me was, they were partying one night, and

Lisa got mad at Tina over something. She started screaming at Tina, telling her she hated her and wished she would have died at birth.

This tirade went on and on, until at one point, Tina crawled under a table, crying, just to try to get away from Lisa. I asked Lisa about this, and she admitted every bit of it. She literally hated Tina.

Lisa even told me that at a party one night, Tina had passed out on the couch. There were several guys there that were friends of Lisa's boyfriend at the time. As Lisa and her boyfriend headed to bed for the night, Lisa told the guys to, more or less, do whatever they wanted to do to Tina, but just to make sure that Tina had her clothes on when she woke up in the morning, so she wouldn't know what happened to her. Tina was only fourteen years old at the time.

After learning about all of this, I felt sorry for Tina, so I began to show her extra attention. Lisa had started telling people that Faye was her favorite and Tina was my favorite. For my part, that wasn't true. I loved both of those girls equally.

Lisa had also admitted to me, that she got pregnant with Joy simply to keep her first husband from leaving her after he caught her cheating on him. Lisa was never married to the twins' father.

Levi's father was just a live in boyfriend, and Lisa had also cheated on him as well, with someone else. Thinking there was a chance that she was pregnant, Lisa started having unprotected sex with the boyfriend to cover up the affair.

I should have seen what kind of person Lisa was, but she convinced me that she was just looking for a chance to prove she wasn't that person anymore.

I loved Lisa, and she did seem like a totally different person than what I was hearing about her, so I thought she really had changed. She even quit drinking after we got married. I was willing to give her a chance to be this better person.

I called Lisa from work around 4am one morning. Faye was at the house with her, and Lisa said they had been spring cleaning all night. It was only January, so I thought it strange that it was referred to as "spring cleaning," but I let that go.

I mentioned to Lisa that I was pretty tired, and couldn't wait for the night to be over. I was off for the next two days, and it looked as if I was going to sleep one of them away. Lisa said she had a little something to "help me out." She wouldn't say what exactly this was, but she did mention that I would like it.

When I got home, Lisa pulled out a small baggie of meth from her pocket. This is the first meth I had seen since that one night in California. Lisa asked if I knew how to smoke it, which I didn't. She showed me how to smoke the meth off a piece of aluminum foil, and after that, Lisa, Faye and I spent the rest of the weekend smoking meth together. It was great!

I wasn't surprised in the leased that Lisa would allow her fifteen year old daughter Faye to do meth with us. I knew that both of the twins had done meth, coke, pills, weed, and alcohol since they were fourteen.

Lisa and I started getting about a half a gram of meth every weekend, and we'd smoke it with Faye. This became a regular thing, and soon enough, we were up to a gram on the weekends. At first, I didn't want to do any meth during the week, in case I was drug tested at work, but I eventually decided that I couldn't pass a piss test anyway if I was getting high on the weekends, so we started doing meth during the week also.

At first, I didn't mind how much we were spending on meth. I made pretty good money, so it wasn't much of a problem. Once we started buying meth during the week however, and I started running short on bill money a couple of times, I decided that it might be a good idea to learn how to cook meth myself. My life would never be the same again.

Chapter 11

While it was my growing addiction and the cost of feeding that, as well as Lisa's, addiction, that inspired me to learn how to cook meth, it would be my love for the whole process that would make it impossible for me to quit using, as well as cooking, meth.

There is a ritual to everything involved in the process of making and doing meth. With smoking meth off of aluminum foil, (also known as "chasing the dragon") you have the ritual of folding the foil to the exact specifications of the person doing the folding. Some people call the folded piece of foil a "boat". Some people want the shiny side of the foil up, while others prefer the dull side. There are a lot of people who incorrectly believe that one side or the other has waxes on it and said waxes account for the difference in the look of the two sides. They don't want these "waxes" in their dope while they smoke it, so the foil has to be turned a certain way. "The waxes" are just one of many meth related urban legends.

Some people don't want you to touch the foil with the lighter flame, because it blackens the foil as you smoke. Others simply don't care. Most meth addicts, who smoke very large amounts, like to carry their own piece of tubing used for smoking meth from foil this is called a "tooter" and is usually a piece of disposable ink pen that has been cut to about four inches long. Occasionally, people will get fancy with their tooters, and make them out of glass or pieces of metal with engravings on them. I've made really nice ones out of wind chimes, myself.

To understand why people like to use their own tooter, you have to understand how to smoke meth from foil. First, the foil, (usually Reynolds' Heavy or Extra Heavy duty are preferred because of the quality, and there aren't any tiny pin-holes for the flame to burn your dope) is folded into a boat. Then, you sprinkle the desired amount of meth onto the foil. A flame under the foil melts down the meth, and the smoke is inhaled through the tooter. That's all there is to it.

After using the same tooter many times, a layer of meth will build up on the inside, and once enough has built up, it can be scraped out and smoked again. Everyone knows this, so everyone that smokes meth, has absolutely no problems with letting others who have no tooter use theirs. It's basically, free dope.

Unfortunately, people will also steal tooters for the very same reason. Some people will let the meth build up in their tooter, then put it up and start using another one. Once they have several tooters saved up, they scrape all of them, and that amounts to hundreds of dollars worth of dope.

In a pinch, tooters can be made out of anything. A cut piece of a drinking straw is commonly used. A rolled up dollar bill works well also. If you are good enough you can inhale the smoke right off the foil with your mouth. Just be careful not to get too close, or you could burn your lips, or set your hair on fire. I've done both, and it wasn't fun.

One evening, out of desperation, I used the barrel out of my Colt 1911 pistol as a tooter. It was heavy, and I almost chipped a tooth, but it worked well enough. Tasted like crap, though.

When I decided to learn how to cook meth, I didn't think it was going to be any problem. I had heard on the television and read in newspapers, that it was made out of everyday household items. The recipe shouldn't be hard to get, or at least figure out, I thought. If I would have known how long it was going to take me to actually make meth for the first time, and how much money I would have invested in my self-education, I would have probably given up before I'd even got started.

When learning a new skill, the first, and most obvious, step is to find someone who already knows how to do what you want to learn to do. This person must also be willing to teach you the new skill you would like to learn.

Just like with any other skill, most meth cooks were taught their art (and it *is* an art form to a quality drug maker) by someone else. So, step one; find someone willing to teach me.

Lisa had been a meth user for many years, and knew a lot of people in the meth world. Since I was new to the game, I didn't know anyone. Even though we had been smoking meth together for a couple of months, I had never gone with Lisa when she went to buy dope. The way

I saw it was, if I wasn't out buying drugs, I didn't have to worry about getting busted and going to jail.

I sent Lisa out on a mission to find one of her friends who would be willing to teach me how to cook meth. I knew it was going to be a long shot but it was worth a try. Of course, nobody was going to give up the several hundred dollars every week that they were making off of me paying for dope, to teach me how to make my own.

Meth cooks normally don't like to teach others how to cook, because doing so would cut into their profits, and bring more competition into their area. That isn't good for business in a specialized market.

When a cook is willing to teach, it is usually for one of two reasons. Either the student is a very close and trusted friend or family member of the cook or the student is paying a lot of money to learn how to cook. I've known personally some cooks who have charged thousands of dollars to teach someone the vital information.

I just wasn't willing to pay someone to teach me to cook. Since I was pretty much an internet junkie at the time, I figured I would just find a recipe on my own. Having someone else actually show me how to cook would have simply been a time saving idea.

I started searching the net for my first recipe. Believe it or not, you don't find much useful information when you type in "meth recipes" in a search engine, like Google. You do, however, get a LOT of anti-meth sites.

Now, something I did not realize at first is just how much there was to cooking meth that I did not know. To my understanding at this point, all a meth cook needs to do is mix a few common chemicals together and, before you know it, you have meth! That is both accurate and not accurate.

One problem is that, you have to clean, prepare, and/or alter several of these common chemicals into something else. Another problem arises when trying to figure out how to make some of the ingredients that you can't simply walk into your local hardware store or garden supply store and purchase legally, or without suspicions.

As I slowly began to put together the list of ingredients I would need, I was still looking for an actual recipe that would tell me how to put everything together. As I searched chat rooms, online bulletin boards, and even the anti-meth websites, I kept coming across the name of an author, "Uncle Fester."

I started searching for the book I was reading about that was written by this author and was eventually able to purchase two separate books directly from him. Both books had many recipes for manufacturing not only meth, but several other drugs as well. All of this was in easy to understand language.

In my opinion, one of the best features of these books was that if there was a hard-to-get chemical, Fester would have a process to make the chemical yourself with ingredients that could be obtained legally.

Even more valuable to me, other than the information in these books, was a website that was listed at the end of the book. While this site no longer exists today, I was able to meet a lot of people on that site who knew an awful lot about cooking meth. I was able to download over one hundred different recipes from this "underground" site as well as other sites that this one linked to.

I learned all of the processes I would need to break down my pills and to make my iodine crystals. Breaking down pills is the process of extracting the pseudoephedrine, or pseudo as we call it for short, from cold and allergy pills. I actually learned several ways of doing this, and had a couple of problems perfecting my own method, but in the end, I learned from my mistakes.

The only problem I had with this website is that you were not permitted to ask any direct questions. Any questions you had would have to be asked hypothetically. If you were describing something, it had to be described as if it had happened in a dream. There was also a lot of code used. If you posted on the site, you had to word everything correctly, or everyone would freak out and you would end up getting banned. With that in mind, I just used the search engine most of the time to find the answers to my questions, and I had many questions.

One of the first things I ever learned about cooking meth was how to obtain and clean red phosphorus, or "Red P". Contrary to popular belief, Red P does not come from match heads. I only mention this because, while in jail, I have been approached by many supposed meth cooks who wanted to "talk shop".

These people often mention that they use this or that kind of match head for their cooks. That instantly proves to me, that the guy is a moron, because the only place match heads are used in a meth cook, are on television specials occasionally aired on the subject of cooking meth. They do this so dumbasses like these don't figure out how to actually make meth by watching the show.

Would someone watch one of these TV specials and think they could figure out how to cook meth? Of course they would. I actually used to go to the anti-meth websites because they have a lot of pictures of meth labs. I figured out different designs for different components of my labs from these sites when I was first starting out.

There was even a time when I would record the nightly news, in case there had been a meth lab bust. The news always had close ups of all the stuff the cops found during the raid.

Some aspiring meth cooks will often claim that they can cook, just so they can get you to start talking. Once I figure out a person is full of shit, I usually just walk away from them. Most cooks will do the same, because that person could easily be a cop. If the person continues to try to get cook info out of me, I will usually tell them some crappy shit that makes no sense at all. I'm just an asshole like that sometimes.

After a lot of study, I finally knew how the cook works, why "this" is mixed with "that," why different styles of labs are made the way they are, and several different ways there were to cook meth. I knew more about meth as a drug, and also the science of cooking meth, than almost any other common meth cook in my area, and I had still not done my first cook. It was time to get busy and put all of this new knowledge to work to see what would happen.

Chapter 12

The method I decided to use for my first cook was called the "push/pull" method. It seemed like the most commonly used method among the people I had been talking to and learning from via the internet, so I decided to go with that.

Now that I had all of my ingredients gathered together, everything cleaned, prepped, and ready, and my cooking apparatus built, I was ready to become a meth cook. Armed with dozens of recipes from what I felt were reliable sources, I set everything up in my kitchen.

I began mixing and stirring, heating and cooking, and following the recipe I had chosen for my first cook to the letter. Everything was going perfect. I had the right size and color bubbles. I was building pressure like I was supposed to, according to my research. I was happy and excited and nothing could go wrong.

Then it did. Something went completely wrong, because everything in my cook pot suddenly came to a stop. I was looking at my mix and there was no action going on. I was no longer happy, or excited.

I still had at least forty minutes of cook time left to go, but my reaction was dead. I began looking through all of my recipes, my Uncle Fester books, and the internet, and I could not find any mention of anything like this happening to anyone else.

Finally, I was forced to conclude that I had somehow screwed the whole thing up. So, I did the only thing I could do. I dumped everything down the drain and started over.

For months, I would get this same result every time I tried a cook. I became obsessed with trying to make the cook work. When I wasn't at work, I spent all of my time in the basement attempting cook after cook. I experimented with different cook pots and set ups. Nothing made a difference, and the end result was always the same.

After I had tried most of my recipes at least once each, and failed each time, I started taking the best process from each of the different methods and created a couple of my own recipes. At this point, I had spent so much time on my new hobby, and I had studied everything I could find on the chemistry of cooking meth, that I felt like an authority on the subject and more than qualified to create a new method of cooking. This also didn't work, but at least I felt as if I were about to make a breakthrough.

I began to think that maybe I wasn't breaking my pills down in a way that made my pseudo pure enough to convert to meth. I experimented with other methods, but only managed to blow the door off my microwave oven. While that mishap didn't cause a fire, it did teach me the importance of a thing called, "ventilation."

I somehow only managed to have one fire in those early days. That fire was the result of the same thing that causes most meth lab fires: Stupidity.

When I was first trying to figure out how to extract the pseudo from my cold pills, I found a relatively new method on the underground website I had been visiting. This process was called, "The Tetra Trap."

I'm not going to go into all the details of the process, but it involves mixing several highly flammable liquids together and bringing them to a very high temperature. In a glass container.

For some reason, the budding chemical genius I considered myself to be at the time, decided this would best be accomplished on my stove top. It also seemed more than reasonable to use a Pyrex pie dish as my cooking glassware. I mean, hey, you cook pies in it, right? (Ed. Disclaimer: Do NOT try this at home.)

I had the whole concoction mixed and the flammables were boiling away, when I noticed fumes visibly rolling over the edge of the pie dish and onto the red-hot eye of the stove that I was boiling this liquid bomb. (Ed. Note: If you tried this, told ya so)

Before I could come up with a plan of action the fumes ignited setting the whole dish on fire and sending flames all the way up to my nine foot high ceiling. I didn't panic at that moment because I did prepare a little for just such an occasion. Before starting this experiment, I filled the kitchen sink with water and placed two large mason jars, also full of water, on the counter next to the stove.

I immediately grabbed the two jars and threw the water on the fire. Little did I know that was my next mistake. The Pyrex shattered spilling the burning, oil-based liquid contents all over the stove, countertop, and floor. Now is when I started to panic.

I ran to the bedroom and grabbed a blanket which I then soaked in the sink water. I used the wet blanket to smother the fire; disaster averted.

The kitchen and dining room were full of a black smoke, so I closed all of the bedroom doors, and turned on the central air, to get fresh air into the house. I didn't think about the smoke getting pulled in through the air return vent, then getting circulated throughout the house, but that's what happened. I repainted the next day, every room of my house.

As I continued to try to figure out why my cooks were not producing results, Lisa thought she knew what was wrong. Her theory was that I actually knew too much about cooking meth to ever be able to do it myself. To me, that was just about the dumbest thing I had ever heard, but it made sense to her.

Lisa wanted me to give up. She even started refusing to help me do any of the prep work I needed done, but I didn't care. The twins helped when they were at the house, and when they weren't, I'd do everything by myself.

In truth, I was getting pretty discouraged at this point, but I had the inescapable feeling that I was about to make a breakthrough. I just knew in my heart I was overlooking one tiny detail, and that that detail was right in front of my eyes. All I needed to do was see it. I tried explaining this feeling to Lisa, but she wasn't buying it. She was done.

I was watching the news one evening because I had heard there had been a meth lab bust in Johnson City. Suddenly, I had a great idea. I would bail the meth cook out of jail in exchange for him showing me what I was doing wrong with my cooks. This, dear reader, is a great example of a meth addict's mind in action. Lisa, of course, said "Hell no," to that idea and I was trying to talk her into it, when a buddy of mine stopped by for a visit.

Joey was a parking lot security guard at The Sound, where Shane worked, and one of only a few people who knew I was trying to learn to cook meth. Joey also had a sideline job as the helper of a meth cook in

Johnson City. I had asked Joey several times if he had any idea what I might be doing wrong. He always said the same thing, his cook doesn't let him watch the actual cook process, that way, Joey couldn't learn how to cook himself. Therefore, he couldn't be of any help to me either.

While we were talking about the trouble I was having with my cooks, Joey asked me something about what temperatures (or temps) I was cooking at. Temps? None of my recipes said anything about what temperature I was supposed to be cooking at. Everything I had, told you what to look for during the cook. When "this" happens, do "this." When "that" happens, do "that." Whenever this or that didn't happen the way the recipes said it would, I would assume the cook was screwed up. Only now, I'm hearing about temps?

When I questioned Joey about this, he said his cook always cooks at three specific temps for three specific periods of time. I knew about the three stages the cook goes through for certain amounts of time. It was the rest I didn't know about, and luckily, Joey just happened to know what the temps were, and he passed that info on to me.

After Joey left, Lisa and I started watching television. I couldn't get the thought of the cook temperatures out of my mind, but I knew if I jumped up and went to go cook, instead of spending some time with Lisa, she would have a fit. I came to a decision.

I told Lisa that, since I had everything ready anyway, I wanted to try a cook with the temperatures that Joey had given me. If it didn't work this time, I quit. She agreed, and I went to the basement where I had set up my mad scientist starter kit lab and brought it all up to the kitchen. That way, I could just dump everything down the sink if it didn't work, and I was pretty sure it wouldn't.

I took all the pseudo, Red P, and iodine crystals I had and just threw it all into the cook pot. Since this was likely to be my last cook, I wasn't worried about weighing everything.

I got the cook going on my first temp. It cooked perfectly for fifteen minutes, like it was supposed to. My next temp was set, and I sat back to let it cook for thirty minutes. After only about ten minutes, the cook reaction stopped. Just like always. I had failed again, and this time, I was done for good.

I was getting ready to take the lab apart when I got to thinking; I had never, in this six month period of time I had been trying this, taken a cook all the way to the end just to see what would happen. Normally, when the cook stopped doing what it was supposed to be doing according to all of my recipes, I would just dump the shit out and start over. Since this was my last cook, I decided to take it all the way, just to see.

Without being very careful about what I was doing for the next hour or so, I finished the cook as if everything had gone perfectly. I finally found myself standing there with the jar full of brake parts cleaner I was using as my puller, hoping, but not really expecting, something to be in it.

A "puller" is an oil based solvent the meth will be dissolved in at this point in the cook. Meth is soluble in both water and oil. During a Red P cook, the meth is dissolved in water. There is a point in the cook where the water's pH is raised from a neutral to a high level, using sodium hydroxide or lye. This same process is used in pharmaceutical manufacturing.

Once the water's pH is raised, the meth is no longer soluble in the water. You will have what appears to be cottage cheese in a jar of water. When you add the oil based puller to the water, the meth is pulled into the puller; hence the name puller. Then, you just drain the water layer off and throw it away. The meth then gets gassed out of the puller.

I made my gassing bottle out of an old soda bottle and a length of aquarium air line that I epoxied into the cap. I poured a couple of inches of muriatic acid into the bottle, then dropped in a couple of aluminum foil balls. After a few seconds the acid began eating the foil. This released anhydrous hydrogen chloride gas through the airline.

I put the end of the air line into my puller and watched as it bubbled. I knew that once the gas worked, I was supposed to see what looked like oatmeal swirling around in my jar. So far, I wasn't seeing anything but bubbles.

I was just about to pull the air line out of the jar and give up, when, faster than the blink of an eye, there was something like an oatmeal substance in my jar.

I pulled the air line out of the jar, as the last of the foil was eaten away and the gas stopped being generated. My hands were shaking so much with excitement that I almost dropped the jar before I could set it down. Once the jar was safely on the counter, I just stared at it for a couple of minutes. I had just created something, although, I wasn't sure what. Did I dare believe it was really meth?

Chapter 13

I placed a coffee filter in a plastic funnel and held the funnel over the drain in the sink. Without thinking that maybe I should save the puller to gas off again later, I poured the puller with the oatmeal substance into the coffee filter. The puller went down the drain, and I was left with what appeared to be a slightly iridescent slime in the filter.

I set the filter on the oven rack inside my oven to dry as I cleaned a glass meth pipe, so I could try to smoke whatever the hell this was I had made. If whatever the hell this was, was even smokeable; I had to find out.

The slime dried to a white powdery substance that had kind of a silky sheen to it. I put the dried filter on my digital scales, and minus the weight of the filter, I had less than two grams of powder. I turned and looked at the sink, because, if this was actually dope, I had just poured what I would estimate to be about twenty grams of the stuff down the drain. Damn it!

I put some of the powder into my glass pipe and melted it by applying heat with a cigarette lighter. It melted, just like meth would, then dried to a crystallized form when I removed the heat. I melted it again and smelled the smoke. There was no smell at all. That was both good and bad, good because, if it had a bad smell, I didn't make meth. Bad because, all the meth I had ever smoked up to this point, had at least *some* kind of smell to it.

Finally, I gave it the taste test. I took a small hit off of the pipe, then blew it out without inhaling. I didn't taste anything, and that too was good and bad for the same reasons as before. At last, I took a big hit and inhaled. I held the smoke in for a few seconds, then blew it out. Still no taste, so I wasn't sure what, if anything, I had made.

I stood in my kitchen, smoking for about twenty minutes. I'd guess I had loaded my pipe four or five times, and smoked a half gram of this stuff, but I still didn't know if this was dope. I decided I'd need someone else to try it with me. It was about 3am, so I was going to have to wake Lisa up.

Lisa had been fairly patient with me during all of my experimentation, but I knew her patience was nearly at an end. If this wasn't meth I was waking her up to smoke, she was going to be pissed off; like, seriously pissed off. So, I had to come up with a plan.

The plan was, I would wake Lisa up and say to her, "Hey honey, get up and get in the bed where you will be more comfortable." She had been sleeping on the couch, where she had fallen asleep while watching TV. Once she got up, I would say, "While you're up, try this stuff out, and tell me what you think it is."

With my plan of action in place, I sat on the edge of the couch, and gently woke her up. "Are you going to sleep on the couch all fucking night, or do you want to go to bed?!" Okay, so maybe I didn't stick to the script I had planned out in my head, but she woke up.

Lisa sat up and asked if I was finished in the kitchen. I said that I was, and I had cleaned everything up. I cleaned up before I woke her up so she wouldn't be mad if I hadn't made dope.

Lisa sat there looking at me for a few minutes, (or maybe it was just seconds, I don't know, I was pretty fucked up on the stuff I had just made,) while I jabbered on about the kitchen being clean, and everything being put up. Suddenly, she jumped up and headed toward the kitchen. "Where the hell is it?" she asked.

"Where's what?" I replied. "You're fucked up out of your head! Where's the fucking dope?!"

I went to the kitchen as Lisa was using a razor blade to chop up some of the larger chunks the powder had formed into as it dried. I explained that I had made "something", but I wasn't sure exactly what it was.

Lisa picked up the pipe, which still had some in it, and took a hit. She looked at me and said, "It doesn't have any taste." I told her that I noticed that too, and that was one of the reasons I wasn't sure if this was really dope.

At this time, Lisa had been a meth user for more than 10 years. That's why it blew my mind, when she informed me that not only did I make meth, it was some of the best meth she had ever smoked in her entire life. Needless to say, I was pretty proud of myself. It was the summer of 2004, and I was finally a meth cook.

Now that Lisa had confirmed that what I made really was meth, I grabbed my phone and called Joey. I knew he would still be at work at The Sound. When he answered, I told him to stop by my house on his way home.

Joey got to our place just before 4am, and I handed him the pipe the second he walked through the door. "I finally did it!" is all I said. Joey pulled out his lighter and started taking some hard, fast hits from the pipe, which was his style of smoking. After about the fourth hit, Joey stopped, looked at me funny, then sat down in a chair beside where he was standing.

Joey was quiet for a minute. He just sat there, staring at the floor. Finally, he looks at me and asks, "You made this?"

"Yep, what do you think?" I replied.

He shook his head a little and then said, "I've been using meth for half my life, and I have never, ever gotten a rush from smoking it. Until now." That, to me, was the most awesome compliment I had ever had, and I couldn't wait for him to leave so I could have celebration sex with Lisa.

I want to mention now, that one thing that is more widespread than the manufacture and use of meth are the rumors about the stuff. In fact, most of what many people think they know about the drug and the lifestyle is completely wrong.

Many of these rumors involve the sexual habits of meth addicts. I read a statement once that said, "Meth addicts engage in orgies in front of their children, leaving them to themselves to scrounge for food." This was presented as a fact, as if this was something all meth addicts did.

That statement is just proof of the ignorance some "experts" like to spread. Not that things like that don't happen, because they do. But, if you do a study of people that have orgies in front of their children, I would be willing to bet that meth users would come out at the bottom of the list, under alcoholics, crack heads, and non-drug using perverts for one simple reason; If you get together enough meth addicts to have an orgy, nobody will shut up long enough to get naked. In fact, you'd have a better chance of everyone going outside to mow the grass and trim the hedges at 3am, than you would of having sex together.

Anyway, back on topic... In the meth world, there is a kind of unwritten rule that says, "Do not go around teaching people to cook." More cooks mean more competition, not only for the person doing the teaching, but for the entire area. Also, the more cooks there are, the better the chances of someone getting busted. I should know. More people getting busted, means there are more chances someone will tell on everyone else. Teaching people to cook just brings too much heat on everyone, so, no one likes for anyone to teach.

Since nobody taught me how to cook, I felt like my knowledge was my own to share with whomever I chose, and fuck anyone who didn't like it. Before Joey left my house that morning, I told him to come back around noon. I told him I was going to do another cook, and that I was going to teach him what I knew, since his cook didn't want to teach him. This really seemed to surprise Joey, but he said he would stop by later, and he left.

I didn't know it then, but I was about to be the one who got surprised.

Chapter 14

Once all of the stores opened, I headed out for more cook supplies. When I got home, Lisa helped me get all of the prep work done. She was back on board again as my partner. By the time Joey arrived, everything was set up in the kitchen and ready to go.

When Joey walked into my kitchen, he was acting a little strange. He just stood by the stove, kind of leaning against the counter, looking at the way I had my cooking apparatus set up. Finally, Joey looked at me and asked if he could show me something. I said he could and, in a very serious tone, Joey said, "I'm only going to show you this once. Watch everything I do, and don't say a word, or I'll leave." Okay, Mr. Mysterious, knock yourself out.

Joey began taking my lab apart, and reassembling it into a completely different configuration. The new set up was one I recognized from some of the anti-meth websites I had spent so many hours studying. On the sites, I saw dozens of different set ups of labs and related components. With some set ups, it was easy to figure out how everything worked. Others, I wasn't so sure of. This was one of the ones I wasn't sure of at all. I really hoped Joey knew what he was doing.

After Joey finished setting everything up the way he wanted it, he began mixing the ingredients and started the cook. Lisa and I just looked at each other. I could tell that she was just as confused as I was.

I watched Joey closely, and noticed a few things he did differently than I did. Several times during the cook, Joey would point at what was going on in the cook pot, and show me the temperature he was cooking at.

I watched as he would adjust the temperature up and down. I had never realized the temperature could be lowered at certain times to make the cook do what you wanted it to do. Joey would also point out the times of certain temperature changes. At one point, he even set the timer on the microwave and walked away, to let it cook untouched for a while.

After about an hour and a half, the cook was done, and we were sitting around smoking the meth that Joey had just made. Joey never spoke a word until the cook was finished, and everything was cleaned up.

Now that he was talking, and Lisa and myself were permitted to speak, I asked Joey, point blank, what was up with him knowing how to cook like that? He got serious, and said that the only people in the state of Tennessee who knew he was a cook were sitting in this room, and he expected it to stay that way. He said that the cook he helped out, and even his own wife didn't know that he could cook. To them, he was just Joey the dumbass helper.

When I asked him why he decided to show us that he could cook, he said it was because I offered to teach him what I knew, without asking for anything in return. He said that I was the only person to ever do that, so he decided to return the favor.

One of the most important things I learned from Joey was that, especially when it comes to a Red P cook, the more you handle the cook, the more dope you lose during the various processes. Joey showed me several shortcuts that saved time, and increased yield.

I asked Joey if he would hang out while I did another cook, that way, I could be sure I understood everything and could repeat the new things he had shown me. He agreed, and we started setting things up and doing some prep work, while Lisa went out for more pills. I didn't know it then, but my lessons for the day weren't over yet.

The cook went great, and as I was getting ready to gas off the dope, Joey said he was going to show me something else. Joey took an electric skillet I had, and laid a wire rack across it. Then, he told me to gas the puller lightly so that there was only a thin layer of dope in the coffee filter when I filtered it. I would repeat this step with a new coffee filter, over and over, until no more dope could be gassed out. This was only a half ounce batch, but I ended up using about forty filters.

As I got a filter ready, I handed it to Lisa, who would dry it on the rack over the hot plate, which was turned up pretty high. When the filter was dry, Lisa would set it in a stack with the rest of them. Joey never touched anything.

When we finally finished, we dumped all of the dope onto a plate. There was a huge pile. When I weighed it, I was surprised to find that there was only barely over a gram of dope there. This wasn't possible! How could all of this dope weigh only a gram? I changed the batteries in my scales and weighed it again. No difference. Finally, Joey started laughing his ass off. This was an old scam used by old school cooks when they would "help" a newer cook out.

The scam begins when the old timer makes an agreement to teach the newbie a new trick in exchange for the coffee filters when the cook is over. Coffee filters that have been used for filtering meth, are often used to make coffee with, because there is meth still embedded in the filter. I would sometimes sell filters for five dollars each to someone wanting dope, but who didn't have a lot of money.

The first trick to the scam is to get the newbie to use brake parts cleaner, or some other puller that makes the dope extremely fluffy when it's dried. This way it looks like there is more dope than what is really there.

The next trick is to be sure you, as the old cook, never touch anything. That way you are never suspected of ripping anyone off.

Once the newbie gasses the dope, the filters are dried over heat. The heat draws more of the dope into the filters. After all of the filters are emptied, the old cook leaves with the filters, and most the dope.

Joey showed me how to soak the filters out in alcohol to retrieve the meth. We ended up getting about ten more grams of dope out of the filters, to go with the pile of fluffy dope. This was dope I had never realized I had helped screw myself out of. It was a pretty cool trick, and I was just glad he did it to teach me, and not screw me over.

It had taken about six months to teach myself how to make meth, and I didn't even want to try to imagine how much money I had spent during that time on chemicals and other supplies. I think the worst part of it all was knowing that most of those cooks I had dumped down the drain were actually good cooks. I just didn't know at the time that they were good, because they did not, at least according to all of my research, do all of the things they were supposed to do.

If I had just had someone to tell me, "Mix this with this, then do that." like most meth cooks, I would have been cooking a lot sooner. Instead, I spent my time learning everything I could about cooking, and that is what I did wrong.

While the knowledge I acquired during those early months made me a better meth cook later, it slowed my progress during my learning period. I knew more than I needed to know, and that caused me to make things too complicated. I guess Lisa was right when she said I knew too much about it to do it.

I learned two more things that day I cooked with Joey. The first was that he had dropped the hint about the cooking temperatures on purpose. He said he figured that info would help me. He only hoped I would be smart enough to pick up on the hint when he threw it out there. Thankfully for my meth cook career, I was.

The second thing I learned was kind of weird at first. Joey got me off alone and told me not to trust those closest to me. He looked towards Lisa as he told me this. I figured he was just speaking generally, but if I had known what he already knew, I would have considered shoving Lisa's head into a bear trap.

Chapter 15

My motivation for learning to cook meth was to save money by supplying Lisa and myself with what was basically "free" dope. Forget the fact that knowing how to make it was just cool. Selling dope was never really part of the plan, because I didn't need to sell. I had a great paying job, and Lisa was working as well, so we had plenty of money coming in.

Now that I could manufacture meth, I wanted to cook every chance I had. This was costing money, although not as much as I was saving by not having to buy dope anymore.

Lisa and I were pretty heavy users, but we couldn't even come close to putting a dent in all the dope I was generating on a daily basis. I decided that it might not be a bad idea to start selling a little bit of the excess product I was producing. I just wanted to be sure I didn't get the reputation of being a cook in the process.

At first, there were only a few people that knew I could cook; me, Joey, Lisa, Shane, and the twins. That was everyone who knew, and that is how I wanted it to stay. I also didn't want anyone at all to know I was still cooking at home.

We came up with a story that we were cooking at one of Lisa's meth world friend's houses. When I was going to cook, we would tell everyone we would be gone from home for a few hours. We would hide one of the cars at the mall, or at a grocery store parking lot somewhere, then go back home and do the cook in the basement.

We covered all the basement windows and stayed down there until the cook was finished. That way, if someone came by the house, one of the cars would be gone, and the lights would be out.

I still didn't know anyone in the meth world other than Joey. Shane was just getting into smoking and didn't know anyone except for Lisa and me because we were the ones who got him on it in the first place. Tina's boyfriend, Bernie, was a smoker and knew a few people who bought some from time to time, but it wasn't much. That left us with Lisa's friends for us to try to build a market with.

Lisa took about a half ounce of meth one night and headed out. The plan was to distribute the dope to as many people as she could, for free. She was letting people know there was a new cook around, and giving away free samples was the best way to get a lot of people to try it without asking them to put out any cash for it. If they wanted more, they could call.

The plan worked great, and I began selling everything I could make. Money was rolling in, and Lisa and I were using more than we ever imagined possible. Cooking meth seemed to be taking over both of our lives. Lisa quit her job, and I changed from night shift to day shift, so I could cook at night to keep up with demand. When I was at work, I was constantly on the phone with Lisa to be sure she was doing all of the prep work, and moving product.

My using was way out of control also. I spent so much time at work in the restroom smoking, that people thought I was sick. Since working out was a thing of the past, and I wasn't eating at all, my weight loss added to the sickness theories.

Several times during my shift, I would duck down under my casting machine with my meth pipe to take a few hits. A few times I even went as far as to bring glass tubing to work so I could blow my own meth pipes using the torches on the assembly line.

I would be getting ready for work and smoking so much, that by the time I ran out the door and hauled ass to work, I was clocking in with only seconds to spare. On the days I did manage to leave for work on time, I would sit in my car, in the parking lot, smoking meth until I had to run inside to clock in for work just in the nick of time.

The company I worked for had a points system when it came to attendance. If you were up to four hours late, you get half a point. If you were more than four hours late, you got a full point. Once you hit ten points, you lost your job. Because of being late, and sometimes not even coming in at all, I was up to nine points in early November of 2004.

Lisa and I had been up all night arguing about something. I had not been to sleep in a couple of days, and I hadn't cooked, so I was out of dope.

Needless to say, I wasn't exactly happy or motivated in any sense of the words. I was so tired, I was about to fall over, but I had to go to work.

As I was getting dressed, Lisa pulls out a gram of ice. Ice is the crystallized form of meth, which I was not making. I wasn't sure where she got it from, and I really didn't care, I had to wake up.

We smoked the gram in record time, and I left for work wired out of my mind. I was halfway to work, when I noticed I had five minutes to get there and I still had ten minutes of driving time left to go. Suddenly, it seemed like a great idea to call in and quit my job. Hell, I was going to end up fired within a week anyway with the way I was going. Besides, I could make more money than I could spend if I cooked full time. That again, would be another example of the mind of a meth addict's logic.

So, I called in, quit, then turned around and headed home. When I got there, I told Lisa I had been fired, then I went to the basement to cook.

There were several problems with this idea that I didn't foresee happening. One of the problems was that the yield on my cooks weren't very high. Red P cooks are notorious for producing low yields as it is. With me still being a new cook, I didn't yet know all of the tricks I would learn later on that would get me more dope out of my cooks.

In those early days, I was getting about a 40% yield. That meant, for every ten grams of pseudo I started a cook with, I was getting four grams of finished product. That isn't very good when you consider the fact that Lisa and I were doing three to four grams each a day, every day. We were also smoking with the twins, Bernie, Joey, and Shane.

We had a lot of bills, with the mortgage payment, three car payments, and insurance on everything. I was also paying $100 bucks a week for child support. It didn't take long for us to start missing better than $1200 bucks a week between the two of us from what used to be our jobs.

Another huge drain on our supply was Lisa smoking with, and giving dope away to, everyone that she was supposed to be selling to. She would go on a run with several grams to sell, then come back several hours later with no dope and enough money to pay for about a half a gram.

Her excuse was always that she had smoked it with "this" person, or "that" person, to try to generate more customers. This normally would have been okay with me, and not bothered me at all. Unfortunately, this dope was now our only source of income, and we really needed the money.

Even though meth addiction is a lifestyle, I was treating it as a business, and trying to live life by the everyday rules of a working man, where home, family, and paying the bills come first. Since I did not work my way up the hierarchy of the meth subculture to become a cook, I didn't really understand how things were done in that world. I was about to watch two worlds collide, and I don't know how I ever survived it.

Chapter 16

Lisa and I were starting to argue all of the time. The arguments were always about the dope she was giving away and the amount of time she was staying gone from home when she was supposed to be out selling dope. I was never allowed to know where exactly she was going when she left to go sell and that was a huge issue for me as well.

When Lisa would get a call for some dope, she would say she was going to see "her friend on the mountain," or, "running over to Milligan Highway". These trips, that used to take less than an hour, started turning into four and five hour ventures, and I'd never hear from her.

There was always an excuse about why it had taken her so long. One night, while the twins were at the house, Lisa left to sell some dope. As soon as she left, I told the girls she would be gone at least two hours, and when she got back, she would have one of three excuses:

The person wanting the dope had to go somewhere, and she had to wait for him to get back.

By the time she got there, someone untrustworthy had shown up and they had to wait for the person to leave before doing the deal.

She was waiting on the money to be delivered.

When Lisa walked through the door, about five hours later, she started with her excuses. She gave not one, but all three of the excuses I told the twins she would be using. The girls started laughing their asses off, and when I told Lisa why they were laughing, she got mad and left. She didn't come home until the next day.

With so much dope going out, and so little money coming in, I was really in bad financial trouble. My truck, and one of the cars had been repossessed, and the house payment was two months behind. I told Lisa we needed to make some changes. It was time for me to meet some of her "friends", so that I could take over the business end of things, since she didn't seem to be doing a very good job of it herself.

Lisa said that she would talk to her people and ask if they would be willing to meet me. She told me these people were very careful about who they let into their little circle, and that the only reason they dealt with her in the first place, is because she had grown up around most of them. They knew she could be trusted.

That was good, because, as I explained to her, since they knew she could be trusted, then they should have no problem at all trusting someone she trusted herself. Especially since that person is her own husband.

I gave her a few days, and she finally said that a few of her friends would be willing to meet me. It just couldn't happen right away. These people were mostly truck drivers, or had out of town jobs, and they would all be gone for a few weeks. But once they got home, we could meet.

I know, I know. Could I really be that stupid as to believe a bunch of bullshit like that? You'll have to understand, around this time I was so strung out that I was pretty easily convinced of anything. I accepted her story as fact, and it went back to business as usual. It never even crossed my mind to wonder where Lisa was going with all of the dope, if everyone was out of town.

One day, Lisa gets a call from someone wanting to trade some ice for some of my dope. While ice is supposed to be a purer form of meth, mine was definitely stronger, and you got a more intense high from it. I told her to go ahead and make the trade, since we had not done any ice in a while.

Lisa left, and after a few hours, I started calling her cell phone to ask where the hell she was at. Her phone was off, but I kept calling anyway, and leaving voicemails. Finally, Lisa calls me back and says she is almost home. I asked what was taking so long, and she said she would explain when she got home. There was something weird about her voice, so I didn't ask any more questions.

Lisa got home a few minutes after we hung up. When she came in the door, she looked really freaked out. I asked if she was okay, and she said she was, but she just needed to think for a few minutes. "Did you get the ice?" I inquired. She did, and she handed it to me.

We sat and smoked the ice, while Lisa told me what had taken so long. She said that she had stopped to pick up Faye to ride with her. Once they got to the friend's house, they had to wait for her husband to get there with the ice. He had gone to North Carolina to get it. A fairly short drive from where they lived.

While they waited, the husband had called. The truck he was in broke down, and he asked for them to bring a tool box. They all got into Lisa's car, and headed to where he had said he broke down. When they got there, there were two cop cars pulled in behind the truck.

The friend gets out, then walks over to the truck with the tool box. After a few minutes, the friend walks back to Lisa's car. She leans in the window, and drops a package with two ounces of ice in it onto the floor, and tells Lisa to "go wait at our house." So, she did.

Once the people got back, Lisa did her trade, then dropped Faye off on her way home. The reason she was so freaked out she said, was because her friends had almost been busted. That sounded reasonable, so I left it alone.

Later that night, Lisa said, that while she was at her friend's house, they told her to tell me to stop buying so many pills at the Wal-Mart in Elizabethton. They also said I needed to get all my cook stuff out of the house.

I asked Lisa, how the hell do they know I'm cooking at home? No one but me, Lisa, and the twins, knew I was cooking at home. She said she didn't tell anyone I was cooking at home, and she could not explain how they would know where I was buying my pseudo pills. I decided to ignore it, despite the fact that this would turn out to be an unwise decision on my part.

Lisa got off the phone one morning, and said she had to go over to Milligan Highway. It was important. I was just about to start a cook, so I didn't really care where she went. I was focused on work. She took what dope we had, and said she would get rid of it while she was gone. Good idea, since we were completely broke.

Sometime late the next day, Lisa had finally come back home. I was ready to kill her. This was getting ridiculous. She had never been gone for over twenty-four hours before. I had spent most of the time she was gone freaking out because I was convinced she had gotten busted. Now that she was standing there in front of me, acting as if she had done nothing wrong, I was convinced she had been out whoring around all night.

I went off on her, and we started fighting. This went on for hours, when I suddenly remembered all the dope she took with her when she left. I told her to give me the money, and she handed me a hundred dollar bill. I told her she had taken a hell of a lot more than a hundred bucks worth of dope, and she had better come up with the rest of the money. Lisa, trying to act excited, said she would explain everything to me, if I would just calm down and stop screaming at her. In my defense, I wasn't really "screaming." I was speaking in a tone, and with proper volume, as to convey my unhappiness with her un-thoughtful actions. Fine, I quit screaming.

She said she had some great news, and that, once I calmed down, we would discuss it. Sure, I'll calm down for some great news. I couldn't wait to hear this.

Chapter 17

Lisa had said that when she got to her friend's house there was someone there she had never met. She was introduced to Bob, who she was told, was an old-school cook who had quit cooking a long time ago.

Bob told Lisa that he was still heavily connected with the meth world, and that he had the means and the money to supply and run a high volume lab. He said he wanted to make high quality meth, and after seeing the quality of the dope Lisa was selling, arranged for them to meet.

Bob had a plan. He wanted to teach someone to cook, his way. Once the cook was trained, that person would show up where directed, do the cook, and then leave. Everything would be at the cook spot waiting to be cooked when the person got there.

When the cook was completed, everything, including the finished product, would be left at the cook spot, and someone else would come in to collect the dope and do the clean up. Payment for doing the cook would be picked up later. No one but Bob would know who the cook was.

For a cook in my situation, this sounded like the opportunity of a lifetime. There was only one hitch; Bob didn't want to teach another cook. He wanted to teach someone who had been around a cook enough to understand what was going on in a lab, but didn't actually know how to do a cook; less bad habits to break. He wanted to teach Lisa.

This was complete bullshit, and I was not going for it at all. I was just about to unload on Lisa and tell her exactly what I thought of the idea, when she pulls out this bag of pure pseudo and said it was a gift from Bob. It weighed a hundred and fifteen grams. Sure, honey, take the job!

Bob was extremely paranoid. Lisa said he had been busted once, and he wasn't looking forward to having it happen again. For security reasons, Bob would call Lisa and tell her where to meet him to learn whatever step in the process he was teaching her. When he called, he would give her the meeting place, and a certain amount of time to get there. If she was late, the lesson was over until next time.

This was Bob's way of being sure Lisa wasn't working for the cops. If Lisa got a call at 4 a.m. and had twenty minutes to dress and drive from Elizabethton to Johnson City, that left no time for her to get wired by the cops. It was not uncommon for the phone to ring in the middle of the night, and Lisa would jump up and run out the door. It pissed me off a time or two when she got a call while we were having sex, but that was business.

I started having problems with this whole arrangement when Lisa started staying gone for several days at a time. Many times she would be gone to sell dope, and would get a call to go to a "cooking lesson." As usual, she would come home with barely enough money to resupply for another cook. Since I would be out of dope myself by the time she got home, just knowing I was going to get to cook soon would be enough to keep me from being too pissed off at her.

Normally, Lisa would go to sleep right after she got home, and I would go buy supplies for another cook. By the time Lisa woke up, I would be finished cooking. She would take all of the dope, except for what I was keeping for myself, and leave. It was the same process over and over again.

Joy, Lisa's youngest daughter, had a birthday coming up, so we decided to put everything else on hold, so we could have a birthday party for her. We scrubbed the entire inside of the house and stashed the lab. Lisa spent two days decorating for the party, and also buying food and Joy's presents.

During those two days, I started piling dozens of trash bags full of cook trash into a small space under the basement stairs. I had let the trash build up, because I really didn't have anywhere to dump the shit. Once all of the trash was packed in, I built kind of a false wall around it, so it was somewhat concealed.

These couple of days were great. We were so focused on making Joy's day special, that we never argued about anything the entire time. I wasn't cooking, and Lisa was there with me, so it was almost like our early days together. Since we were also sleeping at night, my head was beginning to clear. I was starting to realize how screwed up we had become, and I wanted to go back to the way things were.

The day of the party came, and besides Faye, Tina, Levi and Joy, we were visited by Lisa's parents, her sisters, Katy and FJ, FJ's daughter Chris, and a few family friends. Lisa had prepared a huge birthday dinner along with cake and ice cream. It was all very normal, considering the circumstances, and Joy had a great time.

By late afternoon, everyone was clearing out. Tina left with Bernie, and Faye, Joy, and Levi were staying with us for the weekend. That left us with one problem. We were out of dope, and we never did a cook with Joy and/or Levi at the house. That was one of the few rules we had that were unbreakable.

While I loved the normal-seeming family thing we had going, I was still addicted to meth. It was decided that Lisa would take the kids to see a movie, while I stayed at home to do a quick cook.

I had to go to Wal-Mart for a few boxes of pills and a couple other supplies. While I was gone to buy everything, Lisa went down into the basement to set the lab up. This was to save time.

I bought what I needed from Wal-Mart, then left. As I was leaving the parking lot, I remembered that I needed cigarettes. I drove to a grocery store in a shopping center that was next to the Wal-Mart. I got out of my car and started walking towards the store. No big deal, just a regular guy with a shit ton of meth supplies in his car getting a pack of smokes. That's when I noticed two cop cars driving through the parking lot, away from Wal-Mart and past where I now was, at a higher than normal rate of speed. This felt wrong.

When I got back to my car with my cigarettes, I just sat there for a few minutes with the feeling that something really bad was about to happen. I got back out of the car, and put the meth supplies I had purchased at Wal-Mart into the trunk of my car before driving towards home.

As I left the parking lot, I stayed alert for anything unusual that might be going on. When I stopped for a stop sign, a police officer approaching from the opposite direction stopped his car just as he passed mine. I could see in the side mirror that he was checking the license plate on my car. He continued to drive on, but I knew at that moment I was in trouble. I just didn't know how much trouble or what kind of trouble exactly.

I kept driving towards home, being very careful to obey all traffic laws and hoping no cops got behind me. Just as I was about to make a right turn onto my street, I saw another cop coming at me from the opposite direction again. Knowing something was up, I hit my turn signal to try to hurry and make the turn.

Because of the way the road was slanted, and the way my car was traveling down the road, I had to hold the signal switch in my car up while making the turn, so my signal light would blink as I made the turn. This was a hell of a thing to accomplish, because I was pushing the clutch with one foot, while using the other leg to hold the steering wheel where it needed to be, while I shifted into first gear. With all this going on, there's no way in hell I could be mistaken about whether or not I signaled.

The cop pulled in right on my ass as I made my turn. He followed as closely as he possibly could, but I wouldn't go over the fifteen mile per hour speed limit on my street. I parked along the curb in the front of my house, and that's when the cop hit his blue lights. Two other cop cars came out of nowhere, and boxed me in. You can imagine my stomach doing flips as I thought, "Oh shit, this can't be good."

I opened my door to get out of my car, but the cop who pulled me over ran up to my car screaming at me not to move and to stay in the car. The cop said he wanted my license and insurance. I gave him the license, but I had to tell him I didn't have insurance. He went back to his car, and I waited.

Within a few minutes, our little party was joined by two more cops. One of these was a Captain with the Elizabethton City Police Department. The captain walked up to the driver's side of my car, while the other cop approached on the passenger's side. The captain asked where I was coming from, and I told him. "I had just come home from buying some cigarettes." Okay, I get partial credit for the partial truth.

The captain then proceeded to question where the pseudo I had just purchased at Wal-Mart was. I lied, as you'd expect one to do in this situation, and said that I had no idea at all what he was talking about. He then asked me if he could search my car. I told him no, of course, he had no right or probable cause to do so at all. He asked what it was I was hiding, and I said, "Not a damn thing, give me my ticket, and leave me the fuck alone." This wasn't fun anymore.

The captain informed me that he believed I was in possession of precursors to manufacture meth. He ordered me out of my car, which I did, locking the door on my way out. This pissed off all of the cops, who then threatened to bust out my windows, if they had to, to get inside. I told them they'd better get a warrant, because, while I didn't have shit to hide (Well I did, but it's a matter of principal at this point.) I wasn't giving anyone permission to search my car.

They called the K-9 unit and, when they walked the dog around my car, the fucking mutt went nuts. This was all the cops needed. They took my keys and started searching my car.

While my car was being searched, I was approached by a couple of guys who introduced themselves as agents with the Meth Task Force. This meant nothing to me, but they seemed pretty proud of themselves, so I took their word for it.

The agent who seemed to be in charge was a short, red-headed dude who seemed a little too feminine. We will call this guy, "Agent W." Agent W asked me what the cops were going to find in my car. I assured him that he wouldn't find anything illegal, and he said that was good, and suggested we go inside the house so we could sit down and talk.

We started walking towards the front door of my house, when I thought better of it, and sat down in a chair on the porch. I offered the agent a chair, but he said it would be better if we went inside. The other agent, as well as several of the cops, were standing there, waiting to go in my house, but I refused to go in, or let them in. At least, in this situation, I knew better than that.

Agent W got pissed off, and walked away. He walked around my house and when he was finished trying to peek inside the windows, he asked me why someone was going in and out of the basement. He said that there were blankets over the basement windows that he said were suspicious enough in and of itself, but he could also see the lights going on and off. I told him that my wife was probably going down there to do laundry, and that the blankets were there to keep perverts from looking in. (Phew, way to think under pressure.) I don't think he got the jab at him with that last line though.

Agent W finally figured out I wasn't going to agree to anyone coming into my house, so he played his trump card. He informed me, that due to some of the items found in my car, he believed there was a meth lab in the house. He said he was going to have everyone in the house come outside and wait, while he got a search warrant. This could take hours.

Joy had asthma and got sick fairly easily, so I was worried about her having to come outside. It was getting cold. I figured I had to do something quickly, so I told Agent W, that if he would allow Lisa to leave with the kids, I would sign a "consent to search" form. He was all for it, and told me to tell Lisa to pack a bag, because she would need to stay gone all night while they conducted their search. Little did they know that the bag she was going to pack was going to totally save my ass a lot of trouble; for the moment anyway.

Chapter 18

Agent W and I walked through the door, and Lisa was instantly the scared, confused lady of the house. I told her to pack a bag, take the kids, leave, and I would explain everything later. Faye said she would pack a bag, and within five minutes, Lisa had Joy and Levi in the car. As Faye walked out with the duffel bag full of clothes, she winked at me and said, "Don't worry." Easy for her to say.

Once the consent form was signed, Agent W said, "I want to see the basement first." I told him that was fine with me, and he told the other agent to have the cops look around upstairs.

My basement was pretty big and wide open. You could stand at the foot of the stairs and see everything. Since it was an unfinished basement, the only things down there were the water heater, and the washer/dryer.

Also in my basement, there was an old, "butcher block" styled kitchen table and a couple of tool boxes. The kitchen table was where my lab should have been sitting.

We got into the basement, and Agent W looked around for a second, then asked, "Where is the meth lab?" I looked at him just as innocently as I could and asked him, "What meth lab?" It was GONE! He started to get pissed again, and informed me that he was not there to play games. I told him, I wasn't playing games either. I had agreed to let him in the house to search, and that is what he was currently doing. I never said he would find anything.

Agent W stormed back upstairs to the kitchen, and I followed him. He asked the other agent if he had found anything, and he said he hadn't found anything other than a bunch of clean mason jars in the dishwasher. One must keep one's glassware clean. That's a rule.

Agent W must have been getting worried. Here, he had half the cops in the whole damn town in my yard, and as of that moment, it was basically for nothing. He looked at me and said, "Listen. I'm the guy that decides if you go to jail tonight or not. As of right now, you are not under arrest. I'll make you a deal. Give me whatever you have in this house that's meth related, and as long as you don't have an active cook going on somewhere in here, I'll only charge you with felony possession of drug paraphernalia, and you'll spend the night at home tonight. If I have to search, I'll tear this house apart, and I promise, I will find more than enough to send you to jail."

That threat was very real, because I could go into virtually any house in America, and find three components to a meth lab. Three items are all that are needed to charge you with a meth felony. These items include, but are not limited to; aluminum foil, coffee filters, hydrogen peroxide, glue, tape, aquarium air pumps and air lines, batteries, empty soda bottles, gas line antifreeze, starting fluids, camp fuels, paint thinners, and even the good old fashioned nickel. Yep, the loose change in your pocket can be used, along with your pillow case, (another component) and a few other things, to make meth.

So, as you can see, damn near everyone in America has a meth lab in their possession. Don't worry though, chances are the cops aren't going to crash through your door and bust you. They have to profile you first.

Knowing I was screwed no matter what, and with my lab sitting somewhere in the house just waiting to be found, I agreed to tell him where the stuff under the stairs was. I had to take a chance that he would keep his word and not take me to jail.

Emergency response showed up, with their huge, spot-light covered truck that lit up my house like it was the fucking sun. It was actually around 9pm. There was no mistaking why they were there, since people were running around wearing chemical masks and suits. The truck also said, in huge red letters on the side of it, "STOP METH", just in case someone was left who didn't fully understand it.

While someone started removing the trash from my basement and lying it all out on tarps in my front yard for the whole world to see, some of the cops went to my neighbor's houses and evacuated the area. Not only did they evacuate them, but they also made everyone go to the hospital to get blood tests to see if they had any medical issues due to living next door to a meth lab. Apparently, I was extremely popular with the entire county's different forms of police, for giving them something to finally do in this Podunk town, and I was suddenly very unpopular with most of my neighbors.

I would find out later that a cop was at the emergency room that night bragging that the lab they found was *big enough to fill the whole E.R. waiting room*, which, as you and I know is complete and utter bullshit because they never got a lab at all. The only thing they got was a bunch of cook trash from several months' worth of cooks. The lab had gone out the door in the duffel bag Faye had packed, then proceeded to carry out right in front of all of those stupid ass cops. That's one hell of a fifteen year old girl.

It took several hours to bring all the trash up out of the basement, lay it out, inventory it, and seal it all up in fifty gallon drums. Just about the time they were finishing, the local news showed up. Agent W told me that since the news media had showed up, he was going to have to arrest me, even though we had a deal. Personally, I think the cock-sucker called them himself; double-crossing son of a bitch.

I spent four days in jail, before Lisa's mom and sister could get me out on a property bond. When Lisa picked me up at the jail, she said that the drug agents had called her and told her that nobody was allowed to go inside our house until I got out of jail. They didn't care that Lisa was my wife, and had every right to go in and out whenever she wanted.

Surprisingly, the cops didn't fuck up my house when they searched. They did however, take every piece of Pyrex, and every glass jar out of my kitchen.

I found a binder that had all of my meth recipes, as well as other related research, lying on a shelf in the linen closet under a blanket. Lisa said that was where she had hidden all of my Uncle Fester books. I'm guessing, some idiot, had found the recipes and then found the books, and had gotten so excited with his find, that he laid the binder down and completely forgot about it.

That was absolutely retarded, because the binder was excellent evidence against me, where as the Uncle Fester books could simply be reordered right off the Internet. There isn't a law that I know of against owning books.

There were a few weird things we did notice right away though, once we got to looking around. The first was that someone had removed a drawer from our dresser and put it on the bed. The drawer contained Lisa's lingerie, so we just figured some of the cops were just being pervs and sniffing the crotches or something.

Since Lisa didn't know who had their grubby little dick beaters on her undies, she decided to wash everything. When she picked the stuff up, a bag, full of various pain pills was lying on the bottom of the drawer. We had lost this bag a couple of weeks earlier, and thought that Tina had stolen them. Once we found this bag of pills in this drawer that was purposefully left out, we figured it was some sort of message.

Our second "message" came when Lisa found a dope baggie, ripped open, floating in the toilet. We both recognized the baggie as one we had some dope stashed in for hard times. When we checked our little stash spot, the dope was missing. This was crazy, because I was not charged with possession of any drugs, yet here was proof that they could have charged me several times.

The strangest find, was the 8-ball, (One-eighth of an ounce) of meth that Lisa found in the vacuum cleaner. There was a large area rug we had put in our living room. Instead of having to move the coffee table to roll up the rug so it could be taken outside and shaken out, Lisa would just vacuum it with an old vacuum cleaner I had in a storage closet.

When Lisa went to vacuum the carpet, she noticed a large lump where the vacuum cleaner bag was. She unzipped it, and found a large ball of aluminum foil. When she unfolded the foil, there was an 8-ball of meth inside. We smoked it, and discovered it was anhydrous ammonia made dope. I was making higher quality Red P based dope, so I knew it wasn't mine. This was a set up.

We straightened up the house, and Lisa went out to the car to get my lab. I couldn't believe she had brought it with her to pick me up at the jail. I figured the last thing the cops would even expect me to do when I got home, would be to cook up a batch of dope. So, that's exactly what I did; business as usual.

Chapter 19

Not long after the bust, Lisa and I more or less split up. I wouldn't call what we had a marriage anymore anyhow, so it wasn't surprising when Lisa had told me she thought we should just have a business relationship.

Things for me got even worse. The electric and water were turned off because the bills hadn't been paid in a couple months, and the house was being foreclosed on. My truck got repossessed, and my car went soon after that.

It was getting into the middle of December, and it was getting very, very cold. I moved a futon out into the dining room with my computer desk, and a kerosene heater. I hung blankets over the doorways to keep the heat in the dining room, and the heater also happened to be my source of heat for cooking meth.

Every couple of days, Lisa would stop by the house for a few hours. We would get cook supplies, something to eat, and we would get a two and a half gallon kerosene can filled. The can would last about forty-eight hours in my little heater. I also had several gallon milk jugs that I would fill with water at the car wash. This water was used for bathing, flushing the toilet, and washing jars, and anything else that needed cleaning. I sure was living high on the hog at this point in life.

One day, when Lisa showed up, I took her phone and keys from her. I was tired of her fucking around. I was tired of never getting anything but excuses for my dope. When Lisa was at home, all I ever heard about was "Bob this" and "Bob that." I was getting tired of that shit too. FUCK BOB!

Although I had never met Bob, I hated the man. This motherfucker, in my way of thinking, was the reason my life was going to shit. Who the fuck did this dude think he was, running around with *my* wife? I wasn't going to take this anymore, and I made sure Lisa wasn't going anywhere.

Lisa tried to convince me that I was only hurting myself by not letting her leave. She was suddenly worried that we were about to lose the house, and she said she wanted to get our lives back on track. Of course, this could only be accomplished by me letting her go back to the same shit she had been up to, whatever that was.

While we argued, Lisa ended up dropping a bombshell on me that I wasn't expecting. Lisa informed me, that not only did she know how to cook now; she had already done a very large cook for Bob. I didn't believe her, but decided to test her, so I set up the lab, did all the prep work, then told her to have at it. To my surprise, she pulled it off. Now, I'm not sure if she had learned from Bob, someone else, or if she had just seen me cook so many times, that she figured it out, but, regardless of how she learned, I was a little bit impressed.

We talked for a while, and Lisa seemed to honestly want to go back to a normal life. I ended up telling her she could go sell the dope she just cooked, but she had better bring back *all* of the money from the dope she was taking. I also told her, if she saw Bob, she could tell him she wouldn't be around anymore. Lisa said she would be fine with all of that, so I gave her the car keys, and she left.

I really didn't expect Lisa to show back up for at least a couple of days, no matter what we had just talked about. That's why I didn't know what to think when she actually pulled back into the driveway just a few hours later. She said she had dropped the dope off with someone, and that she'd have to go pick up the money later.

While we waited, Lisa gave me a few boxes of pills that she had gotten while she was out, so I started a small cook just to kill time. While I was finishing the cook, Lisa's phone rang. I figured it was someone calling to tell her to come pick up the money. Lisa walked into another room to talk, and I couldn't hear what was being said.

When Lisa got off the phone, she said it was Bob. I was immediately pissed off and asked her if she told him to fuck off. She said she didn't get a chance to, because he had called to ask a favor from *me*.

According to Lisa, Bob needed four ounces of dope cooked right away. Since Lisa didn't have much experience, he didn't want to trust the cook to her, so he wanted to know if I would do the cook. He said he had a camper set up in a secluded area with everything I needed. All I had to do was cook, then leave. I would be paid fourteen hundred dollars per ounce when the cook was completed. The only catch was Bob wanted to be there for the cook.

I was a little skeptical about this whole thing. Bob, supposedly, was a cook himself, so why not do his own cook if it was that important? According to Lisa, Bob was an anhydrous ammonia cook, not a Red P cook, and he needed Red P dope for his customer. Red P cooks were rare in our area, and I was actually considered to be the best they had in the area, so I was the one he wanted for the cook.

This brought about a new question. If Bob didn't know how to cook Red P dope, who had Lisa been learning from? This started one hell of a fight, because Lisa's only answer to that question was, "Don't ask me a question you don't want the answer to."

Finally, I told Lisa to tell Bob I would do the cook. She had convinced me that this money would be what we needed to save the house and start over. That's all I wanted anyway, so the rest was unimportant.

Lisa was about to go pick up Bob. As she was about to leave, I was getting my 9mm out of my curio cabinet, so I could get it loaded and ready to go. Lisa asked me what I was doing, and I told her that I didn't know or trust this "Bob" dude, so I was taking my gun. That way, if he tried something stupid, I could protect myself. She seemed a little freaked out about it, but she left to get Bob. She never showed back up to go do the cook. I wasn't surprised, and luckily, I still had all of the dope from the small cook I had done earlier.

Lisa disappeared for about a week after that. During that time, I got a hold of my old workout partner, Harley, to see if he could give me a ride to The Sound, so I could move some dope myself. I wasn't sure if I would be able to, but I figured Shane or Joey would help me out once I got there. Shane and Joey had stopped coming around my house. I'm guessing this was in part because of my bust, and probably in part because of my overall condition. I was in pretty rough shape with the weight loss, and going days and days without sleep.

Since Joey had been a meth user for so long, he knew that staying awake as long as possible is just a part of being a meth addict. Something else common among meth users are hallucinations. These hallucinations are more of a side effect from lack of sleep than from the actual drug use. While it would be difficult to find a meth addict who has not experienced at least one, very real seeming, hallucination, a lot of meth users do not like them at all. Fortunately for me, I enjoyed them very much.

Chapter 20

When meth addicts get together to talk, the talk always turns to the things they have seen after days of partying with no sleep. Some hallucinations are so common that they are experienced by meth users everywhere. The most common of these are universally known in the meth world as "Shadow People."

Shadow people come at night when all the inanimate objects take on a whole new life of their own. To a person who's been up a little too long, shadow people can be anything from a cop, to a nosy neighbor, to a roving band of ninja assassins. In reality, all the person is seeing is nothing more than the shadows cast by cars, bushes, garbage cans, and other things you'd expect normal casting of shadows from.

When we get in this mental state, we can get pretty delusional; most of the time, we think we are being watched. Sometimes, we even think there are other people in the house. I've even thought there was someone in the same room with me and I just couldn't turn around fast enough to catch him standing behind me. As ridiculous as this sounds you will never convince us that what we are seeing isn't real, because, well, we can see it.

It is not uncommon for others to start to feed off of someone else's hallucinations. An example of this is one night when Lisa and I were "geeked out" together. If you are geeked out, you have been up long enough to be seeing shit, hearing shit, and most likely, doing really stupid shit. If you are "shot out," you are just basically a zombie in retarded mode. I tend to get shot out on occasion.

This particular night, we were doing a cook in the dining room, on the kerosene heater. Lisa got it in her head that someone was trying to break into the house through the basement door. She would say, "Shh.... listen, can you hear that?" It didn't take long for me to "hear it."

I went quietly into the basement and tied a string to the door, then ran the string up through a water pipe access panel in the upstairs linen closet. I then took the opposite end of the string and tied it to an empty soda bottle, and once I pulled it tight, I laid the bottle in the middle of the dining room floor. Thus, my Meth-Addict-Platinum Security System was complete.

I took the cook pot off of the heater and Lisa and I laid in the middle of the dining room floor, staring at the fucking bottle, all throughout the night. Every few minutes, one of us would say, "Did you see it?! It moved!" I don't know what the hell we would have done if that bottle would have actually took off across the floor right in front of us. I'd venture a guess that crapping our pants would come to mind.

There was another incident that happened, during the day, where an intense paranoia and hallucination were caused by an outside force. Lisa and I were arguing, she was in the kitchen, and I was in the living room. Suddenly, there was this incredibly loud sound from right outside the dining room window. It sounded like someone was tearing a hole through the wall.

The problem with actual sounds is, when they really happen, we can't tell when it's an actual sound, or just another hallucination. Following this logic, Lisa grabbed a large knife from a kitchen drawer. I had my gun. Lisa climbed into the cabinet under the sink to hide. I got in the fireplace. The fireplace didn't work, because the chimney liner was falling apart, so I was "safe" there.

We stayed like that for hours, whispering back and forth, then decided to try to make it to the dining room without whatever it was that had made the loud sound "getting" us. We agreed, tactically I might add, to meet up again under the dining room table. By the time I belly crawled to the French doors that separated the dining room and living room, Lisa had made it safely to the kitchen doorway. We agreed, on the count of three, we would make a break for the table. One. Two. Three. GO! GO! GO! Crawling as fast as possible, we made it. (Phew.)

We stayed under that table all afternoon. Finally, gun in hand; I decided to try to get outside to see what the hell the noise had been. For some reason, I had felt that if I could get out the door and onto the front porch, (Where "it" was,) I would be safe. The tricky part was just getting out of the house without "it" knowing.

Keeping my back to the wall and pistol at the ready, I slowly made my way towards the front door. Once I was at the door, I unlocked the deadbolt, and backed out onto the porch to "safety." I walked around the porch to the side of the house, to find that one end of the vinyl soffit had fallen down. This pulled the rest of the soffit down, and it was still attached at the far end of the house. As the soffit fell, it scraped down the side of the vinyl siding, causing a hell of a lot of noise.

Now that I knew we were safe, I couldn't help fucking with Lisa. I walked over to the window and started beating on it, while yelling as if a bear was eating me. Lisa started screaming, then her face appeared in the lower panes of the window. She looked terrified, and I started laughing. She got mad, and called me every kind of motherfucker she could think of, but we were both relieved that the tension was over.

Chapter 21

Harley picked me up at my house and we headed to Johnson City. Harley said he had heard about my bust. No big surprise there, as it had been all over the news for at least a week. "The Big Bust," is what it was being called by the local media. Biggest meth lab bust in the history of Carter County, TN., as of then, 2004. Five years later, the feds would refer to that bust as one of the largest recoveries in the eastern United States. Whatever the hell that means.

Harley asked me how much I actually knew about the bust. "Well, quite a lot, actually. I was there after all." I had told him. He said that what he meant was, do I even know how the cops got onto me? I admitted that I didn't. All I really knew was that the news had said that the cops had been trying to pull me over to bust me, for five weeks now, but each time, I had "eluded" them. I didn't even know that they had tried to get me; I didn't even know I knew how to "elude" anything. Hearing all this, made me feel like a real criminal. Mama would have been proud. Sometimes, I even impress myself.

Harley had a lot of friends who ride Harley's, and Harley was a good bike mechanic, so several of his friends would bring their bikes to him for tune-ups and repairs. Some of these friends are cops, and one of these cops told Harley, (Not knowing we were friends,) a story about my bust.

According to the cop, Lisa, and one of her kids, was in Unicoi County conducting a drug deal, when SHE got busted. The cops threatened to throw her in jail, and take her kid, if she didn't give them some info. She gave them a cook. I'll leave you to guess who that cook might be, but in case you're mistaken the first time, it was ME.

At first, I didn't believe it. Then I remembered that night she told me "her friend" almost got busted. She had Faye with her that night. That night was also about five weeks before I got busted, and if the story was true, it would explain why "a friend" knew so much about where I was cooking, and buying my pills. Was Lisa trying to warn me with that story? I don't know.

We got to The Sound, and Harley dropped me off, telling me to call if I needed a ride home. I started walking around the parking lot until I found Joey who was sitting in his car getting high. Unfortunately, he had a shitload of dope he was trying to sell for his cook, so he couldn't move any of mine.

We talked for a while and I told him what Harley had said. Joey told me he believed it. He also told me that the day he had shown me he could cook; Lisa had told him that she would be willing to work with him instead of with me to try to break into the meth market, but he had refused. Joey said he had "heard things," and that I needed to avoid Lisa if I could.

I went into the club and found Shane. He was able to sell a couple grams for me right away. We hung out and drank a few beers, then I hooked up with someone else I knew from the club, and we decided to go out to his car to smoke a little dope. As we walked out the door, a large, bald dude was coming in. He stopped, and said to me, "Hey man, you need to call me. It's been a while." I didn't know who this guy was, and figured he was drunk, and simply mistaken me for someone else, so I just said, "Alright, I'll do that," and kept walking.

Jerry (the person I was going to get high with) and I, got to his car and he said something like, "I'm just going to go ahead and leave." Or something to that effect. I said that was cool, and we could get together some other time to get high.

I went back inside and found Shane. We were standing by some pool tables with a few other guys when that bald dude yelled my name and waved at me with a smile. I looked at Shane and asked, "Who the fuck is that?"

He said, "Drug Task Force cop..." I then noticed everyone in our little group looking at me a little funny, so I decided to leave.

I had to walk everywhere I needed to go buy cook supplies, so I was really limited on how much I could buy. This meant I had to do small cooks, which was barely enough to cover my own use.

I went out and bought supplies for a cook one day with the last of my money. When I got home, I realized I had forgotten to buy kerosene. There was still a little in the heater, so I just hoped it would be enough.

Of course, it wasn't. I ended up having to take an aluminum pot out of the cabinet, put a roll of toilet paper in the pot, and then poured in some acetone. I lit the roll of toilet paper, and used the flame to finish the cook. It worked, so I was pretty happy with that.

Once the cook was finished, I stashed my lab outside. I started doing this after my bust. I put the cook trash in a bag to dump in the dumpster at the car wash and after doing so, I went to the store to sell a gram of dope to the girl working there. She had wanted some, and this was the first chance I was able to get back to her.

After the sale, I was walking back home, when the cops stopped me. They searched me, and said they had orders to detain me. They claimed they didn't know WHY they were supposed to detain me just that they were told to do so; your tax dollars at work. After waiting almost an hour, who else would pull up, but good old Agent W. He jumped out of his vehicle and immediately started accusing me of going to Johnson City to buy several cases of meth cook supplies.

Agent W and I argued for a few minutes about his accusations, and I pointed out the very obvious fact that I had no fucking vehicle to go to Johnson City in. Lisa and I were split up, and she had her car. The rest of the cars had been repo'd.

This, as you might expect, wasn't convincing enough for Agent W. He said that he believed I had been cooking at the house again, and he wanted to search my house. I said he could, so we got in the car and went to my humble abode, followed by the two local cops who had detained me.

When we got to my house, I signed yet another "Consent to Search" form, and we all went inside. Agent W walked around and slowly made his way to the closet where the vacuum cleaner was. Mysteriously, he knew exactly where specifically to search, and decided to pull out the vacuum cleaner and unzip the bag. I then knew, if it wasn't blatantly obvious in the first place that the dope left in there had been a set up by the cops.

When Agent W didn't find the dope, he went down to the basement for a few minutes, then came back upstairs and told the cops they could leave. Once the cops were gone, Agent W and I had a nice little heart to heart.

He said, "I guess you think you're pretty slick finding that dope."

I told him, "Well, you shouldn't have left it there if you didn't want it smoked."

Agent W sat down and was quiet for a few minutes. Finally, he asked me if I realized he had done me a favor on the night I got busted by not charging me for the drugs he found. I did acknowledge, (although I didn't really want to) that yes he did do me this favor, and I thanked him. Agent W said I could thank him by returning the favor. "How?"

Agent W began to ask how well I knew Bob. "Not at all," I had said I told him I knew his name, but that's about it. Agent W said that Bob had once offered to work for him, in exchange for getting a walk on a meth charge several years earlier. Once Bob got his walk, he screwed him over, refusing to work for him. Agent W wanted revenge.

I told Agent W, I couldn't help him with that. I simply didn't know the guy. Agent W then told me he knew Lisa was screwing around with Bob. If I would be willing to set Lisa up, he could get Bob through her. I told him, that wasn't happening. Our marriage was shit, true, but she was still my wife, and I loved the whore regardless.

Agent W said I had two weeks to think it over before he'd be back to throw *me* in jail, if I didn't cooperate. On his way out, he told me that Lisa had been going around, claiming that all of the dope she had been selling was made by her. That kind of pissed me off, her taking credit for my dope.

The last thing Agent W told me that day freaked me out. He said that word had gotten back to him that Bob was planning on killing me. Instantly, I thought back to Bob's "generous offer" to do his cook for him, and how Lisa's stories just weren't adding up. If I had not insisted that I was going armed that day, I might have gotten killed, instead of paid.

Agent W left, and I was fucking pissed. I walked to the store to call Shane, and basically told him to get to my house right then, or I would kill him. He got there pretty quick. Shane's cousin Frank knew Bob. We went to see Frank to find out where Bob lived. Frank said that Bob lived at his parent's house on Rockhouse Road in Johnson City. That's the sign of a high roller right there, still living with Mommy and Daddy. My Hero.

Shane and I went to find Bob's house. It ended up being an old trailer that sat back off the road a little ways. We pulled in the driveway, and Lisa's car was there. I jumped out of the car and told Shane to keep it running. I walked to the door and started kicking the shit out of it. After about all of a minute, Lisa opened the door, ran out, and grabbed a hold of me as someone else slammed the door behind her.

Lisa was crying and begging me to calm down, saying Bob's parents were old, and I was scaring them. I kept kicking the side of the trailer, and yelling for Bob to come out. "You wanted to fuck my wife, now come on out and face me, you pussy! You want to take me out? Here's your chance!" I was lividly screaming.

Shane got out of the car to help Lisa drag me off the deck before someone called the cops. Once I was off the deck, Bob walked out the door yelling "What's your fucking problem?" I pulled my gun, pointed it at him, and that pretty much let him know that my current problem was *him*.

Bob froze, as you'd expect one to do when a gun is pointed at you, Lisa backed away, and Shane kept saying, "Don't do it. Don't do it." over and over. I really don't know how long we stood there; seconds, half-seconds, milliseconds. I don't remember what, or even if, I was thinking. All I know is that right in that moment, I wanted this dude to die. Slowly.

Bob's mom walked out the door then. She started talking to me, but I don't remember what she was saying. I just remember something about them not knowing Lisa was married. She then turned to Lisa and said, calmly, "Please leave, and don't come back, if you have a husband." I told Lisa to get her ass home, then Shane and I left. We took back roads to my house, in case they called the cops. When Shane dropped me off, I told him to hang on to my gun for a few days. Again, in case someone called the cops.

Lisa got home right after I did, and wanted to know if I had lost my fucking mind. I told her what Agent W had said about Bob planning to kill me, and that I believed she was trying to set me up that day she tried to get me to cook for Bob. I also told her what Harley and Joey had told me, and of course, she denied everything, just like I knew she would.

Finally, I told her about Agent W wanting me to set her up, to get her, to help him, get Bob. Out of everything, above all else, this was the thing that worried her. Of course, I should know that, because this would involve her going to jail, and not me for once. She said that Bob was leaving his parent's house, to go to a house owned by a friend of his, named Mark, when she was leaving. Lisa wanted to go tell him all of what Agent W had said. It was only right to let someone know the cops were out to get them, she reasoned.

Everything Lisa owned, except for a duffel bag full of clothes she kept in her car, was still in the house. I told her she could go warn the piece of shit, but if she wasn't home, in one hour, I would burn all of it; every single thing that was in my house that she owned. She was back, in forty-five minutes.

Chapter 22

Lisa and I ended up getting back together again for a little while. I think Bob told her to stay with me as a spy to be sure I wasn't trying to help the cops bust him. That was fine with me; I didn't care why she was back, just as long as she was there. Ah, the joys of marriage.

Shane was moving a little dope for me, and I had started selling some to Lea, a friend of mine I had worked with for about five years. Lea was also the person I had bought my house from, and she was planning on getting it back from the bank, once it was foreclosed on.

Joey was buying a little dope for personal use also. Between him, Shane, and Lea, we were doing a *lot* better financially than we had done since Lisa started fucking around with Bob. Of course, every time I would bring this fact up, which was every chance I had, it would end up in a huge argument.

The two weeks were up, and I was expecting the cops to show up at any moment. Lea came by one day to buy our 60" Big screen TV. It was a few days before Christmas, and we were going to use the extra money to buy the kids some presents. As Lea and I were loading the TV into her truck, I saw three undercover cop cars drive by. I knew this was it, and I told Lisa we had to get out of there, so we jumped in the car, leaving Lea to lock up for us, and we hauled ass. We went to Bristol, VA., where we spent the day buying pills and other supplies to do a big cook.

We got home late that afternoon. I ducked down in the seat as we drove down our street. After Lisa parked, I waited for her to go inside, then I got out, and crawled into the house through one of the basement windows. Within minutes, two cop cars pulled up in front of our house. Lisa answered the door when they knocked, and told them they could not come in without a warrant. They then proceeded to show her the warrant. At least they were prepared this time. The cops came in, led by Agent W, and arrested me.

I asked Agent W what I was being charged with, and he said I was charged with "Manufacture of Methamphetamine."

I said, "You can't do that. The grand jury already changed my drug paraphernalia charge to '*Attempt* to manufacture meth' which was true; either I was doing it, or I was attempting to - it couldn't be both.

Agent W agreed that I would get it thrown out when I went to court. The only problem, for me currently anyway, was that I was going to have to sit in jail through the Christmas holiday before I got to go to court to see the judge. I guess this was revenge for me not agreeing to work with the cops.

It was three days before Christmas when I went to jail, and, due to my bail being set at thirty-six thousand dollars, I wasn't getting out before I went to court a couple of days after Christmas. Once I finally got in front of the judge, he agreed with me that I should not have been charged and arrested twice for the same incident.

The D.A. said that there was nobody from the Drug Task Force (DTF) available for court that day. She asked the judge to continue the case until the next month so she would have time to get some answers about why I was charged the way I was. The judge agreed to the continuance, then he dropped my bail to a thousand bucks, so I could afford to get out.

Lisa was in court and said she was calling a bondsman right away to get me out. I expected to be out within an hour, but by early evening, I was still in jail. I called Lisa to see what was up. She said everyone she tried to get to bail me out would take her money, go in to get me out, then come back out, give her the money back and leave. No explanation.

Finally, Lisa got someone who was willing to get me out. As I was signing out, I was telling the bondsman about the trouble Lisa had been having all day. That's when the bondsman told me that the trouble was a DTF agent out in the office telling them they shouldn't get me out. He told the DTF agent that no one was going to tell him how to run his business, or who to get out and who not to. I thanked him and left.

I met Lisa in the lobby, and after a hug and a kiss, she looked at me and asked, "Are you ready to go cook?"

Hell yes I was!

We tore out of the jail parking lot and Lisa headed towards Johnson City. "Why are we going to Johnson City?" I asked.

"We're going to Pigeon Forge," she replied.

Chapter 23

Pigeon Forge, Tennessee, in the heart of the Great Smokey Mountains, is a great summer vacation location for families from all across the United States. During the fall season, tens of thousands of people descend on the small town and the surrounding area to see the turning of the colors of the beautiful foliage on the mountains. The Christmas season brings visitors who want to shop at the hundreds of specialty shops, craft shops, and manufacturer outlets. The Christmas decorations and lights alone are almost worth the trip.

After Christmas, everything in this town dies. The tourists all leave and many of the motels close their doors until spring. Most of the motels that do stay open drastically reduce their room rates for nightly, as well as weekly, stays. These low rates draw meth cooks to Pigeon Forge like moths to an open flame.

Lisa knew that it probably wasn't going to be a good idea for us to cook at the house again, at least not right away, so she brought the lab and some cash with her when she came to get me out of jail. That was fine with me, because the DTF obviously didn't want me out of jail, and they weren't going to be happy I was out.

I knew our house was most likely going to be watched closely for a while. Pigeon Forge was just far enough, about ninety miles, from home for both of us to feel safe, so off we went, making a few stops along the way for pseudo pills for the cook. Once we picked a motel, we checked in, asking for a room in the rear of the building. We wanted to be as far away as possible from anyone else in the motel, in case the smell from the cook escaped our room.

We brought the lab into the room and hid everything we didn't immediately need as we did some prep work. This included making the iodine crystals, breaking down the pills, and getting fresh red phosphorus from matchbook covers. Once all of this work was completed, we put everything up until we were ready to do the cook. I wanted to wait until late before starting the cook, that way there was less of a chance of anyone being awake to wonder what the hell we were doing.

Lisa had a little dope with her, so we got high and relaxed while we waited for time to pass. Once I felt like it had gotten late enough, I set everything up in the bathroom. I hung a blanket over the door, then closed it to make a seal around the cracks in the door. This was to reduce the chances of any smell getting out. Since I wasn't used to cooking in motels, I was being extra cautious.

I planned on doing most of the work on the back of the toilet. Since the ventilation fan was directly over it, setting up there took care of most of the fumes. The bathtub was there for water, and to wash anything that needed to be washed. The toilet would dispose of any liquid or paper waste I generated during the cook. I hoped I didn't have an episode similar to the one I had not long after I first learned to cook.

It went like this. It had been a long night, and I was doing a really big cook. Big enough in fact, that I actually did it as two simultaneous cooks. I had finished up around four in the morning, and started to clean up. This cook, because of its size, was being done in the kitchen.

I had several jars of leftover chemicals that included, camp fuel, lye water, denatured alcohol, and iodine, just to name some of them. I poured all of the chemicals down the sink drain as I loaded the jars into the dishwasher. Lisa was there, and I told her to open the front door to air out the house. She opened the door and said, "Come look at this, what is it?"

I walked to the door and looked outside to see a layer of what looked like fog covering the street. The fog only existed from our house, to about three houses down. Then I noticed the "fog" was coming from the sewer drains along the curbs. This wasn't fog; it was the chemicals I had just dumped!

I told Lisa to turn on all of the water faucets in the house, while I got a water hose and started to run water through the sewer drain. Then, I jumped into my car, and drove up and down the street as fast as I could to try to blow the fog away before anyone, like a cop, noticed it and got suspicious.

In case you have been wondering, this incident is the main reason why I had all that cook trash, which included many gallons of chemicals, built up in my basement. There just wasn't anywhere safe to dump the stuff.

Back in the motel, it was Lisa's job to sit and listen for anything unusual going on in the parking lot. She was also supposed to tell me if she could smell anything from the cook. This system worked great. When the cook was finished, I put all of the glassware in the tub and turned on the shower. The hot water would wash the glass, while the steam, along with a can of air freshener, would get the smell out of the bathroom.

We spent the next day in the motel room smoking a whole bunch of meth, and fucking. In the late afternoon we headed out to collect a few boxes of pills for another cook. We did the cook the same way as the night before, and everything went perfectly. The next morning, we cleaned the entire room with some cleaners we had bought, and checked out to head home.

After we got home, we got some kerosene for the heater and a few cook supplies with the last of our money, and Lisa took off to sell some dope. I knew she would be gone for a while, so I didn't get in much of a hurry to do the cook. Besides, I was still nervous about the DTF watching the house, but I had thought that since we had been gone for a couple of days, then maybe they'd still be thinking that no one was home.

Lisa's dad and brother had been by the house and had moved just about all our stuff to storage, because we were down to just a few days before being evicted due to the foreclosure. All that was left was some of our clothes, the computer desk and chair, the futon, and the kerosene heater. There were sheets hung over the windows to replace the curtains that had been removed and packed up.

To my surprise, Lisa showed back up about an hour after she had left. I was laying on the futon, about to get some sleep before cooking, when she came in. She was messing around in the bedroom, then I heard her go back outside, and heard her car leave shortly thereafter.

Curious, I got up and looked around to see what she was doing in the bedroom. The bitch had gotten her clothes, and left. I was pissed! I went to the pay phone to call her in order to find out what the fuck was up, and to tell her she had better bring me some money, or some of that dope back. She wasn't answering the phone, of course.

I ended up calling Lisa's sister, FJ, who came and picked me up. FJ was happy to let me crash at her house for a while. She always seemed to want whatever Lisa had, and this was her chance, she thought, to have me. At the very least, it was a chance for her to piss Lisa off by giving me a place to stay, and I was all for that.

In truth, FJ saved my ass that day. I was stuck with no money, and nowhere to go. While Lisa was getting her clothes, she also stole the Red P, pills, and the iodine crystals, so I couldn't even do the cook! I was so pissed off that I busted the rest of the lab stuff up, cut the tubing, and dumped everything else out.

I stayed at FJ's for a few days, then I decided I needed to get my shit together. After all, I was still out on bail, and I had court dates coming up. I called my friend Lea, who I had bought my house from, and asked her if she knew where I could get a job. She said she could hook me up with a good job, working with her. She also said that if I wanted to come stay at her place, with her and her girlfriend, then I was more than welcome to. Luckily for me, Lea was bi-sexual.

I moved in with Lea that night. She and Casey put me up in one of the extra bedrooms, bought me a carton of cigarettes, and gave me $20 bucks to put in my pocket. Coming off the meth wasn't bothering me at all, but I was eating like a horse. Since Lea had been a meth addict before, she expected this to happen, so she kept a lot of pizza around the house for me.

As I got settled in, I finally asked her what the job was that she said she could get me, and was she sure I could get hired. She was positive I would be hired. She couldn't find nearly enough people to sell those Kirby vacuums. I thought she was joking at first, but as it turns out, she was serious. I was about to be a Kirby vacuum cleaner salesman. This couldn't suck any worse.

Lea, being something of the "man" in her relationship with Casey, just happened to have plenty of men's dress clothes, in my size, for me to wear to my new job. All of my own clothes were full of holes and iodine stains; definitely not appropriate attire for a door to door salesman.

I went for my first day, and as Lea assured me, I was hired and put into training right away. Training basically consisted of sitting around watching videos that told us how we could get as rich as we wanted to get, as long as we sold, sold, sold those expensive vacuums to little old ladies who might not be able to afford meds, but they can afford a Kirby with one of our easy payment plans. In fact, they couldn't afford *not* to buy one, and I was about to be paid to go out and help the people of the world fight the dirt their old vacuums left behind. By doing so, I would be helping these people save their health. I already was not liking this shit, but I didn't really have a choice in the matter. I was staying with Lea and I pretty much had to do what she wanted me to do right now, and she wanted me to sell these fucking Kirby's.

It quickly became apparent that I needed to get out of Lea's house soon. I spent a week riding around with Lea as she did her demonstrations for people who were only interested in the free carpet cleaning, or the free steak knives (their choice). We would be doing this for 14 hours a day and I knew that once my training period was over, I would be expected to do the same thing, and I just could not bring myself to do this shit.

When Lea told me I was about to be sent out on my own, I realized I had an even bigger problem that neither of us had thought about. I didn't have a car. Without a car, I didn't have any way to get around to do demo's. At first, I was secretly happy as hell about all this. Then, I kind of began to worry. Without a job, there was no way Casey was going to let me stay with them for more than another week or so. I had to think of something fast.

The only thing of any value I had immediate access to was the new Dell computer I had recently paid $1800 bucks for. The only problem with that was the computer was sitting in a pawn shop, and I didn't have the cash to get it out. I mentioned this to Lea, and she said she would pay to get the computer out of pawn, and then we would see if we could trade it for a car.

Lea is quite a dealmaker, and by the end of the next day, she had found me a Chrysler 5th Ave. that someone was willing to trade for the Dell. I checked the car out, and it ran great. Other than a little faded paint, it looked really nice as well. I got the title and tagged the car with some money I borrowed from Lea. That night, I assured Lea I would see her the next day at work, and then I hauled ass. There was no way in hell I was going back to that Kirby store again. I left to go visit the twins.

Chapter 24

When I got to Lisa's parent's house to see the twins, they were gone but Lisa was there. We went to the girls' bedroom and Lisa had some dope, so we got high. I had gone without getting high for almost two weeks and here I was, right back at it. Lisa and I talked, and she started with her bullshit "I love you" crap, and making it out to be *my* fault I had not heard from her, because I moved in with FJ, and then with Lea. Forget the fact she took her clothes, and left me stranded with no money, and nowhere to go.

Lisa asked if I wanted to take off and cook. I figured that I might as well, since I didn't have anything else to do at the moment. I told her that we could go cook, but that I was keeping half of the dope. I would try to sell it myself at the bar. Lisa borrowed some money from her dad, and we took off in her Saturn. We left my car there at her parents' house. Lisa's lab was in the trunk with some clothes we had packed. We were heading to Pigeon Forge again to get a motel for a couple of days. We decided to take the old highway to Greeneville TN., because it would save us about forty-five minutes of driving time.

It started to rain slightly as we rode toward Greeneville, on Hwy 107, which dead ended into State Hwy 81 in Greeneville. From there, we would get on I-81 to Pigeon Forge. As usual, we were arguing about something, and when we got to the end of Hwy 107, neither of us noticed the 3-way intersection until we were halfway through it, going at about 50 mph. Lisa hit the brakes, but on the slippery road, they didn't do any good at all.

We hit the slight embankment and the ditch directly in front of us at full speed. For some reason, I threw my hand up on the dash to brace myself, not thinking about the airbag. I ended up dislocating my shoulder when the bag deployed. I also twisted my ankle pretty badly in this crash.

I must have been stunned, because before I realized what was going on, Lisa was already out of the car with the trunk open, yelling about the cops coming. I got out of the car, and pulled my shoulder back into the socket. That hurt like a son of a bitch. I looked around, but thankfully, there was no traffic due to the late hour.

I tried to find a place to hide the lab, but the only thing around was a huge area of red clay mud that had been leveled for construction work. I grabbed the lab, and found a low area to put it in, then I covered it in mud to help it blend in. Since Lisa's lab was in a bright pink duffel bag, it needed a lot of mud. I walked back to the car, but my ankle was really starting to hurt.

As we checked around the inside of the car to be sure nothing incriminating was left in it, someone pulled up and asked if we needed him to call 911. Even though we probably didn't want to say it, we told him yes, we did. The cops eventually showed up, and sent a wrecker for the car. The car was completely totaled. The cop noticed my footprints in the ankle deep mud, and I told him I walked out there to piss. Luck was on my side, and he believed me.

As the wrecker loaded the car, the cop offered to drive us to a motel. We accepted the ride, and when we got there and checked in, Lisa called her dad, and he said he'd come pick us up in the morning. The next morning, I could barely walk. Lisa's dad came and got us, then took us back to his house. We jumped in my car to get me to the hospital for my ankle. That's where we said we were going, anyway. Really, we went back to the crash site in Greeneville to retrieve the lab, which luckily, was still there.

Lisa didn't care that I couldn't stand to put pressure on my leg; she refused to get dirty by walking out into the field to get the lab. I ended up hobbling out there, and getting it myself. When I got it back to the car, we went to get the stereo, and a few other things out of the Saturn. Once we got everything, we went to Pigeon Forge, to go and do the cook that we originally set out to do.

Lisa pretty much slept the entire time we were at the motel. That was fine with me, because I could tell she'd been up for a few too many days, and she was beginning to be a total bitch. I definitely preferred her sleeping, than bitching. I got the cook done, and I let Lisa sleep until I had the room cleaned, and the car packed and ready to go.

Once we got started on our trip back to Lisa's parent's house, Lisa asked me if I wanted her to go sell the dope. This would mean she would need to borrow my car, and I was not about to play that game with her. I told her, I'd take care of it myself. Lisa blew up at me, a favorite tactic of hers to get what she wants, and started running her mouth, saying I'd never be able to move it without her help. I said we would just have to wait and see.

When we got back to her parent's house, the twins were there. I gave them some dope, and asked them to go sell it, which they were happy to do. Lisa was pissed off, because I trusted the twins more with my dope than I did her, but that was how untrustworthy she proved herself to be. I explained to her, that I never had to worry about the girls ripping me off, like I did with her, but in her mind, she never stole from me, so she thought I was in the wrong. Well, fuck her.

I ended up giving Lisa two grams, instead of half the dope, for the money she had put up for the cook and for the room. I left as soon as the twins got back with my money. Lisa tried to get me to take her with me, since she had no way to get anywhere, but I didn't want to be stuck with her. Besides, it served her right for leaving me stuck without any way to get around a couple of weeks ago.

We would end up hooking up again several days later, when she showed up at another motel I had checked into. She said she saw my car in the parking lot, and asked the owner of the motel which room I was in. The dickhead actually told her. When Lisa showed up at the motel, she was driving a beat up Buick that she said she traded some dope for. She saw that I had my lab unpacked, and asked me if I wanted to split a cook. She would supply half of the supplies, and do half the work, and we'd split half the dope. That was fine with me.

I was nervous about cooking in this motel. It was a mom-n-pop motel that was owned by an Indian family, and they pretty much watched everything that went on around there. Another problem with cooking in this motel was that the bathrooms didn't have vent fans to pull the smoke and fumes out during the cook.

Despite all that, we did the cook anyway, and after we finished, we opened the door to let the room air out. I went to the store for something to drink, and when I returned, I ran up the stairs as fast as I could to get back to the room. Something I didn't notice until I had gotten out of the room for a while was that there was a foot thick cloud of smoke floating in the room near the ceiling, and it started rolling out the door, as if the room was on fire. I shut the door, turned off the lights, and peeked out the windows until daylight waiting for cops, and fire trucks to show up. They never did, so as soon as it was daylight outside, we grabbed our shit and left the motel. We left the door open so it could air out while we were gone. Thankfully, the smoke wasn't as noticeable during the day as it was at night.

Another thing that happened at this motel occurred one night when I ran into Lisa while I was out buying supplies for a cook. She wanted to split another cook, and I figured it wouldn't hurt. Besides, I wanted to get laid, and Lisa is a guaranteed fuck. We went to the motel, and while I was setting up the lab and breaking down the pills, Lisa decided to take a bath. She was in the tub for a few minutes, when she started screaming, then ran out of the bathroom dripping wet and completely naked. I ran into the bathroom to see what the hell made her react like that, and as it turns out, the water handle for the cold water had broken off in Lisa's hand, and a heavy stream of cold water was shooting across the tub at face level.

It scared the hell out of her, but I thought it was hilarious. The only problem now was that we had to pack the lab back up, and go get the motel owner, who turned off the water and gave us a new room. These kinds of things would happen all the time at this place. It's a wonder why we cooked there at all. I guess it was just inexpensive, and convenient, and it seemed like a good place to avoid the cops pretty good. And, for awhile, it was.

Chapter 25

Lisa had a brother, Donny, who lived across the road from their parents in a house he had been building, albeit slowly, for years. The house didn't have running water, or electricity, but he made do with water from the spring that ran along the property line. This spring was a source of water for many of the houses in the area.

As for electricity, Donny had run several, hundred-foot long drop cords, end to end, down the hill and across the road to his parent's house. This gave him enough electricity for a lamp, a stereo, a TV, and hot plate. Unfortunately, he could only use two of the appliances at a time, or he'd trip the breaker. There was a wood burning stove for heat, and cooking. Since there was no plumbing, he had to piss and shit in the woods, but other than that, the place was great. It sat high on a hill that was covered with trees, which made it kind of scenic. The trees blocked the view of the house from the road, but you could see the road from the house.

The day Lisa and I got back from the last cook in Pigeon Forge, I went to visit Donny after the girls got back with my money. Although Donny was a bit of a hermit, I knew he loved to drink, and smoke a little meth. I took Donny to the liquor store and bought him a bottle of vodka, and then we went back to his house to party. By the next morning, Donny was suggesting I start cooking at his house. The place was secluded, he pointed out, and the wood burner was perfect for getting rid of cook trash.

It wasn't an accident that I went to visit Donny that day. The truth is I knew that once Donny got high he'd want me to stay at his place. Since I didn't have anywhere else to go, I kind of manipulated Donny into letting me stay there. My only other alternative was to stay with Lisa's parents, and I definitely didn't want to do that. Not with Lisa staying there, anyway.

Lisa was stuck. She had no car, and the twins weren't stupid enough to let her borrow theirs. After a couple of days, she walked over to Donny's to ask if she could borrow my car "for just a few minutes." HELL NO! Eventually, she got someone to come pick her up. I wouldn't see her again until the night she showed up in the beat up Buick, and found me at the motel, which was a couple of weeks later.

Even though I was staying at Donny's, and it was a great place to cook, I still liked to get out of there to go cook in a motel from time to time. Sometimes I would go find Trina, Shane's ex-wife, and take her to the motel to play with while I cooked. Sometimes, Donny was just way too wigged out for me to want to be around, so I would go to the motel just to get away from him.

For a while, things were going good. I was selling enough dope to keep me going, and Lisa and I were getting along, most of the time. Even though neither one of us considered us to be "together," I still loved Lisa. When we would hook up to do a cook, I enjoyed our time together. She learned to keep her phone off when we were together, because if some dickhead called her during "our time," she and I would start fighting again.

It was during this time that I started noticing that I was being followed quite often. Lisa said she was noticing the same thing. There were certain cars that would follow us, everywhere we went. If I sped up, they sped up. If I stopped to get gas four times in thirty minutes, they would stop and do the same. There were several different cars, but after awhile, we got to know all of them. Once we figured out what was going on, we turned the whole thing into a big game of "Follow the Leader."

The Drug Task Force has a super-secret hidden lair in Johnson City where they hang out and hide their super-sneaky undercover cars. IT'S IN THE OLD KROGER'S BUILDING ACROSS THE STREET FROM ONE STOP! Oops, did I just let the secret out? My bad.

What Lisa and I would do is drive through the parking lot at Kroger's around midnight. As we pulled out onto the road, two or three cars would come out behind us. Now, the object of the game is to get away from the pursuers, and hide from them. If they find you, they usually keep driving around so they will see when you take off again, and its game on.

We had quite a few tricks. Lisa's favorite was to get on the twisting, turning roads out in the Limestone Cove area where she grew up. She could drive these roads blindfolded, and knew where a straightaway ended in a sharp curve. Lisa would be hauling ass, kill the lights, and then use the emergency brake to slow down for the curve. A few seconds later, you would hear the cop lock his brakes up to keep from crashing. Sometimes they ended up in the ditch. It was great! My favorite move was to get far enough ahead of the cops, so they couldn't see me driving with no headlights, then kill the engine and shoot across a couple yards and come out on another street. You kill the engine to keep from waking people up.

One night, I was being followed by several under-covers, and I couldn't seem to get away from them. I pulled into a small neighborhood and parked behind a church. There were only two roads in and out of the neighborhood, and the under-covers, I knew, would be waiting for me at both of them.

Earlier in the day, I had bought several cans of white spray paint, and they were still in the trunk. I got out of the car, took off the hubcaps, and painted the steel rims white. Then, I painted the lower part of the car white to make it two-toned, broke off the radio antenna, and drove out of there like nothing was wrong. It actually worked. I got away from those dumbasses.

Occasionally, Lisa and I would chase each other around town. I honestly don't know why I would chase her, which is how it usually started, because when she would finally pull over, I would keep going. Then she would chase me; probably to ask why I was chasing her.

One night, for no reason, Lisa blocked the road I was driving down. I stopped and rolled down my window. "Move," I said. She just sat there and said, "Go around me." I started to pull around, but she backed up to block me again. Okay, so I just rammed her car and pushed her out of my way. That obviously pissed her off but that was kind of the point. Well, that and I just wanted to show her that I could act just as ignorant as she could.

Once, Lisa picked up three grams of meth from me to go sell. I met her at a mobile home sales place to get my money. She pulled in, and parked her car nose to nose with mine. I got into her car, and she gave me the money for two grams, then handed me a gram of the dope back. I got back in my car, and was about to leave, when I looked up and saw Lisa laughing her ass off in her car. She put her hands up to her face, as if she were holding a camera, and taking a picture. I freaked out thinking the cops were watching, and I left in a hurry. Lisa says she doesn't remember doing that, but I damn sure remembered it.

Lisa came by Donny's house one afternoon while we were getting ready to do a cook. She had some dope, maybe half an ounce, with her and started smoking it with us. It was anhydrous ammonia dope, which meant it didn't have the same kick as what I was making, but it was free, so I didn't bitch.

Lisa asked if I was moving any dope, and I told her that I was. She assumed the twins were moving it for me, but in reality, her cousin David was buying a lot of it. Shane was selling some for me as well. My sources in the meth world were still extremely limited at this point. Before Lisa left us that day, she asked me if I had any dope I wanted to sell. I said I had a little I would sell, but she had to have cash. I let her know that I didn't need to get rid of it bad enough to have to front it to her. She said she had cash, and I sold her three grams.

I don't know why she was buying my dope, especially at full price, when she had so much of her own. Maybe it was like I said; her anhydrous dope didn't have the same kick my Red P dope had. I guess it didn't really matter all that much to me, even then. Money was money, and nothing else mattered to me at that point.

While I was out running around town, I would often run into Lisa. During one of these encounters, we were both at the same store buying cook supplies. Lisa asked what I thought about getting a motel room and splitting a cook. I was all for it, and we agreed to split the dope evenly, with a gram off the top for whoever paid for the room. We did this, and the next morning we left the room as... friends... maybe. Well, we were laughing and parted in good spirits at least.

Lisa had a court hearing over the custody of her kids coming up, and we went together as a united force. She got her kids back, but unfortunately she had no home of her own to bring them to. I think this bothered me more than it did Lisa. I hoped that getting her kids back would make Lisa want to go back to having a family, but all she did was take Joy from her sister's house and dump her off at her mom's with the rest of the kids. Sorry to say, I didn't have a place for them either, I was still staying at Donny's.

Chapter 26

The more I think about it, the more I want to say, "Fuck Lisa, I LOVE TAYLOR SWIFT!!!!!!!!!!!"

Chapter 27

One day, in April of 2005, I began to cook at Donny's. Donny and I had been awake for about a week straight with no plans of slowing down. We were both pretty much shot out at this point.

Just about the time I got the cook started, Lisa showed up with Faye. We all sat around bullshitting for a while and Lisa asked if I was going to want to sell anything out of the cook when it was finished. Sometimes I did cooks that were for personal use only, and since this was a small cook, she must have thought this was one of them.

I told Lisa I could sell her some when it was done, if she had the cash. Even though Lisa had been buying a lot of dope from me, I still didn't trust her.

I know it seems unusual for Lisa to be buying dope from me all the time, when she was a cook herself, but the truth is, she wasn't a very good cook. That's why she liked to split cooks with me. She did the prep work and the clean up, and I did the actual cook. We really made a great team back then. Many times, Lisa would pull out a wad of cash and pay me full price for as much of my share as I wanted to sell.

Anyway, Lisa said that she and Faye had to go somewhere, but they would be back by the time the cook was done. As they were leaving, I had a thought.

"Where's your lab?" I asked.

"In my car," she replied.

I told Lisa that I didn't think it would be such a good idea for her to be driving about with Faye in the car and a meth lab in the trunk. Lisa said she didn't have anywhere to stash it, so I told her she could put it in my car until she got back. Since I obviously wasn't going anywhere for a while, the lab would be safe with me. Lisa agreed, and they left.

I finished the cook a few hours later. Lisa and Faye showed back up about the time we were airing out the house, and I was bagging the dope up when they walked in. Lisa walked over to the bar stool I was sitting on in front of a window, and said she wanted two grams. I handed Lisa two baggies, each containing a gram of meth. Lisa held the baggies up and asked, "You sure there are two grams here?" I pointed to the scales and told her to weigh it herself if she didn't believe me. She weighed it.

Something about Lisa is she's a creature of habit. If she does something different than what is normal for her, I pick up on it pretty fast. When Lisa opened her wallet to get the money out to pay me, I didn't realize I was expecting her to pull the money out of the top of her wallet, until she pulled it out of the *side* of her wallet.

I knew something wasn't right, but since I had been awake for so long, I guess it just wasn't enough for me to worry about. Lisa had a stack of brand new twenty dollar bills. I held my hand out, and Lisa started counting out two hundred dollars by holding up each bill as she counted out my money and laid it in my hand. I thought she was just being stupid at this point, and all I wanted was for her to pay me, and get the fuck out.

Lisa's cousin, David showed up and I was about to break out some dope for all of us to smoke, when Lisa suddenly said she had to go. As she and Faye were leaving, I had asked her if she had gotten her lab out of my car. She had said "yes", so I forgot about it. After all, a meth cook's lab is their livelihood, and even though Lisa wasn't a very good cook, it was still her way of making money, and dope, when there was no other way to get it anywhere else. She also had money invested in that lab.

As they were leaving, Faye walked over to me and asked what I was planning on doing the rest of the night. I said that I had to go see someone, and I also had to pick up some more pills for a cook I was going to do the next morning. Faye started acting a little strange, and started telling me that she thought I should go to sleep. I insisted that I was fine, but she asked me to promise her that I would go to bed and not go anywhere that night.

Faye was more than my step-daughter, she was my friend. Even though my life was crazy as hell, I could always count on her to be the same, and I would not lie to her by making a promise I wasn't about to keep.

Finally, I said that I would go meet who I needed to see, and then I would come back and go to sleep. I would worry about the pills in the morning. She didn't like this, but she knew it was the best she was going to get. Faye asked me something strange then, she asked me to go through Carter County, instead of Unicoi County when I left. When I asked her why she wanted me to do this, she said it was because some of her friends had said there were road blocks out and she did not want me to get into trouble.

After Lisa and Faye left, Donny, David, and I started talking about getting some liquor. It was getting late, so Donny and David decided to go to the liquor store before it closed. While they did that, I was going to go drop off four grams of dope to someone.

Since it had been raining, Donny's driveway, which was dirt, was too muddy to drive up, so everyone had to park at the bottom of the hill. While Donny locked up, David and I walked on down to our cars. Just as we got to the bottom of the hill, we both heard something take off running through the woods. I thought it was a deer, but David had said it was a person.

David grabbed a flashlight out of his car to take a look, but whoever, or whatever, it was, was gone. I was just about to ask David if he thought it might be Donny messing with our heads, when Donny came down the hill behind us. It wasn't him. When we told Donny what we heard, he thought we were imagining things. I don't think we could have imagined the same thing, at the same time, but it's possible, so I quit worrying about it. They got into David's car, and left.

Something I never did at Donny's was shoot up, my preferred method of doing meth. While I sat there in my car, I decided I needed to go do a shot of dope. I went over the hill from where I was at, and started to drive to a secluded area at the end of a road on Escape Mountain. As I drove, I passed two vehicles that were parked on the side of the road. One was Lisa's piece of crap Buick. The other was Agent W's Explorer.

Needless to say, seeing those two cars together sent me into another world. I drove to the secluded spot I was heading to, as fast as I could. Once I got there, I just sat there, remembering. Remembering that Lisa held the dope up in front of the window, and asked if I was sure there were two grams there. Remembering how Lisa held up each bill as she counted out my money.

I knew something was up when she pulled that money out of the wrong place in her wallet. I just wouldn't have thought she would set me up. Not in her own brother's house, anyway. I wondered if Faye was in on it then. If it was a controlled buy, then Faye would have been there when Lisa got the money from the agent.

I needed a shot of dope; I was beginning to wig out. I drew up a big shot, and did it. I sat there waiting for the dope to calm me down, but it wasn't having any effect on me at all. I did a second shot, and then forgot whether or not I actually did that shot, so I did another, just to be sure. Now I was high.

I was calming down quite a bit, but I was still extremely paranoid. I was looking down through the trees at these three street lights a ways down the road. Suddenly, I thought there were three people walking towards me through the woods. Each person standing at least ten feet tall, and each carrying a flashlight.

I told myself I was seeing "tree people," but that did no good, because I didn't believe me. Tree people are kind of like shadow people. The difference being, tree people move around because what you are seeing are tree limbs that in a sleep deprived mind look like people moving through the woods when the wind moves them.

One night, Donny was looking out the window. He hadn't moved for several hours. Finally, I asked him what he was looking at, and he said. "These two guys at the end of the road are the hardest working people I have ever seen. They've been digging that hole all night."

I had him point out what he was looking at, and it was nothing more than a tree limb bouncing because the overflow pipe for his parent's water reservoir was tied to it. I told him this, and pointed out that no one would dig a hole in the middle of the night. He just said, "I know, but I still see them," and he kept watching 'til daylight, when he announced, "they're gone."

I once watched what I thought was a ballroom dance, complete with 1800's era ball gowns, tuxedos, and horses, going on in Donny's neighbor's backyard.

That's the way of the mind of a meth addict. You know what you are seeing can't possibly be real, or isn't logical, but that doesn't matter. You know it's just a hallucination, you tell yourself it's just a hallucination. You remind yourself of the thousands of other things that you've seen that turned out not to be real, but in the end, you never convince yourself because what you think you see is right in front of you. If it's not real, how can I see it?

I started my car and hauled ass off of that mountain. When I passed the area where Lisa's car had been, there was no one there. The vehicles were gone. Once I got to the bottom of the mountain, I made the biggest mistake of the night, I didn't trust Faye.

Chapter 28

I'm not really sure if I thought Faye was in on setting me up, or maybe I wasn't thinking at all, but I turned towards Unicoi County, despite her advice. This was when the three shots of dope started to kick my ass.

Aided by being awake for days and days, I started to hallucinate that I wasn't even in my car. In my mind, I was sitting on the couch in someone's house. I've no idea whose house it was I thought I was in, but I wasn't driving down twisting, turning, mountain roads anymore. I don't even remember driving to Johnson City.

After I made the decision to go through Unicoi County, I must have just shut down mentally, because the next thing I would remember is stopping at a red light by the One-Stop liquor store in Johnson City. There was a cop right behind me. Oh shit!

I made a right turn towards Elizabethton, thinking that if I got to the county line, the cop would turn around. I was being very careful not to speed or swerve. The cop stayed right on my ass, so I just had a feeling that he was going to pull me over for something. I was approaching the Milligan Highway exit off of the Elizabethton Highway I was traveling on, and decided to pull off the highway.

As I turned up the exit ramp, I reached into my pocket and pulled out the four grams of dope I was on my way to sell. I also got out my personal stash. I ate all of it, as I turned right off the ramp, then turned into the Shell station. When I parked at the Shell station, the cop pulled in behind me and turned on his blue lights. He walked to my window and asked me, "Sir, are you on drugs?" I responded that I most certainly was *not* on drugs, and then he asked me to step out of the car, which I did.

The cop wanted to know where I was going so late, (it was about midnight.) I told him I was on my way home from a friend's house or some shit, and that I was stopping at the store for some cigarettes. The cop then asked if he could search my car. "Sure, go for it," I said. Hell, my lab was at Donny's and I just ate my dope. My syringe was tucked into a hole in between the front seats, where he would never find it. I didn't have shit to worry about.

The cop instructed me to step to the rear of my vehicle while he searched.

He opens the back door of my car, and asks, "What's this?"

"What's what?" I asked.

That's when he held up the bright pink duffel bag. I almost shit my pants on the spot. It was Lisa's lab. The one she had already said she had gotten out of my car.

I told the cop it was a meth lab, and he arrested me. After I was cuffed, the cop got on the phone. He was on the phone for less than thirty seconds, which I found unusual, then he hung up and informed me that the DTF was on their way. I shit you not, less than two minutes later, there came a line of four cars, three Drug Task Force, one DEA, and an SUV pulling a trailer, with the "STOP METH" mantra printed all over it; pretty fucking convenient that they all arrived so quickly. And, at the exact same time, even.

One of the DTF agents, dressed in a chemical suit and respirator, took everything out of my car, and laid it all out in the parking lot. Everything was sealed in metal drums, then locked in the "STOP METH" trailer. After it was all cleaned up, I was taken into the trailer, where I was ordered to take off all my clothes, and throw them in a metal drum, which was then sealed up. I was given a paper suit to put on, then I was locked in a police car.

I'm not sure how long I was in that cop car before I started to shake and jerk violently and uncontrollably. The cop asked if I was okay, and I said I wasn't sure. I started nodding out, and the next thing I remember was being taken into the Washington County Detention Center, in Jonesborough Tennessee.

The cops took me into a room where the arresting officer filled out the arrest affidavit, and asked me basic questions, (address, employment, etc.) I was sitting in a hard plastic chair, and from time to time, I would look over to say something to the twins, whom I saw sitting there with me. This freaked the cop out, and they brought in a nurse to see if I was nuts.

Sometime during the night, I was put into a holding cell. I would be held in that holding cell, for five days, but I only remember maybe an hour or so of it. There was one day when I remember looking out the window, and I saw Lisa's car pull into the parking lot. Later, a cop told me she was trying to get me out, but she didn't have enough money. I was also told that she said she would get me out after I went to court and my bond was lowered.

Just to be clear, I didn't sleep during any one of these days that I was being held. Once the hallucinations really kicked in, I saw Lisa crawl in the window of the holding cell I was in. A few minutes later, this girl named Michelle crawled in also. Michelle was a cute little meth whore with beautiful, long, brown, wavy hair that went down to her ass. She was really, really sexy.

Lisa and Michelle sat on the bunk, and we talked for a while. I had always wanted to have a threesome with Lisa and Michelle, and although I had done this with Lisa and other girls, I never got the chance with Michelle. I'm so happy that I didn't get the chance then. I can only imagine what the cops would have seen if they looked in that cell while I thought I was having a threesome. It wouldn't have been pretty.

After the five days, the cops finally decided I had come down enough to go to court. I got a pretty good lawyer, and when I walked into the courtroom with him, I saw Lisa sitting in the front row behind the defendant's table. She held up some cash to let me know she was going to get me out. That was quite a relief to know, after what I had thought I was going through.

My preliminary hearing started, and the arresting officer was put on the stand. The prosecutor asked what happened, and the officer basically said he pulled me over because there had been a call from a "concerned motorist," stating that I was driving down the road, hitting myself in the head. Even as fucked up as I was, I'd remember doing that if it was true, which it wasn't, I don't think. My lawyer gets his turn, and asks the cop if *he* personally witnessed me doing anything unusual. "No." Why did the officer ask me, when he first approached me, if I was on drugs? Isn't it common to ask if someone is drunk? No answer to those two questions.

The judge was beginning to take my side. He told the cop that if he couldn't give some good reason for pulling me over, then he was dismissing the charges and turning me loose. That's when my mind was blown after the cop said the following, with resignation in his voice: "Your Honor, we had an anonymous 911 call that there was a meth lab in that vehicle." WHAT?!? Did I hear that right? Was I still hallucinating?

I turned around just in time to see Lisa running out the door. THAT FUCKING BITCH! She got me again.

Chapter 29

By the time I got my new lawyer appointed to me in criminal court, I was over the impression I might actually be getting out of jail any time soon. Lisa sure wasn't planning on getting me out. It wouldn't have really mattered much at that point anyway if she tried, because my other two bonds got revoked as soon as I appeared in front of the criminal court judge.

My new lawyer, Ms. Whiting, asked the judge if he would agree to hear all three of my cases together as one. This judge was my judge on the Elizabethton charges as well as this new one in Johnson City. He agreed, and Ms. Whiting said this was good for me, because the prosecutor in Johnson City didn't give a shit about the Elizabethton charges.

This ended up being very true, because just a few weeks after my first criminal court appearance, Ms. Whiting came to me with an offer of two years probation for all three charges. I was all for that, but Ms. Whiting asked me to turn it down. She said that if I gave her two weeks, she could get all of the charges dismissed. I decided to trust her.

Two weeks passed, then three, four, five... It was almost two months before I heard from Ms. Whiting again, and when I did, it wasn't the good news I was expecting. Ms. Whiting told me that she had been taken off of my cases, because all of my cases were on hold. The feds, she said, were in the process of investigating, to see if they wanted to pick up the charges, and charge me federally. I was a little worried at this point.

In the end, the feds didn't charge me. I don't know why they didn't, but I'm guessing it had something to do with me being charged two times for the same crime in Elizabethton. Once the feds dropped their investigation, my Elizabethton charges got sent back to Carter County criminal court. I went to court again, finally, in Carter County and got my new lawyer there, Bobby. Bobby told me when we first met, that Ms. Whiting had called him and told him how she was planning on beating all of my charges. He said he would stick to that plan.

Bobby filed a motion to suppress all of the evidence in the Carter County cases. The basis for the motion was that the original traffic stop was bullshit, because even if I didn't signal, that would not have been illegal as long as there were no other vehicles behind me on the road. Tennessee law states, when making a right hand turn, you have to use a turn signal to let the cars behind you know you are turning. If there are no cars, you are not expected, by law, to signal.

Bobby also stated in the motion that I was harassed by the Drug Task Force when I refused to work for them, by searching my house a second time. Even though I signed a Consent-to-Search form, they had no right to even ask me if they could search again, because a crime wasn't being committed. By the way, when I say "DTF", I mean Agent W specifically.

The day of my hearing for the motion came and I went to court. One of the first witnesses against me was the K-9 officer from the night of my bust.

"Did your dog alert you to drugs in the defendant's vehicle?"

"Yes."

"Did you find any drugs?"

"No."

My lawyer asked about how many times the dog had searched, both in training and on duty, for drugs. I believe the answer was close to two thousand times. "Has your dog ever given a false alert like he did on the defendant's vehicle?"

"Yes."

"How many times?"

"Two times previously."

What do you want to bet those other two times the cops found other shit to arrest the person for, after using the false positive alert as probable cause?

The cop who pulled me over got on the stand and proved to have a wonderful memory. Not only did he remember there was a vehicle behind me when I supposedly didn't use my turn signal, he actually remembered there were *three* vehicles behind me. Not only that, he could tell you the color, make, and model of *all three*, and *what order* they were in behind me. Did I mention it had been *fifteen months* since that night? Could he tell us the color, make, and model of the *last* three cars he pulled over? "No." Get off the fucking stand!

Agent W got there next. Long story short, he lied also. He claimed he never asked me to work as an informant.

"Agent W, isn't it common practice to ask people you've arrested if they are willing to work with you in order to help themselves?"

"Yes, it is."

"But, you didn't ask the defendant?"

"No."

"Any reason why not?"

"No."

Agent W claimed that he never harassed me, never searched my house the second time. In fact, he claimed he never even *saw* me again after the night he arrested me the first time.

"Why is your name on the second arrest affidavit if you never saw the defendant again after the first arrest?"

"I signed the affidavit, but did not participate in the arrest." BULLSHIT! He was the motherfucker that arrested me!

I got on the stand at long last. I gave the judge the whole story. The truth. I even informed the judge that Agent W was lying about not participating in the second arrest, and that my wife was there at the time. She saw the whole thing.

The prosecutor got up and asked me, "Is your wife here today?"

"No."

"No more questions."

When I was finished and I got off the witness stand, the judge was quiet for several minutes. When he spoke, he asked me if I had any way of contacting my wife to ask her to come be a witness for me. I told him I didn't know where she was, because we hadn't spoken since my arrest.

"I have a problem," the judge said to me, "I believe you. I believe your story of the events as you say they happened. My problem is that I have all these officers telling me a different story. It's your word against all of theirs, so what do I do?" Again, the judge was silent.

"Sir," he addressed me, "Do you have any witnesses at all you can bring to this court to back up your story?"

"No sir."

"Are you certain? If you can bring me one witness, just one, I'll rule in your favor and dismiss all charges against you."

"Sorry sir, I don't have one."

The judge had no choice but to rule against me and said he would get me back in court in two months and get me sentenced. If my lawyer could get me a good deal, I could get all this behind me. I was taken back to jail to await my fate.

In early February, about two weeks after my motion hearing, I was awakened by one of the jailers, and told to get ready for court. This was a little confusing, because I didn't have a court date for another six weeks. I got ready, and I was transported to the courthouse. It was around nine in the morning when I got there, but court hadn't started yet.

As soon as I walked into the courtroom my lawyer led me to an interview room.

Bobby handed me a piece of paper and said, "Read this. I'll be right back," then he left.

I read the paper, and tried to make sense out of it. Bobby walked back into the room, and I asked, "What does this mean?"

He smiled and said, "It means they fucked up, and they know it."

What Bobby had given me, was a letter, from the prosecutor, to the judge. The letter stated that, after the motions hearing, Agent W "had his memory refreshed" and now remembered that some of the events I described in my testimony might have been closer to the truth than he originally thought. The judge wasn't happy. According to him, I had been in jail "for nothing" for almost a year. Now, we all know that I wasn't in jail for "nothing." I just wanted the manufacturing charges dropped. They had me dead to rights on the rest.

The judge set a new court date for April 2006, and then released me on an O.R. bond. It was a good day, and I was happy; in shock, as you can probably imagine, but happy. My court appearance that day had been in Carter County, so I had to wait until the jail could arrange to transport me back to Washington County, where I was still being housed due to my Washington County charge. I arrived back in Washington County at about 1 a.m. I told the jailer that I had been given an O.R. bond, and he told me I would be taken back to my cell to pack my stuff while they got the paperwork done.

I went back to my cell and packed. My roommate and I talked for a little while, and I started to think it was taking them an awfully long time for them to come and get me to let me out. I asked what the problem was, and was told that there was a case number on my file that wasn't listed on the O.R. bond. I would have to wait until the courthouse opened to get it straightened out. That'd be on Monday, and unfortunately, it was only Saturday morning then. I had to spend the whole weekend in jail waiting. It was a very, very long weekend.

Chapter 30

When I did finally get released from jail, in February of 2006, I was pretty much screwed. I was sitting in booking while the cops got my release papers in order, not knowing where I was going to go, or what I was going to do. I didn't even have any clothes to wear since the DTF destroyed everything I was wearing the night I got arrested. The cops took me to a room with a bunch of clothes I could look through to see if anything in there would fit me. Everything in that room looked like shit the Salvation Army rejected in 1974. I was starting to wonder if I really wanted to get out of jail after all.

Minutes before I signed out of the jail, a cop walked through the door with a shoe box and several shopping bags. These were dropped off to me by my first wife, Karen, whom I had been writing for the last couple of months of my incarceration. Karen had gone out and bought me several pairs of jeans, some shirts, shoes, and just about everything I needed at the moment, right down to a toothbrush. The cop said Karen would be waiting out front for me when I got out. Things were suddenly looking up.

I left the jail, and Karen was parked in a handicap spot right outside the jail. I had Karen drive to a store next to the jail, so I could cash the $30 check the jail had given me for the money I had on my commissary, account. This money was given to me by the roommate who I had sold the television too that Karen had dropped off for me. I went into the store, and bought some cigarettes and a Coke. The two things I had been dreaming about for almost a year. When I got back in the car, Karen asked me if I wanted to go get something to eat. I did.

We headed to Greeneville, TN. to eat. Since Karen was engaged to her long time boyfriend, she didn't want to take a chance on anyone seeing us together if we were hanging out in Johnson City. After we started talking about where I was going to stay, I suggested the Salvation Army in Johnson City. Since it was close to a day labor place, and since I needed to work, that seemed like the best idea.

Karen dropped me off at the Salvation Army around 4:00 p.m. to check in. She said she would be back in the morning to pick me up. The rules of the Salvation Army said that everyone who was not in the long term program had to leave the building at 7:00 a.m. and could return at 4:00 p.m. The long term program was for people who were working and who paid a fee of $50 per week. In exchange for payment, the residents received three meals a day, and a semi-private room with a locker. Paying residents also didn't have to leave the building on their days off.

When Karen picked me up the next morning, we went to go get breakfast, and then we just hung out together all day. The second day was a repeat of the first, but Karen got me a cell phone that day so I could find a job, or call her if I needed to. When Karen dropped me off at the Salvation Army on the second day, I told her I would be going to the day labor place the next morning, to see if I could get some work. I would need cash, and eventually, a vehicle.

The first day I went to the day labor place, I got sent to work at a new hospital that was being built in Greeneville TN. Since I didn't have a car, I caught a ride with someone else who was going to the same job. I gave the guy 5 bucks a day for letting me ride with him. Before long, I ended up getting assigned to another job with a company that waterproofed basements of new built homes. Every evening, Karen would pick me up at the Salvation Army and take me out to eat. It didn't take too long, (or a rocket scientist) for me to figure out she was thinking about us getting back together again.

One evening, after work, one of the guys at the Salvation Army was telling me that he had a friend who had just bought a company with her boyfriend, and they were looking for a new employee. He said the couple's company would install seats in baseball and football stadiums, movie theaters, auditoriums, and just about anywhere else large groups of people needed to sit down. This guy, (I don't remember his name) told me I could find his friend, Shala, at a small bar and grill where she was working as a waitress to help out her friend who was the owner of the restaurant. The bar was called "The Cottage", in Johnson City.

On my day off, I got Karen to take me to The Cottage for lunch. Shala was easy to spot, with her bleach blond hair, and huge tits. Karen and I ordered our lunch, and I also ordered a beer. When Shala brought me the beer, she dropped it on the table in front of me, spilling it all over. From that day on, I used to tell people, when talking about how we met, that she "threw" the beer at me.

After Karen and I ate, I told Shala I was interested in the job I heard about. She said she and Mike, her boyfriend, did need to hire a seat installer. The only problem was that the last person she hired didn't work out, so she wasn't going to do any hiring without Mikes input and approval first. Shala took down my number, and said someone would be in touch. Right before Karen dropped me off, that same day, I got a call from Mike. He asked if I could be ready to leave town first thing in the morning for a job in Greenville, SC. I said that I could, and he hired me right away.

Mike showed up about 8:00 a.m. the next morning in a white, diesel, Ford van and I got in. We took off and headed for Greenville. Along the way, I explained my legal problems, and I told him I would have to come back long enough for court, until I got everything straightened out. Mike understood, because he had been in trouble a time or two himself he said.

We got to the job site late that afternoon, after several stops. There was supposed to be a truck waiting when we got to the site, but it had not arrived yet, so we went to the motel where Mike got a room we would be sharing for a few days until Shala got there. Once we settled in, we left to get something to eat. We stopped at a liquor store on the way back to the motel. I was about to find out that Mike had a serious drinking problem. When we got back to the motel, I drank a couple beers, while Mike downed a pint of Jim Beam. I had not drank hardly any alcohol in almost a year, so I had a little bit of a buzz when we got the call that the truck we were waiting on had finally arrived at the baseball stadium where we would be working.

When we got to the stadium, I don't know exactly what I was expecting, but I wasn't expecting a 53 foot box trailer that we had to unload, by hand. Mike got a forklift from somewhere, and unloaded a few of the pallets of parts from the back of the trailer. Once he pulled everything he could reach, Mike put a pallet jack in the trailer, and I would move the pallets to the back of the trailer. Since I had not worked this hard in a long time and maybe partly due to the beer, I got sick before half of the truck was unloaded. For a while, I didn't think that I would make it. I almost quit before that truck was unloaded, but I needed the job and the new start, so I pushed through and got the truck unloaded; job well done.

The next day, we went to the stadium and started putting seats together. Mike had gotten pretty wasted the night before, and he was still pretty drunk, even at that time in the morning. Most of the concrete anchors for the seats were already set. Mike and Shala had already been on the job for about a week, and that was what they had gotten done so far. That first day, Mike and I just got hinges put on the seat pads and set out parts where they were supposed to go. On the second day, we started installing the seats.

By the time Shala got there, Mike and I had gotten a lot of work done. I really liked this kind of work. I was being paid cash, and my motel was paid for. I was saving money, and I knew I would be able to buy a car soon. I was also drinking more than I ever had before. Shala and I took to each other instantly. Every day was a party at work, and it wasn't unusual for Mike to call me over to the van to "talk" about what we needed to do next. That was what we called going to the van to have a couple of beers at break time. Shala was a heavy drinker also, but she didn't drink on the job. I guess she understood that, as sub-contractors, we could, and most likely would, be run off the job if we were caught drunk on the job.

After a few weeks, I had a court date. Karen drove to Greenville to pick me up for my court appearance. I went back to Greenville after that, and after 7 weeks we finally finished installing 4200 seats in the Greenville Drives new stadium. We had another job waiting as soon as we were finished with that one, and so we drove straight from Greenville to Branson Mo. to install 1000 seats in the Dick Clark Rock 'n Roll Hall of Fame Theater. This was a quick job, and we finished with enough time to stop in St. Louis to see the Arch on our way back to Tennessee. Did you know you can go up inside that thing? It's cool!

We returned to Tennessee a couple of days before my final court date. Instead of spending my money on a motel for the time we would be back in Tennessee waiting for our next job, I went to see FJ. I knew she would let me stay at her place as long as I gave her a little cash. I also bought an old Bronco II from Shala for $800 bucks, so I had transportation as well as a pocket full of money.

Court day arrived, and I met my lawyer at the courthouse. He told me he could get me three years probation for everything if I was willing to plead guilty to all charges. I was tired of the whole mess, so I agreed. I appeared in front of the judge that morning and entered my guilty plea.

The judge accepted it, and talked about sending me to a six-month rehab program. I started to panic. If I had to go to rehab, I would lose my job. Luckily, the D.A. spoke up, and informed the judge that the plea agreement was for probation only, no rehab. The judge said he did not like it, but would agree to it. He also said he believed I would go back to using meth without the rehab. I assured him that was never going to happen.

After sentencing, I had 72 hours to report to my probation officer. As it turned out, I had a good P.O. who understood that my job working out of town would make it difficult for me to report on a regular basis. He worked with the judge to get me a work travel permit, so I could leave the area, and he gave me a stack of probation forms. I was to mail a completed probation form along with my $35 monthly fee to the probation office every month. This was going to be easy.

I ended up not having to leave town right away for another job. According to Mike, the jobs were lined up, but the contractors weren't ready for us yet. Mike decided to work around Shala's house, and he had me showing up early every morning to help. We would spend a couple of hours every day doing various household maintenance chores, then we would start drinking. Around 5 p.m. I would go back to FJ's house. This went on for about two months, and Mike paid me for forty hours of work a week, every week, saying it wasn't my fault the jobs were not ready, so I shouldn't have to go without a paycheck. Mike, Shala and I were becoming like family. Shala even took to telling people I was her brother, and the funny thing is, I felt like it.

Chapter 31

The whole time I had been out of jail I had not heard from Lisa. I wasn't trying to either. I did speak to Tina a few times on the phone, and I accidentally mistook Faye for Tina one day at Lisa's other sister's house, but I hadn't seen Lisa. This would soon change.

The jobs finally started rolling in again, and we headed out on the road again. Mike and I had to go to Ocean City, NJ to build a grand stand on a community soccer field. The job only took us one day. That night, after the job was finished, Mike and I decided to go get a steak at a nice restaurant. A habit of ours when we got to a new job site was to find a local bar and grill close to where we would be staying. We would go there to drink, shoot pool, and eat every night after work. On a job where we only stayed in town a day or two, we would usually find the best steakhouse in town to eat at. That's exactly what we did our only night in Ocean City; a beautiful area, by the way.

Right after we ordered, I got a call. It was Lisa. She was crying, and saying the twins were treating her like shit, and how she was stuck at her parents' house 24 hours a day with no way to get anywhere. She said no one would take her anywhere, and all everyone did was yell at her; blah, blah, blah. Typical "feel sorry for me" Lisa bullshit. I spent twenty minutes on the phone with Lisa, trying to explain to her that, even if I wanted to come get her, I couldn't because I was out of town. I don't know why Lisa thought that after not hearing from her for a year, and after her setting me up and everything else, I would give a shit how anyone was treating her. Fuck her.

Another month passed by, and one day while I was driving to work, I got a call from one of the twins. We were talking, and it sounded like she was in a car full of people having a good time. I asked her, and I was right. I also heard Lisa "asking" Tina (at least, that's who I think it was, I always get those girls confused..) who she was talking to. She said it was me, and Lisa said she wanted to say "Hi". I guess I'm supposed to think this was all spontaneous and not planned at all. We had a short conversation, and then hung up. Lisa started calling me a couple of times a day after that. When I told her I would be flying home, (we were in NYC for a week) she asked if we could get together when I got in. Since I told FJ I wouldn't be coming back to her house again to stay, I knew I would either be staying at Shala's house or in a motel for a week. I told Lisa I would come and pick her up, when I got back into town.

I got back to Johnson City at around 3 a.m. after a long delay at the Atlanta airport, and I called Lisa to let her know I was on my way to pick her up. We got a motel for the week, and everything went just fine. We got along great, and even picked up some ice and a gram of powder meth. I hadn't done any meth since I got out, hadn't even thought about doing any, actually, until Lisa suggested we get some. So we did.

The day before I was to fly back to NYC, I took Lisa home and dropped her off. I wasn't going to have time to do it before I had to get to the airport. Around midnight, someone was pounding on my door. I had been asleep for an hour or so, and didn't know who this could be, unless it was Lisa. Since she couldn't get a ride anywhere, I was pretty sure it wasn't her.

I opened the door a little, leaving the chain-lock attached. There were a couple of guys standing outside, and I didn't recognize them until the biggest one said, "Why don't you go ahead, and drop that chain, and open the door." It was the fucking Drug Task Force. I opened the door, and 3 DTF agents stepped in. I could see several Johnson City cops outside also. The DTF agent, "Tank", said he had gotten an anonymous phone call saying Lisa and I were cooking meth in the room. I told him that since Lisa wasn't there, then the call was obviously bullshit. They looked around the room, saw there wasn't a lab, and left. To this day, I know it was FJ who called them on me. Luckily, I didn't have shit in the room for them to find.

I went back to NYC, and we finished the job. Lisa was calling me every night now, and we would talk for hours. She seemed like her old self, the Lisa I had fallen in love with before the dope fucked it all up. I also had started buying the occasional box of pseudo and putting the pills in vitamin bottles. I kept telling myself that I was not going to cook again, but I knew I was lying to myself.

After we finished another job, we went home for a week off. I spent the week with Lisa again, but this time we got a room in Bristol, VA in case someone decided to call the DTF again. The second day I was back Lisa suggested we cook. I said I was up for it, so we went to a few stores, and got everything we needed to do a small cook. When we were done, we had about ten grams of meth. I sold some of it to Shala, who used to be a meth head a long time ago, and who had told me several times she wanted to get her hands on some of my Red P dope. Lisa sold a couple of grams to someone she knew, and the rest we smoked ourselves.

When we went back to NJ for a couple of other jobs, I made a habit of buying pseudo at every store I went to that sold it. Up north, they didn't go through all the bullshit that they do down south to buy a box of cold pills. In NYC, all you did was tell the cashier what you needed, and she gave it to you. In Tenn. you showed ID, signed a ledger, and got put in the computer system. I guess meth wasn't as big a problem up there.

I also began buying matches while I was on the road. At night, I would get the Red P off of the covers, and throw the matches away. The Red P I kept in an empty Advil container. I had to be careful buying pseudo and matches on the road. I didn't take my own vehicle, so most of the time when I was at the store, Mike would be also, and I couldn't let him see what I was buying.

If he ever saw me buying pseudo, he would suspect that I was planning on cooking. I worried more about disappointing Mike than what he would say, or do, if he thought I was cooking again. Mike was like a brother, and he was proud of me for how well I was doing staying clean. The fact that I was drinking damn near a fifth of vodka everyday was okay with him, but if he knew I got high or cooked again, he would have been really upset.

Thanksgiving was coming, and we were just starting a job in historic Williamsburg, VA. Shala usually never stays on the job for holidays. She always spent them at home with her family. This time though, she decided to stay on the job. I, on the other hand, had Lisa wanting me to come in for the holiday. Mike didn't have a problem with me taking off for the week, and even rented a truck for the week, so I could use his van to drive home. On the way back to the job, I was supposed to bring a new guy Mike had hired on, as well as Lisa. Lisa had wanted to go out on the road with me and Mike even offered her a job, so I was bringing her back with me.

I got back to Johnson City and rented a motel. The only money I had was the week's pay that Mike had given me right before I left. I had been spending money as fast as I made it, and my bank account was empty. I picked Lisa up and we spent the week together. I went with her to her parents for Thanksgiving, and Lisa ended up in a huge fight with the twins. We ended up leaving before the dinner was even finished cooking. We got the lab stuff, Lisa had put up from the last time we cooked, and went back to the motel to cook. When we were done, Lisa started calling around for someone to buy the dope. I had to buy some stuff to do the cook, and I wasn't going to have enough money to be able to get back to Williamsburg in a few days if we didn't sell some right away.

Lisa got ahold of a regular customer of hers who said he would take everything we had, if the price was right. I set a price and he said he wanted the dope. We met at a small restaurant in Unicoi, and when I walked in to get something to eat, the guy walked over to the van to deal with Lisa. He asks to see the dope, and when Lisa handed it to him, he jumped out of the van and hauled ass with it. Lisa was flipping out when I got to the van. We took off trying to find the dude, but he was gone.

We spent the next couple of days trying to track the dude down, but he was nowhere to be found. We were supposed to leave for the job the next day, and we checked out of the motel. I only had about 20 bucks on me, and that wasn't going to get us to Williamsburg. I couldn't call Mike for money because he would ask too many questions. I decided to take one more chance, and cook.

Using the last of my money, I bought a few boxes of pills and some HEET to break them down. Since we didn't have the motel anymore, I had to find a place to cook. Mike had an old camper parked outside Shala's house. I decided that would be the best place to do the cook. I set the lab up, and ran extension cords, from the house to the camper, so I would have electricity for lights and the hot plate. I waited until it got late before I started the cook, so none of the neighbors would be able to notice activity in the camper. By morning, I had about 5 grams of dope, and I had to hurry and sell some or all of it. As we were cleaning the camper, Mike called. He wanted to know if I was ready to leave yet. It was still early, but I could hear in the way he was slurring his words that he was either already drunk, or had been up all night drinking. With Mike, it could easily have been one or the other.

I told Mike that I had a few things to take care of before I left, and that I had just gotten out of bed myself. Mike started getting an attitude about me still being in Johnson City. I guess he was thinking I should have left at midnight and arrived back in Williamsburg at sunrise. I assured him I would be there soon, and he didn't need to worry.

We started calling around to see if we could move any of the dope we had. Nobody had any money it seemed. There were several people who said to call them later that evening and they would buy a couple of grams, but that was too late. I needed cash right away. The twins were so mad at Lisa that they refused to sell anything for me that would benefit Lisa in any possible way. I was fucked.

I started considering calling Mike and having him wire me some money for fuel if I could come up with a good excuse for why I didn't have money to get back. While I was trying to think of something, Mike called again. This was now a couple of hours since his first call. When I told Mike I hadn't left yet, he went crazy. I could tell he was shit-faced, and he was screaming that I had stolen his van, and if I wasn't back in one hour he would call the cops. I told him that, #1, there was no possible way for me to be able to be there in one, or even two or three hours, even if I wanted to be, and #2, he better NEVER threaten to call the cops on me. Then I hung up on him.

After I calmed down a little, I answered the phone again when Mike called. He actually had been calling continuously since I hung up on him, but I just kept hitting the "ignore" button. When I answered, Mike was still raising hell. Now he was going off about me driving into Johnson City to spend Thanksgiving with Lisa. I told him that Lisa was family, and it was none of his fucking business who I spent Thanksgiving with. As long as I was at work when I was supposed to be, he had nothing to complain about. He didn't see it that way and said something about he should have never "let" me go see "that bitch" and how I was going to get dragged down by "that whore."

Now, I don't care who you are, you are not calling my wife a bitch or a whore, unless you really know her and have reason, as most people who know her do, to call her that. Besides that, I'm a grown man and Mike doesn't "let" me do a fucking thing. It was on, and I was pissed! We argued for a few minutes, and we both said things I'm sure we both regretted later, but I ended up hanging my phone up and turning it off. I looked at Lisa and said, "It doesn't look like we are going to Williamsburg." I was so pissed off that there was no way in hell I was going to work for Mike anymore.

The guy that I was supposed to take back up with me had been with me the entire night while I did the cook. I told him to just tell Mike that I never picked him up, so his job would be safe. I had about a half a tank of gas in my Bronco and a little less than a half tank in the van, so we used the van to do some running around to see if we could get rid of some of the dope.

After a while, I turned my phone on again. There were several voicemail messages from Mike; none of them very nice. I sent him a text message saying I was on my way. Mike started texting me and cussing me out again. Every hour or so I would send a text saying I was in a certain town and making good time.

He was expecting me to show up around midnight, or a little after, but I had never left Johnson City. I really needed to come up with a plan.

As it turns out, I had been in contact with my brother, who was living in Grand Bay, Alabama. My mother and sister were also living in the area. I called Kevin, my brother, and asked him if he thought I could get a job down there, and told him that Lisa and I were pretty much stuck with no place to go. He and our mother got together, and decided to wire me some cash and told me to come on down to Alabama. My mom and step-dad were going to let us stay with them, and Kevin said he could get me a job.

We parked Mike's van in Shala's driveway, loaded up my Bronco, and took off for Grand Bay. It was going to be a little while before they could get the money sent, but Lisa and I decided to go ahead and drive in that direction. We would stop at a truck stop somewhere along the way to get the money.

Mike must have passed out because he stopped texting and trying to call. Shala did try calling me a few times that night, but I didn't answer. At first I figured it was Mike using her phone to get me to answer a call. When I checked my voicemail and found out that it really was Shala calling, I just didn't call back. Shala was really great, and I couldn't bring myself to tell her I was leaving, even though she would have understood.

About 6 months after all this happened, I did answer a call from Shala. She didn't know what had went on between Mike and I that night, and all Mike had said all he could remember was that we talked and that I was about to leave Johnson City. He had gotten so drunk that day, he didn't remember any of the texts or voicemails he left, much less the argument. Shala and I talked a few times after that, and I talked to Mike, who apologized to me. He offered me my job back, but I turned it down. I was happy with the job I had then. He would end up calling me again a month or so later to offer me a 1/3 partnership if I would come back. I had every intention of taking the offer; I even set a date for when I would meet up with them on a job site. A few days before I was supposed to leave, with Lisa in tow, she started her bullshit and talked me out of going. I've always regretted that decision.

The last time I saw Shala, was in 2008, after I was indicted and arrested by the feds. I was in the Greene County jail in Greeneville Tenn., and Shala came to visit. The cops made her go outside to her truck to change shirts before she was allowed in to the visitation area. Apparently, the shirt she was wearing showed too much of her tits. You gotta love her for trying.

Chapter 32

We got to Alabama without any problems around 9:00 p.m. the next night. Kevin met us at a T&A truck stop, right off of I-10 in Grand Bay. We followed him to my mom and step-dad's place, where we were going to stay. They had a room set up for us when we got there. We sat around talking for a little while, then went to sleep.

The next day, there were a lot of visitors. I had been gone for several years, and with the exception of one nephew; Timothy, and two nieces; Sonja and Jessica, I hadn't met any one of my sister's kids, or Kevin's kids. By now, my sister had a grand total of 5 kids and Kevin had 4. That was a lot of kids for me to have to meet and convince that I was the world's greatest uncle.

It only took about a week or so for Kevin to get me a job at the place he was working at, making fiberglass pipes. I had to get hired through a temporary agency in the beginning, and after a short probationary period, I would be hired full time. When I went in for my interview at the temp agency, I had to take a drug test. I hadn't done anything since leaving Tennessee, and I had been drinking a shit-load of water, so I passed it, but I was nervous about it.

During the first few days we were in Alabama, Lisa was being an anti-social bitch. She just wanted to lay in bed and she would ignore anyone who tried talking to her. I made all the excuses I could for her at first, but she was really embarrassing me. Finally, she told me she just wanted to go back to Tenn. I told her that just wasn't possible at the moment, because I just started my new job. I promised her I would take her back when I went to see my probation officer in a few weeks, and this seemed to make her happy. For a couple of days, she seemed to perk up a little. At least now she was eating, and would talk some.

The second week we were in Alabama we got a call that Lisa's dad was sick and had been admitted to the hospital. Now we *had* to go back to Tennessee. I drove to work to explain the situation to my supervisor, and he told me to, "Go take care of family." He said to call him in a few days, to let him know how things were going. When I got back to my mom's,

Lisa had all of her shit packed and ready to go. I knew she wasn't planning on coming back. After the way she had been acting, I really didn't care.

We had smoked just about all of the dope we had brought down with us, so we barely had enough to smoke one foil between us before we left. Another problem was that we didn't have any cash at all. Lisa had $100 on a bank card that got deposited on her account every 2 weeks for child support for one of her kids. She didn't seem to care one bit that we didn't have the money to get back to Grand Bay. When I brought it up, she mumbled something about cooking and selling some dope to get back. Like it had worked out so well the last dozen times or so we had used that plan.

We were passing through Knoxville at about 2 a.m. with 100 miles to go, and it was cold; below freezing cold, and my heat didn't work at all. I don't think I had ever been so cold in my life. We had a blanket in the Bronco, but Lisa was rolled up in it, asleep. It was all I could do to stay awake, and all I could think about was how I could be in a nice, warm bed right then if Lisa wouldn't have had to have been a fucking cunt a few hours earlier.

About halfway to Montgomery, Lisa's mom called to say her dad was going to be fine, and that there was no need for her to make the trip. I told Lisa we should turn around and wait a couple more weeks to go, since I had to go then anyway. I even explained to her it was costing too much to be out of work for no reason, but she started getting an attitude, and I knew that if I turned around, she would be impossible to be around, so I kept on towards Tennessee.

It was around 4 a.m. when we got to Lisa's parents house. There was nobody home, so Lisa crawled in through a window to open a door. We fixed something to eat, then Lisa went to take a shower. Just as she got into the bathroom, the twins pulled in. Tina said "hi" and then headed into her bedroom. Faye sat down with me at the kitchen table and we talked for a while. When Lisa got out of the shower, she went into Joy's bedroom and went to bed. She never said a word to me or Faye, and Faye never said a word to her. There were still a lot of hard feelings between them.

After Lisa went to bed, Faye got up from the table, and told me to come with her. We went into her and Tina's bedroom, where Tina was in the process of cutting out lines of meth for "hot rails." Doing hot rails is basically snorting meth through a hot glass pipe. When the meth hits the hot glass, it vaporizes, and you snort the smoke. You can do very large hits of dope this way, and it gets you very high. It's considered to be the next best thing to shooting up. As someone who has shot up thousands of times, and has done hundreds of hot rails, I can tell you that there really is no comparison. Nothing comes close to shooting up.

When we walked into the room, Faye told Tina to cut me out a hot rail too. Tina said she already did. We did a few hot rails, and talked for hours. Faye wanted me to drive her car and see if I thought there was something wrong with the transmission, so we left for a few minutes. While we were gone, I asked her to try to make up with her mom, and she said she would think about it. We got back to the house, and Faye had to go to work. Tina was going to drop her off, and then she had a few things to do herself. Since she would be gone for most of the day, she gave me some dope to hold me over until she got back later that evening.

I decided to share some of the dope with Lisa when she woke up, even though the twins told me not to. "I wouldn't give her any dope if she was dying." was Faye's parting words as she was leaving. Obviously, she wasn't trying very hard to be nice to her mother.

When Lisa woke up, I told her I had some dope, and all she could do was bitch about the fact that the girls gave it to me. We smoked it, and Lisa got into a much better mood. Her sister, Katy came and took her to see their dad at the hospital while I stayed at the house. The twins got home, and we were getting high when Lisa got back. They invited her in on the little party, and everything was fine for a few hours.

Lisa kept going into the bathroom, and she was pretty messed up. The girls could tell she was a lot higher than she should have been, but they didn't know what was up. I did. I knew Lisa was going into the bathroom and shooting up. Back then, the girls had no idea I shot up, although Faye and I once shot up cocaine together. They did suspect Lisa had been shooting up, but she always denied it when they would ask her about it.

During one of Lisa's trips to the bathroom, she was gone a long time. One of the girls opened the bathroom door to check on her, and she was sitting on the edge of the tub with a needle in her arm. Lisa was so messed up she didn't even realize she got busted by one of her daughters. The girls flipped out, to say the least. The syringe in Lisa's hand was half full of blood where she was trying to hit a vein, but the needle kept coming out. The girls just grabbed a change of clothes and left.

After the girls got to wherever they were going, Faye called to apologize to me for leaving, and not leaving me any dope. She said she had lost a tooter that had a lot of dope caked up in it, and if I could find it, I could have it. I looked around, and I finally found the tooter after a while, along with 2 or 3 other ones, under Faye's bed. When I finished scraping the dope out of them, I had about a half a gram. I got a syringe out of my Bronco and did a huge shot of dope. What was left, I split into two shots for later, one for me, and one for Lisa.

By morning, Lisa and I were fighting again. I got my clothes and left, not knowing how I was going to get back to Grand Bay. I drove to FJ's house to chill out while I got a plan together. The only plan I could come up with was to call my mom, again, and ask for gas money to get back down there. She wired it, and I headed south.

Chapter 33

About halfway back to Grand Bay, I started to feel a lot of vibration in the steering wheel of my truck. I stopped and discovered the wheel bearing on the right front wheel was coming apart. The bearings were literally falling out. I had no choice but to drive on and hope for the best.

By the time I got to Mobile, I had been driving for over 12 hours, and I was only going about 20MPH. I got on I-10 towards Grand Bay, and the wheel was banging so hard, I thought the world was coming to an end. Maybe 5 miles from my exit, I heard something fall off the front. I coasted to a stop, and got out to find that part of the brake caliper was hanging from the brake line. The brakes and half the caliper were gone. I got back in, and drove on, with no brakes. I finally got home, and as I pulled into the drive, my wheel fell completely off. It couldn't have happened at a better time. It would take a few days, but I got it fixed, and I even replaced the heater core, so I had heat now.

With Lisa gone, I was able to concentrate on work. I went a few days without any dope, and was feeling pretty good. Not saying I didn't want any dope, I just didn't have any, so I was sleeping and eating regularly again. With the thought of Christmas coming, I didn't want to go through the holidays alone and straight, so I started thinking about a small cook. I went out and picked up some pills and a couple of other things I would need, although most of what I needed was in my Bronco already, because I was still carrying my lab around.

I made enough to sell, if I found anyone who needed any, and as it turned out, there was a guy I worked with that liked meth. I ended up selling him a couple grams, and this put me in a really good financial spot. Since I basically had no bills, I needed very little money to get by on. With the money from this sale, I didn't need to cash my paycheck that week. The following week, I cashed two paychecks, and pocketed over $1000 that I didn't need to spend, because I had made a couple more sales to my co-worker.

My mom and step-dad ended up buying a camper, and they moved into it. I took over the rent on the old trailer we were living in, and I went into steady production. My nephew, Timothy, moved in with me and started moving dope for me to his friends. I had a small box I kept on an end table in the living room, and I would have grams and half grams in it. When Timothy had someone wanting some dope, he would just take it out of the box and put the money in. When I would go home, I took the money out, and when the supply ran low, I would do a cook to replenish it. It was a very good and easy system, and money was pouring in.

It was through my co-worker that I first met Jimmy. Jimmy was just a strung out junkie when I met him, and he looked the part. Normally, I wouldn't want someone like him around me, but I had a feeling about him, so I started talking to him. As it turned out, Jimmy was heavily connected in the meth game all around the Mobile area. The first morning we met, Jimmy was pretty dope sick, so I told him to get back with me, when he was feeling better. I gave him a half gram before he left.

The next time I saw Jimmy, he looked 100% better. He had shaved, taken a shower, put on clean clothes, and he wasn't covered with open sores from digging into his skin. The first thing Jimmy wanted to know when he got to my house was where the dope I had given him came from. I told him I made it, and he said he never had anything like it. I told him I considered Red P dope to be the best there was, and he said he never heard of Red P dope. I would meet three people in Mobile who had ever heard of Red P dope, and that was all. Not to say there wasn't people cooking Red P dope, I just never met any of them.

The local newspapers in the area around Mobile, and in, and around, Pascagoula, Miss. regularly listed chemicals used by meth cooks. Not one time did I ever see tinchered iodine or matches on the list. I was used to being in Tennessee where the stores would call the cops if you bought more than two or three boxes of 50 matchbooks. But, in the Mobile area, you could buy as many boxes as you wanted, and nobody said anything. Still, I was nervous about buying too much stuff at once. Timothy didn't care. It was like a game to him, to walk into Wal-Mart and see how many boxes of matches he could come out with. One day, we went into a Wal-Mart, and there were stacks and stacks of boxes of matches. Timothy said to give him $100 and meet him by garden supply with the car. I gave him the money, and waited by garden supply like he asked. A few minutes later, he came out with a big goofy grin, pushing a shopping cart overflowing with matches. We dumped them in the trunk, and hauled ass. I asked Timothy if the cashier was suspicious. He said, he told her he was stocking up in case there was another hurricane. I guess after Katrina did so much damage in the area, that his explanation seemed reasonable.

During a cook one night, Timothy was cleaning up for me, while I was drying the dope. I had spilled some sodium hydroxide (lye) on the counter that needed to be cleaned up. Timothy grabbed a large garbage bag full of hundreds of books of matches we had torn the covers off of. He proceeded to brush the lye into the bag. I never would have guessed the lye would react with the sulfur in the matches, but it did, and we had a hell of a bonfire on the kitchen floor. I just sat at the table, while Timothy danced around the kitchen, stomping on burning matchbooks. In retrospect, it was hilarious.

I once did something just as dumb. I had been driving all over town one day, buying matches, I was ripping the covers off as I drove, so I wouldn't have to do it when I got home. As I filled plastic shopping bags with matches, I threw them in the back seat. I wasn't really paying attention when I ripped the cover off a book, and the matches hit a striker on another cover I had in my hand, igniting the whole book of matches. This scared the shit out of me, because I wasn't expecting that to happen, so when the book ignited and I felt the heat, I threw the matchbook. Into the backseat! Luckily, it didn't immediately set the rest of the matchbooks off. I hit the brakes, jumped out of the car, and threw the back door open, just as the first bag of matches started to ignite I reached in and started throwing all of the bags out. The car was so full of smoke, that I couldn't tell if I got all of the burning books or not, but I got back into the car and hauled ass with smoke boiling out of my windows, and matches burning by the side of the road.

Chapter 34

I got a call from FJ a few days after Christmas. Lisa and her new friend, Winter, had gotten pulled over on Christmas Eve with dope, scales, baggies, and several cooking items in the car. They were arrested for possession of meth, drug paraphernalia, and conspiracy to manufacture meth. Lisa's mom and oldest sister, Katy, were putting their homes and land up to get her out of jail, on a property bond.

I ended up calling Lisa, a couple of months after her arrest. Not for any reason in particular, I just started missing the whore. Things were going great for me at work, and I was meeting all kinds of people in the local meth world, and selling quite a bit of dope. I guess I felt like the only thing missing was her. I was about to make a trip up to Tenn. to see my probation officer, and we made plans to hook up.

I got to Tennessee, and brought an ounce of meth with me. I gave the twins a couple of grams, then Lisa and I took off to party with some of her friends. This was the first time I met Davy and Winter. There were a few other people I met that night, but they wouldn't serve any purpose to me until months later when they supplied me with some anhydrous ammonia. I spent the night partying, and left for Grand Bay the next morning.

As I headed back to Alabama, I was stopping at various Wal-Marts, and auto supply stores, to buy chemicals and pseudo. I did this every time I went to see my P.O. By the time I would get back to Grand Bay, I would have enough supplies to last me for several cooks.

As I approached Birmingham, I was pretty messed up. I started thinking I was being followed by the feds, so I began "evasive maneuvers," which consisted of driving fast, then pulling across a couple of lanes and hitting my brakes to see if anyone else did the same. When I saw a car pulled onto the shoulder of the interstate exit, I became convinced this was a fed waiting for his big chance to follow me.

I exited the interstate at the Steele, Alabama exit and ended up on some local roads. I wasn't sure where I was going, but I had to get away from the cars that were, well, chasing me, at least in my mind. I looked in my rear view mirror and saw 2 cars behind me. The speed limit on this stretch of road was 50MPH, so I made sure I didn't go over or under that, that way the "cops" would have no reason to pull me over.

I was starting to nod out as I was driving. I ended up on a long stretch of straight county highway, when my eyes slid closed and didn't blink back open. Suddenly, I awoke to feel myself being bounced almost to the ceiling of the truck, and before I could react, there was a tree right in front of me. My first reaction when I'm about to have a wreck, is to go totally limp. I read somewhere once that a drunk will often walk away from a bad car accident with few or no injuries, simply because he was drunk and limber. So, I go limp when I'm about to crash.

I hit the tree and saw the windshield coming straight for my face, when the seatbelt caught and stopped me. I sat there for a few seconds to make sure I was okay. I looked out the window, and saw that the rear end of the Bronco had spun around and was up on the side of the embankment I had just driven off of. The front of the truck was a few feet up the tree, so all of the wheels of the Bronco were off the ground.

I looked around the inside of the Bronco, and all of the cook supplies I had bought, along with the lab that had been in a plastic tote in the very back of the truck, were scattered all over the place. I grabbed some shopping bags, and started putting what I could back in them. Someone beat on the door of the truck, and asked if I was okay. I said I was, and the dude asked if I had anything I needed to get rid of before the cops got there. I just looked around the Bronco and thought, "You have no idea."

I got out of the truck, and walked up the embankment. The guy who asked if I had anything I needed dumped, took off. The guy who was in the second car that was following me said he had called the cops and they were on the way. It didn't take long for them to show up. Two county sheriff deputies showed up and asked what happened. I told them the truck just veered off the road suddenly, and I couldn't stop it. The cops figured a tie-rod broke, and caused the accident; sounded good to me.

It took two wreckers to pull the Bronco out of the tree and up the hill. One of the deputies left, and the other stayed while we waited for State Police to show up to make a report. As we waited, the cop asked if I was planning on filing an insurance claim. Since I didn't have insurance, I said I wasn't. The cop told me, that if I didn't need the police report, then he could cancel the call to the State cops and we could get out of there. That sounded great to me because I was worrying the cops would get a look inside the Bronco when they got there.

As the wreckers were getting ready to leave with my Bronco, I got in the truck and grabbed my cigarettes, lighter, and dope. The cop drove me to a truck stop, and I called my mom to come pick me up. I said I would be waiting at the truck stop.

It was pretty late when mom got there to pick me up. I asked her if she minded if we just kind of hung around until morning, so I could get my stuff out of the Bronco. She really didn't want to, but agreed, since leaving would mean having to come back later anyway. We went to an all night coffee house for a few hours, and ate and talked. Around 4am we went to Wal-Mart to walk around. Since my clothes were dirty from climbing up the embankment, I decided to buy some new jeans and a shirt.

After I bought the clothes, I went into the bathroom to change. I was in a stall, and someone else was in the other stall taking a shit as I was tearing the tags off of the new clothes. Apparently, the guy in the other stall thought I was stealing, because he left, and when I came out of the stall, there were two cops standing there waiting to see my receipt for the clothes. Unfortunately, I had just flushed it down the toilet with the tags from the clothes. Luckily, the cashier remembered me, and what I had bought, since it was so early in the morning, and she hadn't had a lot of customers.

When the wrecker company opened, we were waiting at the front gate. I got all of the lab stuff packed up, and we headed back to Grand Bay.

Chapter 35

Once I was back in Grand Bay, my cooking kind of died off a little. I didn't have a vehicle, so I didn't have any way to get around to get supplies. Jimmy would come by on occasion with a few boxes of pills and I would cook. My sister brought pills a couple of times every week also, and that gave me a chance to cook too. I just didn't have enough dope to sell. Everything I cooked went to pay for the pills, or other supplies I had to get through other people, and what was left went to mine and Timothy's own habits. I really needed a vehicle, but since I had just bought a shit load of furniture, and I was spending money like it was water on bullshit, my cash situation wasn't good.

While I was wondering how I was going to get a vehicle, I got a call from Faye. She said Lisa was on the run, because she jumped bail on the charges that she and Winter got on Christmas Eve. Faye asked if I would come and get Lisa, and bring her to Alabama with me. I wasn't going to do it, but Faye said the only reason she called me, is because she felt like I was the only person that would help. I couldn't tell Faye no, so I said I would come pick the bitch up.

My mom came to the rescue again, by offering not only to drive me to Tennessee to get Lisa; she also paid for gas for the trip. Mom and I got to Johnson City around 7 a.m. and we met up with Lisa in the Wal-Mart parking lot. We took off from there, and drove straight back to Grand Bay. Along the way, I told Lisa that Timothy was living with me, and that he was family, so I didn't want her to come off with some shit later about wanting us to live alone. She understood, and it never became an issue.

We got back home, and things were fine. I was still pissed off at Lisa over the shit she pulled the last time I had seen her, but she was being decent, so I tried to let it go. Kevin and his wife, also named Lisa, found a Saturn at a local car lot, and paid the down payment on it for me, so I would have my own ride. I had been using Kevin's truck when I absolutely had to go somewhere. Now I could go when and where I wanted.

The next time I got paid, I took Lisa on a pill buying spree. We drove to Ocean Springs, Miss. and worked our way back to Grand Bay, hitting every pharmacy we came to along the way. Once we got back to Grand Bay, I took Lisa on "The Loop." The Loop, was a circuit around Mobile where you could buy pills at about 10 different locations and end up back at your starting point in about 1 hour's time. It was great when you had 4 people in the car making the loop together.

I used to go to these day labor places about 7am to get pill buyers. By 7am, most of the people who are going out on a job that day, already know when and where they are going. There are always a few people hanging around, hoping for a late call, or they just don't have anywhere else to go. I would show up, and grab a couple of guys needing money, and I would give them $100 each to make the loop with me. It's the easiest money they would make all week so people were always happy to do it.

I always looked for people that really were in need of money, so I could get them to buy pills for me. I worked with a young kid who was dating an older girl. He would spend his paycheck on her every week, and be broke by Monday. To get gas money, he would buy pills for me. It was a win-win situation. When I had people buy pills, I always paid for the pills myself. I usually had about $15 in a box, $10 for the person buying them, and then the cost of the pills themselves, which varied from store to store.

One evening, I was going to get a hamburger on my lunch break from work. I saw someone who looked like he was having car trouble, and I drove over to see if I could help. It turned out he was just out of gas. His wife and kid were in the car, and he said he was trying to get someplace where there was a job waiting for him, but he had run out of gas money. I couldn't leave him stranded, so I told him I would pay him if he would buy me some pseudo pills. He agreed, and I took him to buy a couple boxes. To help him out, I paid him about $15 per box. I would give him a $20 bill and tell him what I wanted. He would buy it, and I let him keep the change from the $20. After we finished, I told him to get a gallon jug full of gas, so he could get his car to the gas station. It was a good night for both of us.

Once Lisa got to Grand Bay, we started doing massive amounts of meth again. I was cooking every day and sometimes twice a day. It wasn't unusual for me to take my cooking beaker to work with me. There was a pond that was kind of hidden by some trees, beside where I was working. After work in the morning, I would drive over by the pond and mix my Red P and iodine, so it could smoke all it needed to during the initial reaction and nobody would notice. Before I left, I would add my pseudo and put a stopper in the beaker, and when I got home, I would do the cook.

The initial reaction of a Red P cook is usually the worst part, because it smokes so much. One morning around dawn, I kicked off a cook in my kitchen. I used the vent fan over the stove to pull the smoke out. This was one of those old vents, where you pulled the chain loose and a flap on the side of the trailer opened and the fan turned on. After getting the cook going, I opened my back door, so I could see anyone driving down the road towards my house. When I looked out, there was a huge cloud of smoke just hanging in the humid, windless morning air. Since I was within viewing distance of my landlord, I flipped out. I ran inside and turned on the fan, and started spraying air freshener through the fan. I'm not sure what I thought this was going to do. I ended up making Lisa and Timothy come out in the yard and we started smoking cigarettes. The plan was, if anyone looked and saw the smoke, they would think it's just from us standing there chain-smoking.

Once I started cooking regularly again, I started getting pretty strung out. Lisa stayed paranoid; she thought the law was going to find her at any minute. This worked to my advantage, because I could still take off and hang out with the people I had been running around with, and Lisa wouldn't ask to go. Lisa became so paranoid, that at one point when she developed a toothache in one of her back teeth, she refused to let me take her to a dentist to get it pulled. Instead, she got in my tool box, and found a pair of pliers. She grabbed the tooth with them, and just as I was about to tell her she wouldn't do it, she did it. Lisa squeezed the pliers so hard that the tooth shattered. I damn near passed the fuck out. She never said a word. She went and got a pair of needle nose pliers out and started plucking the pieces of broken tooth out. That's one tough bitch.

Jimmy started staying at our place most of the time, and before long, his girlfriend, Tara, started staying with us too. I had one other buddy, Bull, who used to come by a lot, and that was just about the only people in the meth world in Alabama that Lisa had met for the first couple of months she was in Grand Bay.

Most of my cooking was done in my own kitchen or in one of the bedrooms if there was a chance someone might come by. When I got finished with the cook, I would either give the dope to Tara, Jimmy, or Bull to go sell, or I would just take off with them. Not all of the meth got sold. I was always willing to trade for anything of value. Sometimes I wanted certain items, and I would put out word that I would give top dollar trades for these items.

One day, after I had passed out for about 24 hours, I woke up to Lisa standing beside me with a gun in her hand. It was a little .25 caliber auto pistol. She was asking me if I would take the gun and $200 for an 8-ball of meth. If you'll remember, an 8-ball is 3.5 grams, or 1/8 of an ounce of meth. I told her I would, so she did the deal while I went back to sleep. When I woke up again, I had this weird urge to trade for all the .25 autos I could get my hands on. I guess I just wanted to see how many I could get.

It didn't take long for me to get quite a collection of .25's. We had a night stand beside our bed with a drawer in it, and that's where we would store the guns. Late one night, after being awake for way too long, Lisa said something that had me convinced that she had called the cops on me. As a felon, and with a meth lab in the house, I didn't want to get caught with all these guns. I got them out and piled them in the passenger's seat of my Saturn, and left to hide them someplace where they wouldn't be found. I still haven't found them.

Chapter 36

Lisa would venture out on occasion with me to buy pills, and to call her kids, who were back in Tennessee. Since Lisa's brother-in-law was actively helping the cops try to find her, she didn't want to call from close to home, for fear of them figuring out where she was. I came up with the idea of driving over to Pensacola, Florida for her to make her calls. We would get there in the morning, and spend the entire day driving around buying pills. On one trip, my sister went with us and bought pills for me too.

After several trips to Florida for phone calls, Lisa started wanting to go get the kids and bring them down to Grand Bay with us. Lisa called her mom, and told her she was going to come see the kids. Lisa's mom was one of Lisa's cosigners, and was in danger of losing her home and land if I didn't get Lisa back in jail before the six month grace period was up. She trusted me to bring Lisa back, and trusted Lisa to turn herself in, and that says a lot about the lady. She really is good people.

It was late evening when we got to Lisa's parents house. The twins were there, and I gave them a little dope while Lisa talked to her mom and dad. We only stayed at the house for a few minutes, and Lisa had told her mom we were taking the kids to go get something to eat. While Lisa got Joy and Levi strapped in, I was saying goodbye to the twins. As I was walking out the door, Lisa's mom stopped me and said, "Please, don't let me lose my home." I assured her Lisa would be back, and we left for Grand Bay again.

Along the way back to Alabama, we stopped at a couple of Wal-Marts, so we could buy new clothes for the kids. Lisa was high, and I guess she thought it would seem normal to be in a Wal-Mart in the late evening/early morning hours, buying clothes for the kids.

A few days after we got back home, a trailer that was in a lot nicer condition than the one we were living in became vacant, so we decided to move into it. There were two other young couples that wanted to go in together to rent it, but since I was already a tenant, I got first option to rent the place, so I took it. The kids got the run-down place. They weren't really happy about it.

The night before we were supposed to be moving to the new place, I decided to do a cook. Lisa said she didn't want any cooking going on in the new place, so I had to get it in while I had the chance. About halfway through the cook, the people moving in to our old place showed up with a moving trailer with all their shit in it. They knocked on the door, and asked if it would be okay to go ahead and leave the trailer there so they could be ready to move in as soon as we left. Timothy and Lisa were talking to them, and before long, they invited them inside. All of a sudden, all these people I didn't know where sitting in the living room, while I was in the bedroom cooking dope. I just worked quietly, hoping that they wouldn't figure out what I was up to.

Timothy kept coming in and out of the bedroom, and I told him to get rid of those people. The next time he came in, he had the two guys with him. Apparently, they knew what I was doing, and asked if they could watch me do the cook. Timothy took it upon himself to let them in. These guys ended up being good customers for a little while. One night, while I was especially paranoid, I paid one of the guys to lay under his trailer with a walkie talkie to watch the road while I cooked. For half a gram of meth, this guy laid in the dirt for three hours, staring at the highway to see if any cars came down our road.

The good will finally wore off, when one of the guys owed me for a half gram of dope, and I was having a hard time tracking him down. One night, while I was prepping for a cook, I saw the dude's truck pull into his driveway. Jimmy saw him also, and he ran out the door with Bull to get my money. When Jimmy and Bull came back, Jimmy said they had made it clear that I had better be paid no later than the next evening.

The next day, the dude's girl showed up to trade pussy to clear the debt. She was cute but she was also six or seven months pregnant. Since it was only half a gram, I let her "make payment." Afterwards, the dude got pissed off over it, and kicked the girl out, then called the landlord and told her I was running a meth lab out of my place. The landlord didn't believe him, but I sent Jimmy and Bull back to "speak" with the dude about the situation. He "apologized" by "giving" me his DVD player, his Fossil watch, all of his tools, and the JVC stereo out of his car. He also "agreed" to move by morning. That's the explanation Jimmy gave me when he came back and gave me all that stuff he got from the dude, and I didn't question him.

Something I didn't really understand until I got in the meth game in Alabama is that, as a cook, I had a hell of a lot of power over people. In Mobile, people who are closest to cooks will act almost as personal servants, in order to keep their dope connect happy. Jimmy used to wash my car, and clean my house, so Lisa didn't have to. He would go to the grocery store for me, go on resupply runs for chemicals anything I needed was done for me. If I was cooking in the bedroom, and Lisa cooked dinner, Jimmy would make me a plate of food and bring it to me. Dope cooks in the Mobile meth scene weren't just cooks, we were kings.

There would also be a lot of back-stabbing going on to try to push someone to the side, so a cook could be taken over by someone else. One night while Lisa and I were spending a quiet night alone, there was a knock at my door. I answered it, but didn't recognize the person standing there. He said his name was "Fat Head" and that Jimmy had sent him. Sounds like an Italian mob kind of thing, doesn't it?

I had heard of, but never met, Fat Head. According to rumors, Fat Head had a degree in chemistry, but preferred cooking meth to legitimate work. It was easy to see where Fat Head got his name. He was of average height and build, but he had this huge head that was way too big for his body. He also spoke very softly and more mumbled his words than actually spoke them, so it was hard for me to really understand him, at least until I got to know him.

I invited Fat Head in, and he said that he had bought some of my dope from Jimmy, and loved it. He said he had several grams of lab grade Red P, and he wanted me to have it. Fat Head gave me about 10 grams of pure Red P, and I gave him some dope in exchange. He left with an open invitation to stop by again anytime he wanted. As it turned out, Jimmy never told Fat Head to come by my place. He didn't even know how he had found out who I was or where I lived. All we could figure was that Tara must have told Erica, his girlfriend, about me, and Erica told Fat Head.

Fat Head started coming by to trade pills and Red P for meth. Although he was a cook himself, he only cooked using the anhydrous ammonia method. Since he preferred Red P dope to anhydrous, he was happy to trade me some of his pills for a supply of my dope for his personal use.

Jimmy was not happy at all that Fat Head came straight to me, because that cut into Jimmy's supply and distribution chain. This would happen many more times, but sometimes there were consequences for side stepping Jimmy.

Chapter 37

At that time, I was the most important thing in Jimmy's life. I was his friend, I gave him a place to live, food to eat, and I was basically his employer. Although I didn't pay Jimmy for his services, I did give him enough extra dope for him to be able to skim a little for himself, or trade for pills, that he would trade back to me, for even more dope. I was also supporting his and Tara's dope habits, along with mine, Lisa's and Timothy's. Jimmy had a lot to lose if I started working with someone else, and he knew it, so he guarded my identity jealously.

Jimmy also wasn't your average dope fiend. In another life, before meth became his life, Jimmy regularly competed in every tough man contest he could get into. Jimmy loved to fight. Since Lisa wasn't allowing any cooking at the new trailer, unless it was an emergency "Lisa's-out-of-dope" type situation, I had to find new places to go cook. This kept me out of the house for days at a time, and eventually I ended up quitting my job. Jimmy was great at getting me places to go cook.

One night, I was at a house in Grand Bay, cooking. The owner of the house, B.J., was one of Jimmy's oldest friends. B.J. set me up in an empty bedroom to cook, and I would use this room several nights a week. This particular night, I had Timothy with me to help me out, because this cook was unusually large. There were a lot of people at the house that night, and I knew everyone except for one person. The person I didn't know was named Bruce. I would end up being introduced to him by Timothy, who I thought knew him, but I would find out later that he had just met him that night also.

Bruce let me know that he had a good supply chain for pills, and he had a permanent cook spot I could use if I was interested. I got his number, and met up with him in a parking lot later that night. He had a lot of pills on him, and more at the cook house. I followed him to the house, and it really was a good spot, with woods in the back, and windows facing every road. The house was a nice brick home, in a nice area, the kind of place you'd never think to find a meth lab. There was a large garage for our cars, so we could park there, and nobody would see several strange vehicles parked out front.

I started going over to Bruce's place about 3 times a week, for about a month. Bruce couldn't really sell any dope for me, but he was good at getting pills and supplies. I still had Jimmy to move the dope, although I couldn't tell him where I was cooking it. When I was at Bruce's, Jimmy would constantly be calling me. He was worried to death that he was about to be replaced.

One night, I was out of iodine, and Bruce had several boxes of pills for me. Jimmy also needed me to cook, but I told him the same thing I told Bruce, I couldn't cook without iodine. Jimmy had an idea. He called Bruce and had him meet us in Grand Bay. I know Bruce was nervous when we met up, because he never got out of his car, or even turned it off. I was kind of wondering if Jimmy was up to something myself, but I just waited to see what was up. As it turned out, Jimmy did have a good idea. We were right across the street from a feed and seed store that sold the iodine I needed. Jimmy had scoped the place out the last time he was in there to buy iodine, and had discovered that there was no alarm on the door. He told Bruce to go over to the store, kick in the door, and steal all of the iodine on the shelf. This was the kind of thing Bruce loved to do, so he agreed to do it, and meet us afterward at B.J.'s house. Timothy had said he wanted to go with Bruce to be sure he showed up at B.J.'s, but I think he just wanted in on the fun of kicking in the door.

We got to B.J.'s and waited. Bruce and Timothy got there not long after we did, and they said there were no problems with the job. As they stepped on the porch, Jimmy hit Bruce in the mouth, knocking him off the porch and on the ground. Jimmy started beating the hell out of Bruce and told him he better never go around him again to try to steal his dope connect. Jimmy told him to get the hell out of there and never come back. As Bruce left, I told him, "Great work, dumbass. The iodine is still in his car." Jimmy then jumped into Tara's Mustang and somehow was able to get Bruce to pull over and give him the iodine.

I kind of felt bad for Bruce. He wasn't actually trying to "steal" me. I was just using supply lines other than Jimmy, but local politics in the meth world of Alabama didn't allow for Bruce to deal directly with me. It wasn't anything I engineered, it just was.

There were times when I did exercise my power over Jimmy. I got a call one day from someone I knew through Fat Head. This was Chris, and although I knew Jimmy and Bull knew Chris, they didn't do any deals with him if they didn't have to. Chris was very heavily connected with the

Vietnamese who were bringing in a lot of ice into the area. You don't want to step on any toes when the Viets are involved. That is why Jimmy stayed away from Chris. Chris was a middleman. He didn't cook, and he didn't nickel and dime deal. Chris liked to buy quantity, and sell quantity.

When I got the call, Chris said he wanted to meet at his house. We set a time and I showed up alone as requested. Chris told me he wanted me to supply him with Red P dope. He wanted everything I made. I told him that there was no possible way I could do that, because I had suppliers to pay, with dope, and a lot of my cook supplies came through Jimmy or Fat Head, who would go elsewhere if I cut their dope supplies too much. I finally agreed to supply Chris with a substantial amount of dope on a weekly basis to see if it worked out.

When I told Jimmy about my deal, he was pretty pissed off, but I told him I wasn't changing teams, I was just adding to what was going on. Since I needed to cook a lot more dope, I needed Jimmy out there hustling more pills, and a few more different cook spots.

Jimmy ended up taking me to one of his best kept secrets, Amanda's crack house. Amanda was a crack whore who inherited a house after the death of her parents. You could find crack heads and dealers there at any time of the day or night, whether Amanda was there or not. When Jimmy would get hard up for pills, he would go to Amanda's, buy some crack, and give it to crack-heads to walk up the street a block to a CVS to buy a box of pills. Now that we needed a lot more pills, we needed all the crack-heads we could get.

At first, we set the lab up in the garage, but there was way too much traffic in and out of there, with crack whores going in there to fuck for crack. I would be trying to concentrate, while some crack dealer was getting his dick sucked 5 feet away from me. It was disturbing, to say the least.

We ended up moving the lab to one of the bedrooms in the house. I would be cooking a supply of pills, while Jimmy was driving crack heads around in my car buying more pills. One day, I pulled into Amanda's, and Jimmy ran outside and jumped into my car with a gym bag, and yelled, "Go! Go! Go!" I hauled ass, and when we got down the road, I asked what was up. Jimmy opened the bag and it had several dozen boxes of pills in it. When I asked him where he got them, he said he sent a crack head to the store to jump the counter and grab all of the boxes of pills. I don't know if that's where the pills really came from or not, but I never went back to Amanda's after that.

Chapter 38

For a couple of weeks, my deals with Chris were great. I would give him the dope, then pick my money up the next day. Then, I tried calling him one day for my money, but he wouldn't answer or call back after I left voicemail messages. I gave him till the following day, then, when I still couldn't get a hold of him, I told Jimmy to go get my money. This was a very dangerous job for Jimmy, because Chris was protected by the Viets, and was supposed to be "untouchable." Jimmy took Bull, and they got a promise from Chris to have my money later that night.

When we showed up at Chris' that evening, the door was open, so we just walked in with Jimmy in front of me, and Bull behind me. As we walked in, I noticed that right in the center of Chris' beloved big screen TV, there was a perfectly round bullet hole. I just laughed and shook my head. It was obvious how they convinced Chris to come up off my money.

We walked to Chris' bedroom that he practically lived out of. As we all sat down, Chris handed me a stack of 20's Without a word, Jimmy took the money out of my hand and threw it back at Chris, saying "We don't want that shit." What I didn't know, but Jimmy expected, was that Chris had just tried to pay me with counterfeit bills he had been printing off of his home computer. Jimmy told him to pay with legit cash, but he said he didn't have any. Without a word, Jimmy and Bull started packing up Chris's laptop and printer he was using for the funny money. While they did this, with Chris asking for one more day to get the money, another car pulled in. Chris went out to the living room for a few minutes, then came back in the bedroom with a wad of cash, which he handed to me. I checked it, and it was real, so we walked out of the room to leave. As we walked through the living room, we encountered several, very unhappy looking, Vietnamese gang bangers. It was a tense moment, as we all nodded to one another, while Jimmy and Bull escorted me out the door. That was the last time any of us ever went back around there.

Things between Lisa and I were getting bad; again. I was gone from home almost all of the time, and the more strung out I got, the less I cared about being home. I came across an old Coleman camp stove and decided to try a few outdoor cooks. I took Lisa along with me for a couple of these, so we could spend some time together.

I was taking a couple of days off to sleep, which I did once ever couple of weeks. Usually, when I took my sleep days, I could count on not being disturbed. Lisa or Jimmy would basically stand guard at the door the entire time I was asleep. They started "guard duty" after I fell asleep one day with a Pyrex dish, full of dope, laying next to me on the bed. Lisa came out of the front bedroom to catch my sister standing at the bedroom door, with her cell phone, taking pictures of me. This was just too strange, because my sister definitely could not be trusted, and any pictures she took would most likely find their way to the cops.

Anyway, I'm not sure how long I was asleep when I woke up, but I suddenly went from a blissful slumber to wide awake in a split second. Lisa was sitting on me, straddling my waist, asking if I was awake. I just nodded my head to indicate that I was awake and aware. Lisa then held up a syringe and said, "I had to give you two shots to wake you up."

I had only been asleep for a few hours, but Lisa said Jimmy needed me awake right away. He had called to say he had a huge supply of pills from another cook, that the cook wanted me to cook for him. In return, I got to keep half of the dope. This is a common agreement meth cooks will make with someone who has a quantity of pills, but no desire to sell them straight out. Jimmy wanted me to meet him at B.J.'s as soon as possible. Lisa had even taken it upon herself to ask if she could come with me. B.J. told Jimmy he was okay with it, so against my better judgment, I took her with me, leaving Tara at the house to babysit.

We got to B.J.'s, and when we went in, I told Lisa to go in the living room. I headed to the bedroom and started setting up. I had Jimmy and B.J. helping me get the pills broken down and the lab set up. Lisa kept coming in the room, generally being loud and getting in the way. I knew we would end up getting into an argument before the night was over. Lisa needed to sleep.

Once all the pills were broken down, and I was ready to start, Lisa asked if she could do the cook. I told her no, because this wasn't my cook, and I didn't trust her with it. This pissed her off, and she started yelling about how she was a good cook, and so on. I just simply locked her out of the room and cooked.

It took until morning for me to finish, and Jimmy, B.J., and I sat in the bedroom for an hour or two, smoking some of the dope. I split the dope, and gave Jimmy half to give to the person he got the pills from. I gave some to Jimmy for helping, and a few grams to B.J. for letting me cook at his house. Lisa was still being a bitch, and I packed the lab up and put everything in the car, while she stood there and continued to bitch.

When I was ready to leave, I told Lisa to get in the car. She started screaming about me being a "sorry son of a bitch" and how "she hoped I got busted cooking dope," and so on. When she started yelling about cooking dope, Jimmy and B.J. were both ready to kill her. I just grabbed Lisa by the neck and shoved her in the car, telling her to shut up.

I had to go to the Wal-Mart in Pascagoula. Along the way, Lisa kept on and on about anything and everything she could think of to bitch about. At one point she started saying shit about how I had never done anything for her, or her kids; that was way too much for me to put up with. I told Lisa I was going to pull over, and beat her ass. Since I had never laid a hand on Lisa before, I guess she felt confident I still wasn't going to do anything to her, so she looked at me and said, "I wish you would."

I pulled over and put my car in neutral. I just sat there for a second, trying to calm down. Lisa looked at me and said, "I thought you said you were going to beat my ass? You ain't shit." I remember backhanding Lisa once. The next thing I remember is putting my car back into gear, and pulling back onto the road.

Lisa was on the floorboard, knocked out. After a few miles, she got up off of the floorboard, and sat in her seat. She put her seatbelt on, and sat quietly the rest of the way to the store. When we parked at Wal-Mart, I looked at her and asked, "Are you going in?" She simply said, "No!" After I finished shopping, I drove back to Grand Bay. The more Lisa sat there pissed off, the more I couldn't stand to have her near me. I pulled over at a convenience store, and told her to get out. She did, and I took off, leaving her in the parking lot.

Once I dumped Lisa off, I got tired. I went to the truck stop, and parked in the parking lot to get some sleep. I put the seat back, and laid back. Just as I was about to go to sleep, a truck pulled in behind me. I got up and looked. It was the repo man. I hadn't made a payment on my Saturn in a month, and they wanted the car. Fine. Fuck it. I didn't give a shit at this point. I just wanted to be away from Lisa, and I wanted some sleep. I grabbed the gym bag with the lab in it, and took off walking down the road to a house I figured that Jimmy would be at, on his way back from dropping the dope off he was delivering.

I got there about the same time as Jimmy, and he took me to see a friend of his. It was actually his ex-girlfriend, but she agreed to let me stay at her house and cook for a few days. When Jimmy and Tara picked me up to go do some running around a couple days later, Tara said my brother had went and picked Lisa up after she had called him. Since our rent had not been paid in weeks, (We paid by the week,) we were being evicted, so Lisa and the kids were staying with Kevin and his Lisa. I was told that Kevin had sent me a couple of messages to "come get your wife." Fuck her! I didn't have a car, and she only had a couple of days to turn herself in, but I didn't give a fuck. I was done with her for good.

For a couple of days, anyway.

Chapter 39

The day before Lisa had to leave to go back to Tennessee, she tracked me down. By then, I was out of dope, money, cook supplies, and with no vehicle, I had no way of getting my hands on anything to help my situation. I was pretty much screwed as far as cooking dope went, but I didn't really care anymore. I was getting tired of the lifestyle.

I was tired of having money today, and being broke tomorrow. I wanted to go back to work and have a home again. The last 4 years had been crazy, and I had lost everything I had going for me, over and over again. It was time to get the hell out of Alabama, and head back to Tennessee, where life wasn't so insane. It was time to start over - again.

Lisa and I talked about starting over and getting away from the lifestyle together. She said she wanted the same thing I did, but first she had to take care of her charges back home.

My step-dad, Elwood, was driving Lisa and the kids back to Tennessee, so I packed up and went with them. The plan was to get back to Johnson City, spend the night with the kids, and then Lisa would turn herself in the next morning. Lisa's parents would be helping and taking care of the kids.

I wasn't sure what I was going to do for a place to stay. The twins said I could stay with them, but they lived so far from town, that it would be impossible for me to get to work, if I could even find a job from there.

We got to Johnson City around 8pm. Before we got to town, Lisa had called Tina and told her to meet us at the Red Roof Inn. She was waiting with her friend, Leanna, when we got there. We packed all our stuff into the trunk of the car, and headed to Lisa's parents house.

When we got to the house, I went to the twin's bedroom to see if they had anything for me to get high on. They had a little dope, and they smoked it with me, while Lisa told her parents what she was going to do about turning herself in, in the morning.

Lisa eventually came into the girls' bedroom to see them and change clothes. While we were talking, Faye pulled a meth pipe out of a small plastic container. She asked if it was Lisa's, and Lisa said it was. She took the pipe and container and slid it into my pocket. This becomes important later on in this particular night's activities.

After an hour or so of visiting, I was ready to go somewhere. Tina suggested we go to Johnson City and grab something to eat. Faye didn't want to go, so it was Leanna, Tina, Lisa, and I, piling into the car to go eat.

We were only gone about two hours, when we decided to go back to the house to hang out. As we turned onto the road that Lisa's parents live on, Leanna slowed the car and yelled, "I can see a UFO through the trees!" I looked, and sure enough, there was a huge, bright light hovering in the air. Just as we took a sharp curve that would put us in view of the house, I realized what we were looking at; a helicopter.

I pushed Lisa down in the seat and I ducked down. Tina said the helicopter had a spotlight shining on the house, and that there were cops everywhere. I asked if there was room to drive past there, and Leanna said there was. I told her just to drive slowly, and pretend she was just trying to see what was going on. She did, and we made it past without raising suspicion. Once we got out of sight, Leanna hauled ass back to Johnson City.

We didn't know it then, but Joy or Levi had called Lisa's sister, Katy, who was the other co-signer on Lisa's bond, to tell her they were home. This alerted Katy's husband, Rupert, who had been trying to track down Lisa ever since she had left town. Rupert called the cops, and they tried to catch Lisa at her parents.

Since Elwood had gotten a room at the Red Roof Inn for the night, we decided to have Leanna and Tina drop us off there. We would hang around until morning, and then wake Elwood to have him take Lisa to the jail.

Lisa could have just went ahead and let the cops have her, but she just didn't want to give them the satisfaction of catching her. Also, it would look better in court if she had self-surrendered.

Lisa and I laid low, in a small tree line that separated the Red Roof's property from that of another motel. About 4 a.m. a cop car came in through the parking lot, and I got a bad feeling. I told Lisa we should go ahead, wake up Elwood, and get out of there. Lisa wanted to wait a little longer, so we waited until 5a.m.

We walked over to the motel, and got on the elevator to the 3rd floor. When the door opened on the 3rd floor, we were surprised to see two cops standing there with their backs to us, and Rupert, Lisa's brother-in-law, standing there as well, talking to them.

I pushed Lisa against the wall, so nobody would see her, and pushed the door-close button. Before the doors were able to close though, Rupert saw me, and started jumping up and down, literally, while screaming, "There they are! There they are!"

As the doors slid shut, one of the cops turned and saw me. He grabbed the door to stop it from closing, and said, "Step out of there." We got off the elevator, and the cops handcuffed us.

Rupert was bouncing around like he was on crack or something. He kept yelling at Lisa, saying that he knew he would get her, and he was saying that I was wanted for violation of probation. The cops told Rupert to shut up, before they arrested him for disturbing the peace; small consolation.

I'm not sure why Rupert thought I had a warrant on me for violation of probation. While it's true that I had not reported to my P.O. in several months, but since I had a work-travel permit, I was allowed to miss reporting.

The cops got my Alabama driver's license out of my wallet, and ran my name. There were no warrants, so the cop in charge told one of the others to let me go. As the cop was about to uncuff me, he said he was going to pat me down. I didn't mind that, since I was going free and I had nothing on me. When the cop checked my jacket pocket, and pulled out that plastic container with the meth pipe in it, you should have seen the look on my face. I had totally forgotten about it during all the activity, and right then, I knew I was in trouble.

When the cop opened the container and pulled the pipe out, he asked, "What's this? A crack pipe?" Knowing that the law in Tennessee is a lot harder on meth than it is on crack, I just went with it.

"Yep, it's a crack pipe." I answered.

The cop said, "Well, if you had a Tennessee driver's license, instead of an Alabama one, I would just issue you a summons to appear in court. Unfortunately, since you don't, you're going to have to go to jail for possession of drug paraphernalia."

To her credit, Lisa spoke up then to say it was her pipe, but the cop said since it was in my pocket, it's my pipe. They then took both of us to jail.

Since it was a Saturday morning, (isn't it always?) I had to wait until Monday, before I could get anything done about seeing a judge, to try to get out of jail. I wasn't sure, but I believed the twins would get me out if the bail was low enough. As it turned out, I didn't need them to get me out. The judge had granted me an O.R. bond. This, as you well know, meant that I was free on nothing but my word that I would return for my court appearances. I was willing to agree to anything to get out of there, before the probation office found out I was in jail, and hit me with a violation before I could leave.

Chapter 40

As soon as I got out, I called Tina to come pick me up. My plans for a new start were not going well, at all. Since returning, I had caught a new drug charge, went to jail, and I was sure my probation was going to get violated soon. On top of that, I was broke, had no car, and nowhere to go. I didn't even have a lab, to cook some dope to make some money.

I had Tina drop me off that evening at the Wal-Mart in Elizabethton. She gave me $25 before I got out of the car, and told me to call her if I needed anything at all. I thanked her, and went to go get change for the phone.

I called FJ. She said I could stay at her place if I needed to, so I took off walking, and arrived at her house around midnight. I spent a few days at FJ's, trying to figure out what I was going to do. I had her drive me to get my clothes and shaving bag, from her parent's house, where I had left it the night we came back to town.

Friday afternoon, was Lisa's visiting day at the Carter County jail, and the twins told me they had made an appointment for all of us to go see her. Visitation there was all done by appointment. Faye also told me to bring clothes, because I was going to be staying with her and Tina.

The visit went fine. Lisa was crying the whole time, and telling me how she wanted to change, and leave dope alone. It was an Oscar-worthy act of epic proportions. I didn't believe a single solitary word of it. I went back to the house with the twins, and we started smoking dope again. Leanna showed up, wanting the twins to go somewhere with her. They said they would be back soon, and left.

A couple hours later, a car pulled up the driveway. I walked into the living room, and my father-in-law was outside. I was just about to look out, to see who else was out there, when Levi came flying through the living room, and into his bedroom. Only one thing made Levi act like that. Cops! Feeling uneasy, I headed for the front door to make a run for it, but just as I got it open, I heard someone behind me say, "Sir, I need to speak with you." I turned around to find a Carter County deputy standing inside the back door.

My father-in-law was getting pretty worked up. He was telling the cop he had no right to come on his property, which was on the Unicoi County side of the line, and be able to arrest anyone. That was true, but I didn't want a scene at their house, so I asked the cop what he was arresting me for. I expected him to say, "Violation of probation." Instead, he said I was being arrested for possession of schedule two drugs. Since I knew I hadn't been caught with any dope, I went on to jail with the cop. I figured it was a mistake, and we would work it out Monday when court opened.

I got up for court Monday morning, feeling nervous. Surely, my P.O. knew about my arrest a week earlier, and had violated my probation, or at the very least, he would see me in court and violate me then. I sat in a small, windowless room with several other inmates waiting to see the judge. On occasion, a lawyer, or the assistant district attorney, (A.D.A.) would squeeze into the room to talk to someone. When the A.D.A. called my name and asked if I would need an attorney, I got pissed.

When I came to jail a few nights earlier, I asked how it was I was being charged with possession of anything, when I didn't have anything on me. The officer checked the report, and said FJ had called the Drug Task Force to her house, after finding meth in some property that belonged to me. The property was my shaving bag.

I told the A.D.A. that I felt like this charge was bullshit, and I think she knew it too. If they could do this to me, then I could easily plant some dope somewhere, and swear it was hers and get her arrested. There was no PROOF the dope, or even the shaving bag for that matter, belonged to me. The A.D.A. agreed that, if I fought the charge, I would probably get it thrown out. She then asked, "Are you going to get bailed out of jail?" I told her it wasn't likely, and she said I would end up sitting in jail for at least, two months waiting for a court date to plead my case. Unless, I wanted to work something out.

"Working something out" turned out to mean, I plead guilty to simple possession, for a year of probation. Once again, hoping my P.O. didn't know I was locked up, I took the deal to get the hell out of jail.

When I got released, I didn't want to call the twins again to come get me, so I walked downtown to decide on my next move. I finally decided to call Lea, to see what she was doing. Lea was now living in a big fixer-upper house in Elizabethton. I asked if I could stay with her until I got straightened out, and she said she would be glad to have me stay there. She came, picked me up, and took me home.

I got a hold of the twins later that day, and they brought me my clothes. They asked if I wanted to stay with them, but I said I was better off being in town, where I could get around. Besides, once my P.O. started to look for me, their place is the first place the cops would show up at.

I spent the first few days at Lea's house helping her underpin a doublewide trailer she was about to sell. When we were finished with that, we pretty much did nothing except visit with a couple of her lesbian friends, and try to find Lortabs to buy. Lea always had a bad pill habit.

After a week or so at Lea's house, I had to find something to do to make some money. I called Faye, and asked her if she would front me the cash to get a lab together, and supplies to do a cook. She said she would. I got a ride with Larry, Lea's neighbor, to go meet Faye to get the money. I told Faye I would give her a call when the cook was done, so I could repay the loan with dope.

Larry loved meth too, so it wasn't hard to convince him to help me buy pills for the cook. It took us about three hours to buy everything I needed, and then we went back to Lea's, so I could get everything ready. Lea didn't have any problem with me cooking, since she was a meth head from way back. I took everything to my room to do all of the prep work, in case someone came by to visit, or to buy or sell pain pills.

I spent hours getting the Red P ready and the pills broke down. Once that was finished, I had to build my cook pot and get everything mixed for the cook. When the cook kicked off, I set the pot out the window, onto the roof of the front porch. There was a good breeze out which blew the smoke away, so it wasn't noticeable. I laid down on the bed to give the reaction time to settle down. The next thing I knew, it was morning.

I jumped out of bed and ran to the window, hoping the wind didn't blow my cook pot off of the roof. Luckily, it was sitting right where I left it. I brought it inside, and went down to the kitchen to do the cook. The cook went perfect, and I went back upstairs to gas it off. I ended up with several grams of quality meth; seems that a good sit does wonders for the stuff.

I called the twins, and told them why I didn't call sooner, but they weren't worried at all. Tina came by to pick up the dope, and I gave her a couple extra grams to sell for me. After she left, I woke Lea up and we got high. I had some syringes, so we were banging the hell out of some dope that day. Larry came by, and I got him high too, for driving me around and helping me buy shit for the cook.

Chapter 41

By the next morning, Lea was getting a little paranoid. It started around late afternoon, when Lea was washing dishes. She looked outside, and noticed a county work crew, working on the sewer system. For some reason, Lea thought the workers were DEA agents, who were pumping the water out of the sewer system to test it for chemicals, to see if anyone was cooking meth in the area. I tried to explain to her just how ridiculous this sounded, but she was absolutely convinced we were about to get busted.

Finally, the work crew left, and Lea seemed to forget about them. We went to Lea's bedroom, and relaxed for a while by shooting up some more dope. Sometime after dark, Lea suddenly lost her mind. I was sitting on the bed, tapping my cigarette lighter on the nightstand, when Lea jumped up and asked me what the hell I was doing. I didn't know what the fuck she was talking about, so I asked her, "What the fuck are you talking about?"

Lea asked, "Why are you sending Morse Code messages?"

"Morse code? Who the fuck would I be sending Morse Code messages to?" I asked while laughing my ass off at her.

All of a sudden, Lea had gotten it in her head that there were four police officers in the basement, waiting for my signal, to come up into the house and bust us. She couldn't explain to me how the cops got in the basement to begin with, or how she knew the exact number of cops down there waiting for the signal, but they were there; in her mind, anyway.

I decided to have some fun with Lea, so I started tapping my foot on the floor in a Morse Code fashion. Lea flipped the fuck out. She started screaming for me to stop, and I would, for a couple of minutes. Then I would do it again. This was quite entertaining to me; kind of like using a laser pointer to fuck with a cat. When the Morse Code got old, I started telling her I was hearing voices in different parts of the house. Lea, armed with a steak knife from the kitchen, would believe me every time, and she would go investigate to see who was in the house.

At one point, she finally locked the bedroom door and pulled a dresser over to barricade it. The entire time, all of this is going on; I've been kicked back on the bed, enjoying myself at Lea's expense. Lea was bouncing around the bedroom, and peeking out the windows, when she told me to turn off the lights. I did, and asked what she was seeing outside. Lea asked me who put the ounce of dope on the running board of her truck for the cops to find. I got up to look out the window, and when I tried to open the curtain, she grabbed it out of my hand, closed it, and asked, "Who are you trying to let see into the house?"

Irritated, I snatched the curtain back out of her hand and opened it so I could see the driveway as Lea did a belly flop onto the floor, out of sight of whoever it was she thought was out there. The "ounce of dope on the running board" was nothing more than the streetlight, reflecting off the surface of the running board. I tried to explain this, but she insisted she knew exactly what it was, and knew exactly what was going on... She was being set up! That was her explanation anyway.

I finally gave up on messing with Lea's head after a while. She was doing just fine messing with her own head. I walked over to the door, pushed the dresser out of the way, and was unlocking the door, when Lea ran over, grabbed her knife, and demanded to know where I was going. "To take a piss. Want to come watch?" Apparently, she was so fucked in the head, she did. Lea followed me to the bathroom, and stood in the doorway, knife in hand, while I took a piss. Just for the hell of it, I kept pinching off the stream, so I was pissing in a "Morse Code" rhythm. "Hey Lea, I'm messaging the DEA's sewer submarine, so they know where we're at." She wasn't the slightest bit amused.

When I was done, she followed me back to the bedroom. When we got back in, Lea locked the door, and pointed the knife at me, telling me to sit down. Things were going from fun to serious, kind of quick, and I decided it was time I got the fuck away from this situation. Since it was the middle of the night, I couldn't call anyone to come get me. Not that I thought Lea would let me use the phone right then anyway.

I made sure I had my dope, syringe, and cigarettes in my pocket, then I told Lea I heard someone coming in through the living room window. She threw the bedroom door open, and took off running through the house. As soon as I saw her turn the corner into the living room, I took off down the hall, towards the backdoor. Seeing me open the door, she ran towards me yelling, "Don't open that door!"

I took off across the yard, jumping the fence between her house and Larry's, while Lea stood at the door, yelling at me to get back in the house. I ran down the street, not knowing where to go. At this point, I'm pretty paranoid myself, and everywhere I looked, all I could see was tree people, and shadow people. To top that off, I ended up convinced the cops were looking for me for leaving Lea's house, so I was ducking and hiding in the bushes.

It took me a couple of hours, but I finally made it the four blocks to my old house. That was the only place I could think of to go. Once I got there, I hid under the porch. I stayed there until daylight convinced that every car that drove by was a cop, waiting for me to come out from under the porch. The porch was enclosed, except for an entrance hole, cut out near the driveway at the side of the house. This made me feel safe, because the cops couldn't see me. The problem with this setup was that I couldn't see out either, so all I had to go on to know what was going on around me, was what I could hear. What I was hearing, once the sun came up, was the cop on the porch, sneaking around, while he waited for me to come out, so he could arrest me.

I was stuck, but I decided to wait the cop out. Surely, he would leave after a while if I stayed perfectly still, so he couldn't hear me. I lay under that porch for hours, afraid to move. I was so thirsty, I couldn't stand it, and that is what finally made me decide to give up. I crawled to the entrance hole, and prepared to surrender. Before I exited, I announced that I was giving up. I crawled out, and once I was clear of the doorway, I laid face down on the driveway, and awaited orders. Nobody said shit. After a few seconds, I peeked around behind me. There was nothing there, except a piece of rope, dangling from the front porch railing. The wind was making the rope sway back and forth, causing it to make noise every time it made contact with the rail below it. That, is the sound I thought was a cop sneaking around.

I got up, cleaned myself off, and walked to the McDonald's for something to drink. Once I saw that the cops weren't stalking me, my paranoia began to subside a little, and I began to think about what I was going to do. I was practically broke, and Tina would be giving me a little money for the dope she was selling, but that wasn't going to help me much at all. I still had no transportation, and nowhere to live. All of my clothes were still at Lea's house, and so was my lab. Since I didn't know the state of mind Lea was in at the moment, I wasn't about to go collect my belongings just yet.

I walked around downtown Elizabethton all day, visiting several of the "junk" shops, just to kill some time. When it started to get dark, my paranoia started to return. I started to think the cops were looking for me again. This time, I thought they were looking for me, for probation violation warrants. I ducked into a movie theater to get out of the streets, and went into the bathroom to do a shot of dope. By the time I came out of the bathroom, I was now convinced the cops were after me for escaping from jail. I don't know where that thought came from, but in my mind, I had escaped from jail and was on the run.

I called Tina and asked her if she would come pick me up. She was out running around with Leanna, and she said they would meet me somewhere. I told her to park behind a little ice cream shop a few blocks from where I was at, and I would be there soon. By the time Tina and Leanna got there, I was already there. I was laying on the ground, under an old school bus, watching to see if they had been followed. Once I felt that it was safe enough, I made a run for the car. I jumped into the backseat, and ducked down, telling Leanna to get me the hell out of Elizabethton.

We ended up at Tina and Faye's house. I explained to the girls that the cops were after me for escaping from jail. They pretty much humored me, and talked me into taking a nap, which is exactly what I needed. When I woke up, I was much better. I no longer thought I had escaped, or that the cops were looking for me, but I still had a lot of problems to work out. I didn't know exactly how I was going to fix all my problems, but Tina's boyfriend, Billy, said he could help with a place to stay. That's a start at least.

Chapter 42

Billy lived in Johnson City with Angelina, a friend of his from Georgia, in the basement apartment of Angelina's mother's house. The house was a nice, brick, 3 bedrooms in an upper middle-class neighborhood. The basement of the house had been almost entirely finished with carpeting, sheetrock walls, and a drop ceiling. The apartment consisted of a bedroom, living room, bathroom, and laundry room. There was also an area of the basement that was unfinished. It had a concrete floor, and cinderblock walls. The railings for the drop ceiling had been installed in this area, but there were no ceiling panels, so the floor joints from above were still visible. This area was furnished with a couple of couches, chairs, television, and even a small bed.

With its own entrance, Angelina's basement apartment was something of a hangout/party house. People would come and go at any and all hours of the day or night. Sometimes people would stay for several hours, and sometimes they would stay for several days. The first time I went there, it was late in the evening. We parked on the street, in front of the house, because nobody was allowed to park in the driveway or carport, and we walked through the carport, down a narrow set of wooden steps to a large deck area, that once surrounded an above ground pool. The pool area was surrounded by a 10 foot privacy fence. From the deck area, we took a set of steps down to a patio and entered the basement, without knocking, through a door down there.

When we entered the house, I was surprised to see there were five or six other people already there, when there was only one other car and a pickup truck parked at the curb. Someone said that Angelina wasn't there, so Billy brought me a change of clothes, and showed me to the bathroom, so I could get cleaned up and changed. When I came back out, there were three more people there in the living room. Two drunk chicks and some dude who was apparently the boyfriend of one of the girls, a hot blond with big tits. The other girl was a pretty brunette, I'd say around 26 or so. This was Angelina. She was tall, pushing 6 feet easily. She was wearing platform boots, with obnoxiously high heels, so I had to look up at her, and she was wearing a short leather skirt. Sexy! When she lifted her legs, during a drunken fit of laughter while sitting across the living room from me, I also saw that she wasn't wearing any panties. I definitely wanted to get to know this girl.

Billy introduced me to Angelina, as a friend of Tina and Faye's. I found it odd that he didn't say anything about me being married to Lisa, since I had heard repeatedly, from Lisa, about how good of friends Angelina and Lisa were. I still had some dope, so I loaded a foil, and passed it to her. We sat there, passing it back and forth across the coffee table, as we smoked together. I'm not sure why, but neither of us offered the foil to anyone else, and although we didn't speak to each other while we smoked, we pretty much ignored everyone else in the room. It was weird, now that I think about it. Billy told Angelina that I was going to hang out there for a few days, and she said it was cool with her. All that night, I met new people as they came and went. The twins, who had driven Billy and me to Angelina's house, left sometime before daylight, because Faye had to go to work.

One of the people I met that night was John. John was 6 foot 5, and about a buck twenty, soaking wet. At first, he pretty much sat off in the corner, by himself. I decided to go over and smoke a foil with him, and we got to talking. I told him about what went down at Lea's house, and mentioned that my clothes and lab were still there, and I needed to get over there soon to get my stuff. It turned out that the truck I had seen outside, a 2002, 4 doors, Chevy Z71, 4x4, belonged to John. He said he was almost out of gas, but if I could put a few dollars into the tank, he would be happy to take me to get my stuff. It had been a few days since I had left Lea's, so the next morning, John and I left to go to Lea's. John asked me to drive, because he didn't have a driver's license, and he said he had warrants out on him, so if he got pulled over, he was afraid that he'd go to jail. He was probably right, that's exactly what would have happened, so I drove. I knew I would soon have warrants on me, but at least I had a license, and that would get us through D.U.I. checkpoints, or a road block, if there was one.

We got to Lea's house, and I got out, while telling John to wait in the truck. I wasn't sure what state of mind Lea might still be in. As I approached the door, someone called to me from next door. It was Larry. He jumped the fence, and walked over to me. We shook hands, and laughing, I asked if Lea was pissed at me for leaving.

"You haven't heard?" Larry asked me, a little too seriously.

"Heard what?"

Apparently, after I left that night, Lea really flipped out. She started calling her family members, mom, grandma, son, daughter, and begging everyone to help her. She was babbling about the cops trying to set her up, and saying that they were trying to break into her house. Lea's mom, step-dad, and son eventually showed up at her house to see what was going on. They knocked on the doors, but Lea refused to let them in. She, in her altered state of mind, thought they were cops.

Larry came over to see if he could help, and Lea's step-dad asked for a pry bar, so he could get into the house. Larry helped get the door open and as they came in, Lea ran up the stairs and locked herself in the bathroom on the second floor. Larry said they spent close to two hours trying to talk Lea into opening the bathroom door. Lea refused, and finally her step-dad decided to kick in the door. This wasn't very easy, considering this was a solid wood door, in an old, well built home, and Lea's step-dad was probably as old as the house.

After several attempts at knocking the door down, it finally started to come apart. That's when Lea, kicked out the bathroom window, and jumped, barefoot, out and into the yard. I'm not sure if she hurt herself or not, Larry had said he didn't think she did, but once she landed in the yard, she took off running down the street, screaming at the top of her lungs. Larry, Lea's son, parents, and the cops, who Lea's parents finally called, looked for Lea for several hours. Someone finally spotted her, lying under the fallen garage door in someone's garage. Larry said it took some doing, but the cops finally wrestled Lea out from under the garage door, and into the police car that transported her to the hospital where she was sedated. The last Larry had heard, Lea was admitted, involuntarily, into a nut house in Knoxville.

This was the craziest shit I had ever heard. Lea wasn't new to meth; in fact, she had actually been doing meth *longer* than I had, and so I thought it was weird that she would flip out like that. Of course, Lea also did a whole lot of other drugs, so maybe it was a combination of everything that made her go nuts. That last night I was at Lea's, was actually the last time I had ever seen, or heard, from her. I did see in the newspaper a few years later, that she got busted for possession of several different kinds of pills, so I guess she went back to normal at some point.

After Larry told me what happened with Lea, he said Lea's step-dad would probably be showing up at any minute, and it probably wouldn't be a good idea for me to be there. I agreed, and said I needed to get my clothes and lab. Larry said he had packed up my lab and stashed it for me. I ran into the house real quick, to get my clothes, while he went to get my lab. I threw everything into the back of the truck, and left. We went back to Angelina's house to spend the day. I was feeling a lot better since I had my clothes, my lab, and I had a place to stay for a little while.

Chapter 43

John told me that he didn't have anywhere to go, and had no money for gas, food, cigarettes, or anything else he needed. I asked him if he thought he could sell any meth, and he said he could, very easily. We worked out a deal: John would be my helper; helping me collect supplies, sell dope, cook, and whatever else I needed, and he'd also be my transportation. In return, I'd make sure he ate, had cigarettes, and where I stayed, he would stay. Also, I told him I would teach him, slowly, how to cook dope. It was a win-win situation for the both of us.

Right away, I had a couple of problems. I was out of dope, almost out of money, and I didn't have anywhere to cook. I mentioned this to Billy, and he went to talk to Angelina. She came through the house a few minutes later, telling everyone to leave. As John and I were leaving, Angelina told me to wait until everyone was gone, then come back. I took the time to run to a couple of pharmacies, to buy some pills, and a few other cook items I needed. We went back to Angelina's, and she let us in. Locking the door behind us, she asked me how bad it'd smell if I did the cook in the basement. I told her, the only part of a cook that smelled, was the gassing off part. I could do that outside if I had to, or I could put a fan in a window blowing out, and gas it off in front of it. She asked if her storage building in the back yard would be a good place to gas off, and I said it would. "Okay," she said, "do the cook in the house if you need to, but go out in the storage building to gas it. Don't make a mess, and don't burn my mom's house down." I didn't bother to tell her that my way of cooking wasn't flammable.

I did the cook, and ended up with about a quarter of an ounce of dope. I gave Angelina a gram for letting me cook at her house, then John, Billy, Angelina, and I, sat around smoking my dope for the rest of the night. The next morning, Billy made a couple of calls, and I had the rest of my dope either sold, or traded for pills, in no time at all. I did another cook that morning, before people started showing back up again, and once they did, I smoked with everyone who walked through the door.

Tina and Leanna showed up that afternoon. I gave Tina a gram of dope, just because she's Tina, and I started talking to Leanna about her getting me pills from some of her boyfriends. Leanna kept a few guys in her stable at all times, so I figured she would be a good source for pills. She was.

After a few days of staying at Angelina's house, and cooking there, I was getting cabin fever. I wanted to go somewhere, and do something. The problem was I didn't have anywhere else to go. I was worried I would wear out my welcome at Angelina's soon, because now that there was always someone at her place who always had dope, and would smoke with everyone, her place was staying packed with people.

I kept it quiet that I was a cook. I was meeting a lot of people and I didn't know who, if any of them, could be trusted. One night, Leanna got me alone, and asked me if I would be willing to work with someone, besides John, who would supply me with pills and cook spots. I told her that I might be willing to take on another helper but I was helping John, and I wouldn't just up and abandon him for no reason. She understood, and introduced me to Sam.

Sam was the exact opposite of John, it seemed. Where John was 6 foot 5, Sam was more like 5 foot 2. Sam was also well dressed and neatly shaven, where John dressed like a bum and was scruffy as hell. Sam was not a bad looking kid, which explains Leanna's interest in him, and John bore a striking resemblance to the Crypt Keeper. The oddest thing about Sam, was his truck. He drove a huge, long, black, Chevy dually truck. Compensating?

I met Sam at Angelina's for the first time, and right away I said I needed some pills, and a place to cook. "Not a problem," he said. We left, and John and I followed him to another house where we picked up a pretty blonde girl. We all got into Sam's truck, and he drove to a couple of different places, so the girl could buy pills for us. Sam was paying for the pills out of his own pocket, but I told him I'd pay him a half gram of dope for every box. Once we got all of the pills, we went back to the girl's house. When we went inside, Sam showed us to a bedroom, and said that John and I could do the cook there.

When we finished cooking, I gave Sam his dope for the pills, and a gram for the girl. We still had not been introduced, and she never said a word to me the whole time I was there, or even when I left. I didn't know if the girl was Sam's old lady, or what. John didn't know either, but we both kept talking about how we wanted to see her again, as we went back to Angelina's for a little while.

Later that night, while several of us were partying, a couple people showed up. One was the girl who let me cook at her house. She was pretty talkative this time, and I talked to her a few times. As she and her friends were leaving, she gave me a Styrofoam cup she had been drinking out of. "Call me, 'Mallory'" was written on it, along with a phone number. I didn't know if she wanted to go on a date or what, but I was going to find out. I showed the cup to John, with my finger over the phone number. "You lucky motherfucker." was all he said.

The next cook I did was at Angelina's house again. This time, I ran an extension cord out to the outer building, to do the cook there, because Angelina's mom was home. Angelina's mom was born deaf, but had an incredible sense of smell, so I didn't want to take a chance on her smelling anything weird coming from the basement. If she decided to investigate, she might have caught us in the act, although she would not have realized what we were doing. One thing I did do was break my pills down in Angelina's bathroom. It was cold in the building, so the only thing I wanted to do out there was the actual cook. I had the bathroom door open as I worked, and Leanna was kicked back on Angelina's bed, talking to me as I worked. For some reason that I didn't quite understand at the moment, she stated, "You know, I've been with older guys before." Now, I've known Leanna since she was 15 years old, so I didn't take this as a come-on. I just kept working, and she went right back to talking about whatever it was she was talking about before.

When I went out to the out building, it seemed like everyone in the house went with me. There were at least 8 people, including myself, there. Not suspicious at all. I got the cook going, and sat down on a box to wait. Everyone was talking, and it seemed like everyone was having a good time, when Leanna, who was sitting on the floor, said she needed to talk to me alone. I asked everyone to give us a few minutes, so they all left and went inside the house.

"You didn't tell me what you thought about what I said." She stated.

"What did you say?" I asked. I really had no clue at all what she was talking about.

"You know, when I said I had been with older guys before." She said.

"I didn't know you wanted me to say something about it. After all, you've been with lots of guys." I said with a smile.

I was basically calling her a whore, but she knew, while true, that I was just joking. She rolled her eyes, and said something about me never being able to take a hint, as she took her jeans off. Well, that's a bit clearer, and you don't have to tell me twice. There was no way I was passing up this piece of ass. That would be the first time I fucked Leanna, but not the last. Since she and the twins were such good friends, and had been for years, I never let it get back to them that we ever did anything. If they knew, they would have looked at it like Leanna had fucked their mom's husband, without even considering the fact that Lisa had fucked around on me every chance she got, for years. As far as I was concerned, Lisa and I were done. It was time for me to live my life for me.

Chapter 44

I called Mallory, she invited me over, and said that I was welcome to come cook there at her place anytime I wanted. John and I loaded up the lab, and went to see her. When I went in, there was a guy there that looked familiar, but I couldn't place him. He walked up to me and asked, if I remembered him.

"No. Should I?" I asked.

"My name is Scott," he said, "My wife and I worked at the Appco in Boone's Creek. We used to see you every day."

Right then, it clicked. He and his wife were cashiers at the convenience store down the road from the townhouse Elvira and I lived in for 5 years. One weekend, I had tickets to an AC/DC concert in Nashville. Scott's wife started a fight with Scott so she could take off with me. I met her at the mall in Johnson City, and we went to the show. Scott apparently never found out, based on how he was acting towards me.

I went into the bedroom to cook, and sometime during the process, Sam showed up. He didn't seem pissed that I was helping myself to his cook spot, so that was cool. Sam and I talked while I cooked, and I was able to find out that Mallory wasn't seeing anyone. In fact, Sam said I had a good chance at hooking up with her, because I was a cook. Mallory, like all dope whores, loved meth cooks.

When I was finished with the cook, Sam asked if I felt like doing another one. It was pretty late, but I said I would do it. Sam had a shit load of pills, and that was the reason he had tracked me down to Mallory's. He didn't want to do the cook at Mallory's, so he told John and me to follow him. We left, and followed Sam for a few miles. We had to stop and turn around a couple of times, but finally we came to a trailer that didn't appear to be lived in.

Sam got out of his truck, and signaled for us to stay put. He knocked on the door of the trailer, and after a few seconds, the door opened. There was a short conversation, and Sam waved us in, as he walked inside. When we walked in, the living room was lit by a couple of candles. The place was a disaster. There were bags of trash piled in the kitchen, pizza boxes and food containers all over the place, and there were at least 20 milk jugs full of water sitting on the kitchen floor, and the place was heated by a single kerosene heater in the living room. "Make yourself at home", came a voice from the back of the trailer, a 16' by 80', 3 bedroom, 2 bathroom home, with no electricity, or running water.

When the owner of the trailer came out of the back of the house, I saw that it was someone I knew. It was Scott.

"Long time, no see," I said.

"Hell, why didn't you tell me at Mallory's that you were a meth cook?" he wanted to know.

"It's not something I advertise to everyone I meet." I explained.

Scott said he was fine with letting me cook at his house anytime I wanted, as long as I paid him a gram of dope every time I cooked. That was my basic deal with everyone, so I said that was fine. Scott told me he had some fines he needed to pay to get off probation, and he was going to sell the dope to get the money. Whatever, I didn't really care what he did with the dope, but it was nice to know he needed cash. I could exploit that to my benefit.

I cooked at Scott's house the next couple of nights. Sam and John were always by my side, ready to learn something new. They could make the iodine crystals, prep the Red P, and break the pills down. I also showed them how to safely shop for ingredients, and all this made things a lot easier for me.

Before long, I was basically living at Mallory's house. I would sleep on occasion, at Scott's house after a cook, and I spent a little bit of time at Angelina's house every couple of days. But, most of my non-cooking time was spent at Mallory's. Mallory was a sweetheart. Beautiful, sexy, and a damn good fuck, but I swear she would lie about anything. It drove me nuts. She would lie, and when you caught her in the lie, she would lie about lying. "Baby, that wasn't what I said. You must have misunderstood." she would whine. I would get pissed off about this from time to time, and that's when I went over to stay at Scott's for a bit.

One night, before doing a cook, Sam got a call from someone wanting to buy a half gram of dope. Leaving John to do the prep work at Scott's, I rode with Sam to meet the person. This was the first time I met Crystal. Crystal wasn't the one wanting the dope, but Sam was meeting the person at Crystal's house. While Sam went in, I waited in the truck. When Sam came out of the house, Crystal walked out behind him.

When he got in the truck, he said quickly, "Say no."

I had no idea what he was talking about, but right then, Crystal walked up to my side of the truck and said, "Take me with you."

I just looked at her, dumbfounded, not knowing what to say. Before I said anything, she said, "I know who you are, and I know what you do, and I just want to watch." I told her, that I couldn't take her right then, because I wasn't sure if the people at the cook spot would allow it. I promised to take her one day, and we got out of there.

The next day, Crystal showed up at Mallory's. We all sat around, getting high and John kept trying to talk to Crystal, but she wasn't interested. Crystal had known John a long time, and it just wasn't going to happen for him. Before Crystal left, she got my cell phone number, in case she needed some dope.

When we went back to Scott's house, he had company. Scott had been getting quite a few pills for us, and one of the people getting him pills was this guy who was sitting in Scott's living room. His name was Carson, and Scott had taken it upon himself to invite Carson over to watch me cook. This pissed me off to no end, because it's a breach of meth cook etiquette to do this without letting the cook know, but I let it go.

After the cook was finished, Sam, John, and I all went over to Angelina's house to sell some dope. The twins were there, so we hung out a while. Sometime later that day, Mallory showed up. When she walked in, I was sitting on a couch next to Faye. Mallory asked me to come outside, where she proceeded to show her ass about me sitting next to my own step-daughter. Granted, Faye is extremely pretty, and maybe she didn't know this was my step-daughter, but still. Fuck her. I told Mallory to go to hell, and to get the fuck away from me. She left, and a little while later, I took John's truck to her house to get my clothes.

When I walked in, Mallory tried giving me the silent treatment; fine with me. I went into the bedroom, and started packing my clothes. Mallory walked in and asked what I was doing. "Leaving." was my reply. She started crying, and asking me not to leave, and the usual bullshit, but I didn't really care. I got my shit, and went to Scott's.

Chapter 45

The morning that John and I went to Scott's house to move in, we pulled into the driveway to find Scott, slumped over in his car, bleeding and barely conscious. We got him out of the car and into the trailer. Once he got to moving around, he seemed to straighten up a little. We asked what happened, and at first he said he didn't know, but the more we pushed, the more we found out. As it turned out, Scott had gone out the night before, and was apparently stalking his wife. Well, ex-wife. She was with her new boyfriend, and when they discovered him sneaking around outside the house, the boyfriend beat the shit out of him. Okay, so he had it coming.

John and I moved in, and I set up my lab in one of the bedrooms. Scott had gone out and "acquired" a couple of power inverters, so we could run a light and a hot plate using the battery in his car, and in John's truck. This made cooking a lot easier, since I had been doing my cooking at Scott's on a kerosene heater, and on the Coleman camp stove I had bought Scott.

Carson had started hanging around Scott's house all the time, and he was a pretty good dude. Carson knew a few people who could always get a few boxes of pills whenever we needed them in a pinch. Most importantly, he knew a couple of diabetics, who kept me supplied with plenty of U-100's.

I was getting ready to cook one night, when Crystal called. She said she had heard that I had moved out of Mallory's, and she wanted to know if I wanted to hook up. I figured, why not? I sent John to pick her up. When he left, Scott asked me where John was going. I told him, and Scott started to get an attitude. He started with some shit about not wanting people he doesn't know at his house, and that pissed me off. I told him if he wanted me cooking at his house, then he really didn't have a say in who was there when I cooked. In fact, I let him know he was damn lucky I even came back after he brought Carson in without asking me first.

You should understand here, that in the meth world, it is nothing short of a great privilege to have a meth cook do his cooking at your house, building, barn, or whatever. If you have a cook working at your place, you instantly "move up" in the eyes of others in the clique. You are "in" with a cook, and sometimes, that's almost as good as being one. Also, there are certain rules that *will* be followed if you let a cook work at your house. The most important rule is, "The cook makes all the rules." If I don't want someone there, they will leave. If I don't want *you* there, you *will* leave. I have walked into a room and taken everyone's cell phones before, so I could keep an eye on them while I did the cook. I've taken car keys, so nobody could leave until I was finished. I've had people held at gun point while I searched them, because I thought someone was wearing a wire. Hell, I've done some shit to people just because I could. "I'm the cook. Fuck you if you don't like it. I can always go somewhere else." That was my attitude.

Crystal got there, but she wouldn't fuck in Scott's house. I was pissed, because that was really the only reason I sent John after her. I guess I couldn't blame her though, the house was pretty filthy. When Sam showed up, I had him call Leanna, and ask her to come to Scott's the next morning. She showed up, and I told her I would pay her and Crystal a gram of dope each to clean Scott's entire trailer. They agreed, and got to work. It took them all that day, and most of that night, to clean everything, but when they were done, it was spotless.

There were a lot of visitors at Scott's house since I had started cooking there. After the girls cleaned up the place so well, people started to bring better furniture for the trailer. Cyle, one of the local meth heads, and a great electrician, even rigged up some electricity straight from the power lines. I still don't know how he did that, but the meter was gone, and he still got power to the house. These were just a few of the perks of having me there.

Scott got one gram of meth for every cook I did at his place, plus half a gram for every box of pills he got for me. That was our deal. Since I cooked every day, and sometimes twice a day, he was getting well over a quarter ounce every week. During a cook one night, he walked into the room I was cooking in, and said that he felt like he should be paid 2 grams for every cook I did. "Okay." I said. I finished that cook, got my shit, and as I walked through the living room to leave, I threw him 2 grams and told him to go fuck himself. John and I left, and went to Angelina's.

It only took about a day for Scott to start calling me. I wouldn't take his calls, and Sam found me some new places to cook for a while. It was really risky to be running around with the lab, so when Sam suggested we go back and cook at Scott's, I agreed. The only difference this time, was that I wouldn't pay one gram per cook, I'd pay one gram per *day* that I cooked there, no matter how many cooks I did in a day. Scott, having really no other choice, agreed and I started cooking at his house again.

Instead of moving back into Scott's trailer, I ended up moving in with Crystal. She had a small trailer, with a bedroom at each end. Crystal and I slept in the front room, and I would go in the back room to do any prep work I wanted to do before a cook. One night, the twins showed up with Billy. Billy had bought everything he needed for a lab, but he couldn't figure out how to cook with Red P. They wanted to know if I could show him what he was doing wrong. I refused. I was trying to make a living, and I didn't need another Red P cook, who knew all the people I was doing business with, competing with me. They did ask me to do a cook for them, using Billy's supplies, and I agreed to that.

I went with them the next day to "The Hill." The Hill was located - you guessed it - on a hill. The person who owned the property was Will, another meth cook. On the hill, were Will's house, another small house where a dope/crack whore named Kelly lived, six trailers, and four apartments. Will owned it all, and everyone occupying the homes, which were nearly all of them, was involved in some way, in the dope game.

We went to one of the apartments, where Faye's boyfriend, Dirk, lived. After smoking a couple of foils, Bill and I walked next door to an apartment that nobody lived in. His lab supplies were there, but everything needed to be prepped. This was going to be a long day.

I started getting everything ready, and Billy was supposed to help. After all, I was doing this cook as a favor. Dirk was supplying the pills, Billy was supplying the lab, and I was doing the cook. I wasn't getting shit for my efforts, and Billy and Dirk were splitting the dope from the cook 50/50. Every time I told Billy I needed him to do something, he would run off to do something else. Once I finally got everything ready, I told Billy to get me the pills. It was only going to be a six box cook, roughly half an ounce. He got them, I began extracting the pseudo out of them, and once again, Billy disappeared. I was pretty pissed off.

I started the cook, and everything went fine. Or, so it seemed. The weird thing about Red P cooks is that, everything can go perfectly the entire cook, but when you gas it off, sometimes, you don't get shit back. Wouldn't you know it, that's exactly what happened to this cook. I worked this cook for hours, and I didn't get anything out of it at all.

I told Dirk and Billy what happened. They both said they knew there was a risk of not getting any dope back, so everything was cool. The twins had seen me do plenty of cooks, and not get shit back, so they know it happens. I told Dirk I would be by in a couple of days, to bring him a few grams of dope to pay him for the pills. That way, I didn't feel so bad for the cook not turning out. Dirk said that would be great, and I got Sam, who was at a whore's trailer next door, to give me a ride back to Crystal's.

Chapter 46

The next day, Crystal and I rode over to Angelina's. When I walked in, Angelina asked me what happened at Dirk's.

"Nothing, why?" I said.

"Dirk has been telling everyone you ripped him off for half an ounce of dope," she informed me.

Well, needless to say, that cock-sucker never got a drop of dope from me for those pills after that. That was pretty much what ruined the relationship between me and the twins. They know I wouldn't rip them off, but they chose to believe I did. Oh well, fuck 'em.

Crystal and I went to Mickey's house. Mickey is Crystal's brother. While we were there, he said he had a crawl space under his house that he thought would be good for cooking dope. I went with him to look, and his crawl space was the size of a small basement. It really was a good spot to cook. The floor was even dirt, so I could dig little holes to pour my leftover liquids into. I went to go get my lab and some pills, then came back to Mickey's to do a cook. While I was cooking, Billy showed up. He was pissed off at Dirk for him running his mouth. We talked while I cooked, and when I was done, Billy traded me over a dozen boxes of pills he had stolen from Dirk, for dope. Billy asked me to meet with him later, and I said I would.

I borrowed John's truck, and left the pills I got from Billy with him to break down for me. I picked Billy up, and he said he wanted to go steal all of Dirk's pills, which he kept somewhere in a storage building. Billy wanted me to drive him through the storage facility, which didn't require a code to enter, so he could see if he could spot Dirk's unit.

I drove up and down all of the units. Out of the corner of my eye, I could see that Billy was watching me, to see if I was watching him. I just looked straight ahead and kept driving. As we approached the end of a row of units, Billy turned and looked at one of them. I wasn't sure which one he was looking at, but it was one of the last two, and that was good enough. I dropped Billy off, and he said he would call when he was ready to break into the unit. He didn't sound too enthusiastic about doing it, so I figured he wouldn't call.

When I got back to Scott's, Sam was there with more pills. As we worked to prep everything for the cook I was about to do, I told them about Dirk's storage unit. We decided, that when it got late, Sam and John would go to the storage place, break into the last two units and look for Dirk's pills. We also knew this was going to stir up a lot of shit. Not only with Dirk, but with other cooks who got their pills from Dirk. We had to keep this between the three of us, so we codenamed the theft, "Operation: Snake in the Box." Whenever we spoke of the theft, we always said, "Snake in the Box" I don't know how we came up with that name, but it sounded all James Bond-y, so we went with it.

When it got late enough, I had the cook going. Scott and Carson were sitting there, so I said to Sam, "you need to go see about that Snake in the Box." Sam and John left in John's truck. I could tell Scott and Carson were curious, but they asked me no questions. I only expected Sam and John to be gone for about half an hour. All they had to do was open two units, and look for the pills. It was over an hour before they showed back up. John came in and nodded to me. I walked outside, and Sam had two gallon sized glass jars full of pills. Jackpot!

I asked Sam what took them so long, and he said he forgot which end of the row of units I told them to start at. So, they just started at one end, and cut the locks off of every unit, until they found the right one. It turned out to be the one with four locks on it. Duh!

Sam seemed pissed at John when they got back, and I asked Sam what was up. He told me that John almost got them busted. Sam said that as he was looking through the unit for more pills, a car pulled in. John took off, and Sam had to run him down and jump in the back of the truck, before he got left behind. Personally, I didn't blame him for being pissed off.

Everything was going good for me for a while. I was cooking almost every day, either at Scott's, or at Crystal's. I had plenty of pills coming in, and lots of dope going out. Leanna was starting to bug me about teaching Sam how to cook. I told her one day, that I really didn't want to do that so soon. I was still trying to get established, and putting another dope cook in business wasn't the way to do it. I guess she went back and told Sam I wasn't going to teach him how to cook, because the next time I went over to Scott's house to cook, the lab I built and left at Scott's was gone. Sam had stolen it. After finding the lab gone, I was a little pissed. Not so much because the lab was gone, but because, other than a few of Dirk's pills that were left and some Red P, there wasn't anything there of real value, I just don't like being stolen from. Oh well.

I had my main lab at Crystal's house so I went back there to chill out, since it looked like I would be taking the day off. After a little while, I called Scott and asked how many boxes of pills he had. He said he had four, so I told him to bring them to me, and I'd go ahead and cook them. It would only yield roughly a quarter of an ounce of dope, but I didn't care. I was bored and wanted to cook.

I waited, and after about an hour, I called Scott again, because he still hadn't showed up. There was no answer. I tried several times, still no answer. I started to use Crystal's Blazer to drive over to Scott's, to see what was up, but she had a flat tire, and I didn't feel like changing it, so I gave up.

Crystal and I were laying on the couch later than night, when someone pulled into the driveway. I got up and opened the door, just as Scott and Carson stepped up onto the porch. Scott was carrying a two-liter soda bottle full of liquid, that once he stepped into the kitchen, I could see was part of a cook. When I asked what they were doing, neither of them said anything. I could tell they were nervous. I took the bottle and looked at it.

"Are these the four boxes of pills you had?" I asked.

"Yes," Scott said, "John tried to cook."

"John tried to cook?" This blew my mind. He wasn't anywhere near ready to try cooking.

Carson told me, "John has been putting together a lab, and he has been asking Scott and I to go into business with him, instead of helping you. When you left earlier, he talked us into letting him cook our pills, but he couldn't get anything out of them. We brought everything over to you, to see if you would try to get some dope out of this shit."

"Where's John?" I asked.

"Outside in the truck, he's ashamed to come inside," this from Scott.

209

I told them I would try to work the batch, but I would keep half of any dope I got out of it. They agreed, not like they had any other choice.

I worked the batch for a little while, but it didn't take me long to figure out that John had added so much lye, that the dope was lye-locked. I was going to have to add so much muriatic acid, to lower the PH that it was just going to turn everything to salt, so I gave up. I gave them their bottle of shit back, and they left. On their way out, I told Scott to inform John, that since he had a lab and he felt like he was ready to be a cook, he was on his own. I hated doing that, because John was my transportation. But, I couldn't trust him, so he had to go.

Chapter 47

I got around to getting Crystal's tire fixed a day or two later then we rode over to Mark's house. Mark was sort of looked at as the leader of this bunch of people I had started dealing with. Shawn, Mark's right-hand-man, thought it would be a good idea if we met. Well, Mark and I had actually met a time or two, in the past. We had just never met formally, cook to cook. Lisa and the twins however, had known Mark for a couple of years.

When we got to his house, he came outside and Crystal introduced us. We were invited inside and we followed Mark in to one of his bedrooms he had converted into a party room. Shawn and Mallory were there in the room when we got there. On the floor of the room was a big mattress that everyone was sitting on. On the floor beside the mattress was a Pyrex dish, piled high with at least 3 or 4 ounces of meth.

Mark loaded then smoked a couple foils with us. I, in turn, pulled out some of my own dope and loaded a few foils for everyone. We had all been sitting around talking for a while when Mark jumped up and said he had to go to the garage. He told Shawn to come with him to help him with something. I assumed he had a cook going on and needed to check on it. Crystal went out with them, so that left me alone in the room with Mallory.

Mallory was asking why I hadn't been around and I made a few excuses about being busy or something. I wasn't real comfortable with being in Marks house, with him not there, so I told Mallory I was going outside. Before I left the room, I told her to put Mark's dope up before something happened to it. The dish was still sitting on the floor.

I went outside and sat in the car, listening to the radio until Crystal was ready to go. Mallory left a few minutes after I walked outside, telling me to stop by her house later, if I had the chance. When everyone walked out of the garage, Mark walked over to the car with Crystal. He shook my hand and told me to feel free to stop by anytime I wanted, day or night. That was his way of saying I was being accepted into his little world.

As soon as we got back to the house, Crystal got a phone call from one of her friends. When she got off the phone, she told me that someone had stolen about 10 grams of Marks dope. I borrowed her Blazer and drove back to his house. When I got there I saw Shawn and told him I wanted to see Mark. I followed him into the house and to the bedroom I had been in earlier.

Mark was on the phone when I walked into the room. When he hung up, he looked at me and asked, "What's up?" I told him that I hadn't stolen his dope, plain and simple. He looked at me for a second then started laughing his ass off. He said he knew I didn't steal it. He had a camcorder running the whole time. He said he had left the dope there to see if I would steal from him. "Just a test", he said. Instead of catching me stealing from him, he caught Mallory.

I was kind of pissed off about the whole thing for a minute. I wasn't so much pissed that he tested me, that's to be expected. What pissed me off was that Mallory would have known that Mark would have suspected me of stealing his dope and she stole it anyway. I know, although she has always denied it, that she meant for Mark to suspect me so we would never become friends. Fucking bitch. That just goes to show, you can't trust anyone.

One day, while Crystal was gone, and I was at her house alone, this little crack whore, Kelly, stopped by. She lived in a small house on The Hill. She told me that she had left some clothes there, so she wanted to get them. I let her in and she dug through the dirty clothes till she found what she was looking for. When she left, she had a pair of jeans and a couple shirts. She showed them to me so I could tell Crystal what she got, if she asked.

After Crystal got home, I remember Kelly had been by and I told her she came to get her clothes. Crystal started to get all worked up over it. She had obviously been awake way too long and she started saying Kelly had stolen half her wardrobe. I tried to assure her that Kelly only took a pair of pants and a couple shirts but Crystal had it in her head that she was missing a whole lot more than just that. When Crystal gets something in her head, you can't get it out so it's useless to even try.

We ended up in the Blazer, headed to Kelly's house to get Crystal's shit back. When we got there, no one was home. That wasn't going to stop her. She busted a small window pane out of the door so she could unlock it and let herself in. For the next 2 hours, I sat in the truck waiting for Crystal to finish rummaging through Kelly's house. From time to time, Crystal would come to the door, hold something up, and yell, "this is more of my shit". I would just smile and wave.

When she felt like she had finally found all of her shit, Crystal started carrying large garbage bags full of stuff out to the truck and loaded them in the back. These bags not only contained clothing, there were dishes, radios, kids toys, and tools as well. Stuff Crystal damn well knew didn't belong to her. Hell, she practically cleaned poor Kelly out that day and I had a feeling it wasn't going to end very well for her, but, what could I do?

Finally, we could leave. On the way back to Crystal's house, I stopped to pick up some pills to do a cook. Once we were back at the house, I was able to get her to take a nap she desperately needed, whether she admitted it or not. While she slept, I prepped for the cook. Later that night, Shawn showed up with Leanna. Leanna went straight to the other bedroom and went to sleep.

To keep from waking Leanna, I decided to get all of my lab stuff out of that room and brought it all to the kitchen. Shawn hung out in the kitchen with me as I cooked and around midnight, I was done. Before I cleaned up, I decided Shawn and I needed to sample the new batch, so we smoked a few foils.

There was a knock at the door and, not thinking anything of it, I walked over to ask who it was. "Carter County Sheriff Department" came the answer. I almost swallowed my tongue. I turned around to tell Shawn to help me hide all the shit, but he was gone. The bastard had run to the back bedroom and jumped in bed with Leanna to pretend he was asleep. ASSHOLE!!

I turned back to the door and asked what they wanted. "Crystal", was their reply. Okay, I had jars all over the place, the cook pot was sitting on the stove, and chemicals were everywhere. The whole damn place smelled like a fucking meth lab and I just knew I was going to jail. It was time for Crystal to take one for the team. She was going outside, even if I had to shove her out the window.

I told the cops to hang on, then I went to wake Crystal. I told her that the cops were right outside. I explained that I had just finished a cook and that the lab was sitting in the kitchen, in plain view. I told her that they were coming in to get her, and she was going to jail, no matter what so it would be best to just walk on out there and not make them come in, or we would all be going to jail. To her credit, she jumped up and walked outside. She was under arrest for breaking into Kelly's house.

We got her out of jail later that morning, but now I was way too nervous to ever cook again in her house. I went back over to Mallory's house to stay. Leanna, who was also staying at Mallory's, had two vehicles, a Malibu and a Honda Accord. To me, that meant I would have transportation, as long as I kept her high. Not a problem.

I got my stuff moved over to Mallory's and, of course, we ended up hooking up again. Now, Mallory loved to lie, and that shit drove me nuts but I really did love that girl. I started cooking at the house but I also started going back over to Scott's house some as well. Angelina was starting to stay at Mallory's a lot around this time and we were becoming pretty good friends.

Angelina was different from all the dope whore's I had been around. The biggest difference being, she never tried to hook up with any of the cooks. Ever. I knew she was bi-sexual, but for a while, I was beginning to think she was all the way gay. Nobody could get any pussy off of her.

Angelina rode over to Mickey's house with me one night to sell him some dope. On the way back, I got a call from Carson, who was at Mallory's. He said that the cops had just been there and picked Mallory up for violation of probation. Shit! I could not really use her house for a cook spot while she was in jail, so this sucked. We got back to Mallory's and Angelina was packing her shit while I was getting my stuff together.

Carson was hanging out at Mallory's because he wanted to hook up with Angelina. I figured the only way that was going to happen was if they spent a lot of time together, so I brought him over to stay. I guess I was just trying to play matchmaker. After I got my stuff together, I thought I would just lay back and relax. There was no hurry for us to leave so I wanted to get my thoughts together. I figured it was back to Scott's for me and I really didn't want to start staying over there if I didn't have to. Unfortunately, it was looking like I had to.

I must have fallen asleep because, one minute I'm lying there dreading going to Scott's, and the next Angelina is sucking my dick. I had a very short moment of guilt because Mallory and I were supposed to be together. Also, I knew that Carson, who was in the other room, really seemed to like this bitch and things looked like they might have been going good for him. But, I got over all of that and we ended up fucking in Mallory's bed. Carson walked in on us at one point, but he walked right back out and closed the door. I don't think he got mad but, who cares?

Chapter 48

After I had sex with Angelina the first time, she asked me to move in with her. Yep, I'm that good. I agreed to, simply because there was just something about this tall, sexy bitch I really liked. For some reason, and I've never figured out why, I have always felt relaxed when I'm with her. Her house was always a peaceful environment for me. If I wanted to be left alone, she would run everyone off. That was never a problem for her. I didn't like cooking at her house, unless I had to. You just never knew when her mom was going to show up in the basement unannounced.

I had done a cook at Scott's house one night and taken the dope back to Angelina's house so I could package it up for sale. There were several people at the house when we got there so we ended up having a little party. I was sitting on one of the couches with this big mirror on my lap and this huge pile of dope on the mirror. I was concentrating on weighing the dope up so I didn't notice much of anything else going on. For some reason, I looked up to see Angelina's mom standing there, watching everything that was going on.

She had walked down the stairs, and into the living room, with no one noticing her. I just froze. After what seemed like minutes, but was only a couple seconds, Angelina saw her mom and freaked out. She got her mom to go back upstairs after some fast talking, and even faster sign language. Once she was gone, I asked if I needed to get my dope and leave. Angelina said for me to not worry about it.

Apparently, the reason she came downstairs was because she knows what pot is, and smells like, and she doesn't want it smoked in the house. When she came home, she smelled it and came down to get on Angelina's ass about it. She had no clue what meth or cocaine was, so she didn't have a clue what I was doing.

That wasn't the only time Angelina's mom walked in at a really bad time. She came in while some of us were doing hot rails off of the glass coffee table. Leanna had just done a huge hit, and was holding it in when Angelina's mom walked into the room. There was a look of terror on Leanna's face because she couldn't hold her breath forever, and she didn't want to blow all that smoke out right in front of the woman. Leanna, using some quick thinking, grabbed a cigarette and acted like she was taking a hit off of it, then blew the smoke out.

There were times when she walked in and caught people doing things that simply could not be covered up. Tina and Billy were hanging out at the house alone one day when they decided to fuck. Angelina's mom walks in to find Billy with Tina's legs over his shoulders, pounding the living hell out of her. They were both so into what they were doing that they didn't notice her until she was standing right next to the bed. They finally saw her and froze. They stayed in that position for 15 minutes while they got preached to about the sins of premarital sex. To say the least, they were all pretty embarrassed over the incident.

Angelina started going to Scott's with me every time I cooked. That was great because I liked having her around. One night, she scored an ounce of 'shrooms while I was doing a cook. She came into the room I was working in and asked if I wanted any of them. I was at a point in the cook where I had to boil the pot. I took some of the 'shrooms and threw them in as the water boiled. I wasn't sure if it would make a difference but it was worth a try. I liked experimenting to try to make a better product.

The following day, I started getting phone calls from people asking me if I had anymore of the new batch of dope. That batch, I was being told, was causing some really cool hallucinations and people wanted more of it; lots more. All I had left was my personal supply and that, I wasn't getting rid of. I tried to get more 'shrooms, so I could make more of that dope, but I couldn't find a supplier. I had been up so long, and seeing shit that wasn't there anyway, that I don't really know if the dope affected me any differently or not.

One afternoon, while Angelina and I were hanging out at Scott's house, she got a call from a friend of hers. Ron, her friend, talked to her for a few minutes then she started waving me into the kitchen, where she was standing while she was on the phone. She handed me the phone and Ron told me, "I'm standing here with my arms around 2 beautiful ladies. They weigh about 400 lbs each."

I asked Ron if he was crazy or something and he started to laugh. He explained that he was actually standing beside 2 large tanks of anhydrous ammonia. I started to question him about the tanks but he cut me off.

Not wanting to talk on the phone. He told me to stay at Scott's; he would be by after work. I had a feeling things were about to change for me that night, but I had no idea just how much things were going to change.

Chapter 49

Although I was a Red P cook, I knew a little about anhydrous ammonia dope. Just about every cook I knew was an anhydrous cook and even Lisa knew how to make anhydrous dope. Hell, she even taught me the basics of making my own anhydrous ammonia gas. Personally, I never wanted to make anhydrous dope. To me, it was a cheap, dirty form of meth that was full of impurities. I thought that because, all the "Annie" dope I had ever used was dirty and full of impurities.

One of the biggest things that turned me against Annie dope, was all of the stories about meth labs blowing up. Since I knew that the Red P method I used wouldn't blow up, I figured it had to be those anhydrous labs that were doing all that exploding I kept hearing about on the news.

To this day, one thing that drives me nuts is all the bullshit rumors about meth. These rumors are more widespread than the actual use and manufacture of the drug. Incredible as it might seem, much of the general public's lack of accurate knowledge about meth can be directly attributed to the misuse of the news media by so-called meth experts.

These "experts", usually local police officers with "special training", don't always, purposely, try to mislead people. Occasionally, their problem is that they will accept incorrect information as fact, simply because they, themselves, don't know any better. This means that they are not nearly as informed as you would believe, or they would believe themselves, to be. Since they are the expert, no one questions their expertise.

To give you an example, let's go back to my 2005 arrest for Lisa's lab in my car. When the cop was describing the items found in my car, he stated that there were several "D" sized, alkaline batteries visible through the window. He said that, during his meth awareness training, he had learned that alkaline batteries are used to manufacture meth. The officer really should have paid closer attention in class because it is lithium, not alkaline, batteries that are used for making meth.

It is definitely not unheard of for cops or drug agents to make up their own facts just to fill in some of their own blanks. A lot of the times, the facts are not even important, which makes the whole process even more ridiculous. Here is an example of what I'm talking about. After Crystal was arrested on federal drug charges, (we haven't gotten to that yet), she would learn that DTF and DEA agents claimed her nick-name, Crash, came from a supposed habit of "crashing out" at whoever's house she happen to be at. Normally, the tale went, at a meth cooks house. The truth is, everyone called her Crash because the bitch can't drive. She crashes all the time.

Cops and agents who deal with meth people on a regular basis, often do receive accurate information. This is usually obtained while conducting post-arrest interviews. This information, if understood then used correctly, can be very helpful to law enforcement. However, just as often, suspects will give information that is designed to either downplay his or her own part in the criminal activity, or to make the cop think they have some special knowledge of something, or someone. This is done to make the person seem more, or less, valuable to the investigation and, with luck, get a better deal in court.

One of law enforcements greatest tools in fighting the meth epidemic is their use of the news media. The news media is normally given current and accurate information, however, they are also quite often given information that is anything but accurate. They in turn report this crap, unknowingly, to the public. Not to say that the news media is the picture of innocents when it comes to lying to you, because they are not. There are many times when a reporter takes a simple story and goes wild with it.

Let's take the dismantling of a meth lab for example. I have noticed that my local newspaper from Elizabethton, Tenn., when reporting on the dismantling of a lab, has begun to basically give weather reports in their stories. "Captain W., of the Elizabethton Police Department, dismantled the lab while wearing protective safety equipment. It was humid and 87 degrees at the time."

I'm sorry but, who gives a fuck what the temperature was? Is reporting the temperature supposed to make the job seem more dangerous? Apparently someone thinks so. Hell, I worked at Exide for eight years, wearing safety equipment 8 hours a day in temperatures well over 100 degrees. Nobody ever wrote about that shit in the fucking newspapers. Damn, I just wish people would stick to what is relevant and stop making other shit out to be more than it is.

There is a newer method of cooking meth that is getting very popular. It is called the "shake -n- bake" method, or the "one pot" method, Basically, all of the ingredients are mixed together in a soda bottle and the cook happens in that bottle; very easy process. The dismantling of a one pot meth lab basically involves taking the lid off of the bottle. WOW! What a story that would make, right? It would have to be at least 93 degrees outside to make that shit interesting.

While I'm on this rant, I want to address the most common, and widely believed, bit of disinformation there is when it comes to meth labs. Let's talk about meth labs blowing up. While I will be the first to admit that there certainly is a basis for this rumor, I also know that the whole story isn't being told.

With few exceptions, the act of cooking meth is *not* an explosive process. In fact, there are methods of cooking meth that are completely, 100% non-flammable. Of course, you are never told this when the local news reports on the latest meth lab discovered in someone's garage. Maybe the police don't actually distinguish the difference when they give the story to the news reporters. But, even if they did, I'm not convinced the newspapers would report it to the people. A meth lab that is non-flammable doesn't scare people as much, so it's not as good a story.

It is true that there are a lot of fires (fires, not explosions) associated with cooking meth. Most of these fires happen due to someone doing something stupid, or simply not knowing what they are doing to begin with. If you don't know what you are doing, you will end up doing something stupid. A magnificent example of this would be the fire in my kitchen when I was learning to break down my pseudo pills. We all remember that story.

When there actually is an explosion, and there are some (rarely), it is not the lab, or cook pot, that explodes. Explosions happen because of a lack of ventilation. Just like when I blew the door off of my microwave oven. It didn't blow up because I was evaporating alcohol; it blew up because the microwave was in an enclosed area that allowed the fumes to build up then explode; could have happened to anyone.

This kind of thing can, and does, happen in legal work that involves using flammables. For instance, say you are staining a beautiful, antique table in your home workshop or garage. The warning label will quite clearly tell you to use with lots of fresh air but, you decided to keep the windows closed. We don't want the air stirring up dust. Once the table is all stained, you stand back to admire your work. Hell, why not have a cigarette? BOOOOM!! You just ignited a room full of flammable vapor and blew yourself up. Does this mean furniture refinishing is explosive? No, it means, don't be stupid, ventilate.

So, what have we learned today? A) Despite what Captain Hero wants you to believe, dismantling a meth lab isn't quite as dangerous, or difficult, as reverse engineering a nuclear weapon, and, B) If you suspect your night owl neighbor, with the blacked out windows, is cooking meth, because you smell something strange coming from his house, then chances are pretty good that he is ventilating. That means, he isn't about to blow up half the block so, with all that in mind, try to calm down.

Chapter 50

Although Angelina assured me differently, I was beginning to wonder if Ron was actually going to show up at Scotts, like he said he would. Angelina said, "If he said he will be here then he'll be here". Eventually, he did show up. It was about 9 p.m. when he got there with a girl named Rose in tow. Rose was his sister-in-law, and very pregnant at the time, but I found out later, he was doing her.

I asked Ron what was up with the anhydrous tanks. He said that he had been doing refrigeration work that day at a local bottling company when he noticed them. According to Ron, they were just sitting out in the open waiting to be stolen. And, as luck would have it, he was the man for the job.

We jumped into Ron's car, a '67 Fairlane, and took a ride over to where the tanks were at. I wanted to grab one of them right then and there but we couldn't fit the tank into the trunk of his car. We went back to Scotts, collected Angelina and Rose, then we all went back to Angelina's house. Ron and I had some talking to do.

I wanted to know why Ron came to me, a relatively new guy around this group of people, about the tanks. There were people he had known a lot longer that he could have dealt with. Why me? It turns out that he thought about Will and Mark first but decided he couldn't trust either of them enough to deal with them. I reminded Ron that I was a Red P cook, not an anhydrous cook. He asked if I could figure out how to use the gas and I assured him that it wouldn't be a problem.

The truth is, I had been around a couple of anhydrous cooks so I knew *how* to "cold cook", I just had never done it. I asked Ron, what kind of deal did he have in mind about the tanks? He told me he just wanted me to remember him with a little dope from time to time. Hell that was easy enough to do.

Since I was in need of a pick-up truck to acquire the tanks, I was going to have to bring in a partner. I called Cyle. Although he didn't have a truck, he did have an old Jeep Cherokee. I figured that would work just as well.

I took Cyle to show him where the tanks were so we could figure out how we wanted to steal the damn things.

Something irritating about Cyle is that he wants to over complicate things. When I was ready to go get the tanks, he wanted to dress up in camo, face paint and all, then go lay in the weeds and watch the building. Watch it for what?? I waited for Cyle to get off his ass for two days but he kept wanting to stake out the building so, I decided to get someone else to help me. Tweakers are so hard to work with.

Word was getting out that there were a couple of tanks about to be stolen from somewhere. Will, Mark, and a few other people were asking a lot of questions of a lot of people. Everyone wanted these tanks so I had to hurry. I approached Shawn with the idea of letting him help me but his truck wasn't in any shape to try to haul that much weight.

I found myself at Angelina's house going nuts. I needed a truck and it was killing me that I couldn't find one. I even tried finding John's stupid ass but nobody knew where he was hiding. About the time I was considering trying to get the tanks onto the roof of Leanna's car, Michael, a local junkie, stopped by to give me some great news. He said to me, "Cyle and Queeny are on their way to steal two tanks of anhydrous." I could have slapped him.

I was so fucking pissed off. That dirty little bastard was stealing the tanks, *my* tanks, with someone else. I called Cyle. No answer. I called Queeny. No answer. I was on my way out the door, to go to the bottling company, to keep anyone from touching those tanks when Crystal walked in.

"Call Mark!" I said as soon as I saw her, "Tell him I'll split one of those tanks with him, if he helps me get them, but we have to get them right now."

Crystal called him and we set up a place, convenient to both of us, to meet. When we met up, Mark had this pretty little dope whore, Jessie, with him. I was with Crystal. We parked Crystal's car and all of us rode in Marks truck to go look at the tanks. He took one look and said, "we need more help." They were pretty big tanks, weighing in at about 400 pounds each.

We went to Will's house then. The girls went inside to wait while we made our plans for getting the tanks. I suggested we just drive up there like we owned the place, jump out, and throw the things into the back of the truck. It wasn't late so, if anyone saw us, they would most likely assume we were maintenance workers. It was a simple idea and everyone agreed it was what we should do, so, that's what we did.

We got to the bottling company and Mark and I jumped out of the truck. As Will turned the truck around, Mark and I worked on getting the chain loose, that kept the bottles from falling over, out of the rack. We got the chain off just as Will pulled alongside us again. Mark and I lifted the tanks into the bed of the truck and we slammed the tailgate closed. Mark grabbed the dealer tag Will used on all of his vehicles off the bumper then we jumped in and hauled ass.

The whole job took all of 45 seconds, at the most. It was great!! As we rode back to Will's house, Mark asked if I was positive the tanks had anhydrous ammonia in them and not some other gas. Hell no, I wasn't sure of anything. It never even crossed my mind that there could possibly be anything else in the tanks. I didn't actually say this but I thought it and I guess the look on my face told Mark all he needed to know.

Mark turned around in the seat and squeezed through the sliding window to have a look. Once he read the labels, he got back into his seat and just sat there, staring silently ahead. I sat there looking at him pissed off that we had just done all this for nothing when he started smiling. It was anhydrous!!

Back at Will's house, Mark and I loaded the tanks into Marks truck while Will headed inside for a beer. Mark wanted to know how I wanted to pay Will for helping us. I said we would split one of the tanks 3 ways. Mark was cool with it so that's what would happen.

We got Jessie and Crystal, then left. Mark dropped Crystal and me off at Crystal's car and we all agreed to meet up at Marks house within an hour. I had to go to Wal-Mart first to buy a new, empty propane tank, to fill with anhydrous. Just as I was getting into Crystal's car, my cell phone beeped with a text message; "Someone just stole the tanks. Cyle" The dumbass was doing his Rambo bullshit the whole time we were stealing the tanks.

By the time Crystal and I got to Marks house, he had one of the tanks unloaded. He had left the other in the truck, assuming I would want to borrow the truck to take the other tank somewhere for safe keeping. He was right. There was no way in hell I was leaving both tanks at his house, even if it meant I would have to roll the thing down the road to get it somewhere.

I took off in Marks truck and found a place to bury the tank. Since the tank at Marks house had enough gas in it to last 3 people for quite a while, I wouldn't need this one right away. Once I had it safely underground, I went back to Marks house. By the time I got back, he still had not gotten my propane tank filled so he gave me a smaller tank he had, that was full, to hold me over.

Having so much anhydrous at my disposal was only one of the reasons I decided to be a cold cooker. Another reason was, gram for gram, anhydrous cooks produce more finished product from the available pseudo then a Red P cook does. That obviously means more money for me.

My biggest incentive for switching cooking methods was because of a lack of 7% iodine, which I needed to make my iodine crystals. It wasn't that it was getting hard to find, the shit just wasn't being produced anymore. (Damn meth cooks screwed that up too.) Anhydrous labs also use less chemicals, and the cook time is a lot less than that of a Red P lab. Really, for a lot of reasons, I should have switched to anhydrous a long time ago. It was much easier.

Chapter 51

About two days after stealing the anhydrous ammonia tanks, I decided to go ahead and try my very first cold cook. Because the strong ammonia smell associated with cold cooking, I needed to be in a fairly secluded area to do the cook. I went to Scott's house to do it.

When I got to Scott's house, there were quite a few people there so I told Scott to get rid of everyone. While he did that, I began unloading all of my new cook supplies from the trunk of Leanna's Malibu. I had borrowed her car to go do this cook.

Other than Scott, the only people I allowed to stay at the house while I did the cook was Queeny, another friend of mine, Jeremy, and a dude I didn't know, Mitch. Yes, this was the same Queeny who was going to steal my tanks but, in his defense, he didn't know they were mine, so it was all good in the end.

Mitch was new in the circles I had been hanging around in. He was an old friend of Queeny and John, and that is the only reason anyone even let this dude hang around. He definitely was not trusted, especially by Mark who absolutely refused to sell him anything at all. If Mitch wanted to buy, or even trade pseudo pills to Mark for dope, he had to go through Queeny or John. The only reason I even let him stay while I did the cook was because I didn't trust him enough to let him leave. Hell, he might have called the cops or some stupid shit like that.

Knowing that Jeremy had been around several cold cooks before, I asked him to help me out with this cook. He agreed to help me. We set up by the window in the empty bedroom I always liked to cook in when I cooked at this house. One of the best things about cold cooking is that the pills don't have to be broken down to cook them. All you do with cold cooking is, grind the pills to powder in a coffee bean grinder and cook them like that. It's a huge time saver.

We got the pills ground then sprayed them with the ammonia. The odor was horrible and it was all we could do to breathe. Since there was a fan pulling most of the ammonia out the window, we were able to keep working. In case you didn't know, ammonia vapor is attracted by water.

In our case, water meant our eyes and lungs. That means, we were also having a hell of a time seeing, as well as breathing.

When it was time to add the lithium strips, from the "AA" batteries, I realized I had a new problem... I didn't know how to strip the battery. I was standing there with the battery in one hand and pliers in the other, looking at them like I was stupid. I guess Jeremy figured out what the problem was pretty quickly because he took everything from me and started stripping the batteries for me. After that, I completed the cook with no further problems.

I did have a few questions along the way but, even though Jeremy wasn't actually a cook, he was able to answer most of them. After the cook was finished, and the lab stuff was packed up, I smoked most of the dope I had just made with everyone that was there. I really just wanted to see how well they liked it. Since it was free dope for them, they loved it.

That's the thing with meth heads, they are loyal to the cook they are around at the moment. Not all of them but most of them, that's for certain. Besides the girls, Carson was the worst for being two faced. He would do absolutely anything I asked of him, as long as I let him hang around me. As soon as I took off, and he got around another cook, I was suddenly the worst cook he knew. My dope, he would be quoted as saying, wasn't worth smoking. Well, fuck him and all those like him.

During the night, I got to talking to Mitch. He seemed alright, I suppose. He was just really full of shit. A natural born liar. Probably because he was trying so hard to get people to like him. I guess he never thought that people might actually like him if he wasn't getting caught in lies every five seconds. I know it had a lot to do with why nobody trusted him. You just can't trust a fake-ass motherfucker like that. That's all there is to it.

While we talked, he informed me that he had a lot of connections he could get pills through. He said he would like to start supplying me with pseudo. He also claimed to have over ninety acres of land, a huge horse barn, and a work shop, all perfect for cooking in, if I was interested in working something out. Queeny backed up his claim so I said I would come by one day and check the area out. We exchanged phone numbers and left it at that.

The next night, I got a ride over to Marks to pick up the propane tank he had filled for me. While I was there, I ran into Billy Jean Ambrose. Billy Jean was kind of new to the meth world but a lot of the people I was doing business with had known Billy Jean for most of their lives. He was trusted.

Billy Jean was from Erwin, Tennessee and the boy had money. Lots of money. He had only recently been buying large quantities of meth and he was able to work his way in with Mark, Will, and me so he could buy directly from us. He was also trying to push Shawn out of the picture as Marks number one helper. This was beginning to cause a few hard feelings between Mark and Shawn because Shawn began expressing his feelings that something just was not right with Billy Jean working his way in the way he was. Mark just called his suspicions, "jealousy".

So, I was talking to Billy Jean and I mentioned that I needed a vehicle. Leanna never had a problem with me borrowing one of her cars but, she was going through a shit load of my dope as payment. Also, every time I was gone for more than an hour, she would be calling me every five minutes wanting to know where I was, what I was doing, shit like that. It was irritating as hell so I wanted to get my own car; less of a headache that way.

Billy Jean told me he had a really nice Ford Bronco he would be willing to sell me for sixteen hundred dollars. We talked about it and he said he would take six hundred cash and the rest in trade on dope. I told him to bring the Bronco by Angelina's house the next day and I would check it out. The next day, he showed up with his best friend, Kid. I looked the truck over and it was a real nice ride, especially for an '86 model. I bought it and was happy to finally have my own vehicle.

Angelina and I gave Billy Jean and Kid a ride back to Erwin then, after dropping them off, we went to pick Carson up. I wanted him to pill shop for me so I could do a cook that night. Carson, Angelina, and I spent the day buying all the pseudo we could get our hands on. Once we were finished shopping, we went back to the house to wait for night; my favorite time to cook.

I called my friend Davy to see what he and Winter were planning on doing later that night. He said, they really didn't have any plans so, I asked if he cared if I cooked at his barn. Davy was all for it. He knew I would be hooking him up with dope for the use of the barn, like I always did. Angelina, Carson, and I headed out to go to Davy's house at around 1 am. It had started snowing a few hours earlier and the roads were getting pretty slippery, especially in the mountainous areas like where Davy lived. I was glad I had 4-wheel drive for the trip.

About halfway to Davy's house, I hit a fucking deer. The damn thing ran right out in front of me. There was no way for me to avoid hitting it; the road was a solid sheet of ice. Angelina cried like a baby over it and I got my bumper pushed back into the door so that it wouldn't open. I wished I could have run it over again because of that.

The cook was perfect that night but, we all about froze out asses off. There's no heat in the barn. I paid Carson and Angelina with dope, their preferred method of payment, for the pills they bought. Since Christmas was on the way, I gave Davy a pile of dope for letting me use his barn that night. I figured he could sell some of the dope, then use the money to buy Winter a present or something. I also had enough dope left over to pay myself back for the Bronco. See, it turned out to be a good night, despite what the deer did to my truck.

When Angelina and I got home, the next morning, we had a surprise waiting for us. Mallory was there waiting for us to come home. Mallory being out of jail was the last thing I expected but, there she was. I'm not sure what Mallory thought when she showed up there that morning. That we were still together, I suppose. Well, I had news for her, Angelina and I were together. Not to be outdone, Mallory had news for me... PREGNANT!! Oh shit!

Chapter 52

After Mallory told us that she was knocked up, she said she was going home and stormed out of the house. Angelina, being as awesome as she ever was, suggested I go talk to Mallory. She knew there was going to be drama and I was going to have to figure out what I was going to do about the situation. I got to Mallory's a few minutes after she did. When I walked in the house, I figured the best way to start this conversation was with sex; nothing better than that just-got-out-of-jail piece of ass.

Mallory tried playing the hurt, broken hearted role because of me getting with Angelina. In all honesty, I didn't care how she felt about it. She knew what was up when she started messing around with me, I was a meth cook, every dope whore in four counties was throwing it on me, I wasn't about to turn it down.

Anyway, just knowing how Mallory operates was enough for me to decide to lay back and see if she really was pregnant. It would be like her to make some shit like that up just to see if she could get me to leave Angelina. Besides, two weeks before I hooked up with her, she was with Mark. So, if she really was pregnant, it could very well have been his.

I went out and paid up Mallory's electric and water bills. Her mortgage was a little behind too, so I paid that as well. I wanted to be sure she was taken care of, whether she was pregnant or not. Mallory being, or pretending to be, pregnant had one big upside... I could have her and Angelina both without one or the other complaining about it. I was a winner no matter what. I ended up halfway moving back in with Mallory. I was there sometimes, sometimes I stayed with Angelina.

There was a huge difference in the way I treated Angelina and the way I treated Mallory. That difference really was based on how they acted. Angelina was quiet, sweet, and she had a lot of self respect. She never pressured me about where I had been, for days at a time. She never acted like she was available to anyone, but me. Most importantly, she never asked me for dope or money.

Because of this, I treated Angelina with respect. I never talked down to her. I never made slick, off-hand sexual comments to, or about, her in front of other people. When we were together, whether in public or alone, I treated Angelina like a girlfriend. I never treated her like she was a dope whore because, to me, she wasn't one. Angelina was wild, but she had class. I really liked that about her.

Mallory was nothing like Angelina. Mallory thought of herself as a player. That was fine, it made it that much easier to play her for the fool she was. She was very predictable as well. I knew that, when I showed up at her house, after being gone for a few days, she would start complaining about this or that bill she needed to pay. A lot of the time, I had already given her money for the bill, or paid it myself, but she forgot and she would hit me up for more money.

There were times when I would give Mallory money for a legitimate reason. I'd give her the light bill money then send her to pay it. She would claim to have paid the bill, then when the lights got turned off, she would act all surprised. Usually, I would leave her ass in the dark for a few days before getting the power turned back on.

Mallory also presented herself as a whore. She was famous for always saying she could, and would, use what she had to get what she wanted. We used to fuck with her over that. A couple of my buddies and I would wait until she was out of dope, and dope sick, then we would take turns going over there to offer her dope for pussy. She would give up the ass then not get any dope. She would fall for this same scam every time. One time, after three of us had done this to her, we all went back and made her tell everyone who came to the house how we had conned her out of her ass. Then, we finally got her high.

One day, while I was sitting in the bedroom, working out a deal with Scott and Carson, Mallory comes in the room to change clothes. She stripped her jeans off, while not wearing any panties, right in front of everyone. This pissed me off because, this was one of those times when we were "together". Fine, she wanted everyone to see her naked ass so bad, I figured I would help her out. I made the stupid bitch walk around the house, butt ass naked, all day long. Since Mallory was really pretty, and had a great body, we had a *lot* of company that day.

Mallory was always calling me to ask me for dope, whether she needed it or not. I think she just wanted to see if I would give it to her sometimes. Other times, she would be around a couple of her girlfriends, so she wanted to look big in front of them, by getting dope from me. I would help her out occasionally, nothing wrong with letting her feel special in front of the girls from time to time.

I wasn't always free with my dope with Mallory though. One day, I stopped by to see what she was up to. She looked like hell. She said she hadn't gotten high in a couple days and was dope sick. She was laying in the bed so I figured, why not? I got in bed with her and fucked her for awhile. She tried to be a sport, but mostly, she just laid there. I didn't care, I was only screwing her because she didn't feel like doing it.

When I was finished with her, I got up and got dressed. I took a gram of dope out of my pocket, then threw it on the bed next to her. "There's your payment, whore", I told her. She got mad, obviously, then threw the baggie of dope back at me, screaming that she wasn't a dope whore. "I don't fuck you for dope motherfucker, I fuck you because I love you!!" was the one thing I clearly remember her saying. I looked at her and said "I love you, too", then I picked the dope up and left.

Crystal and Leanna, both, moved into Mallory's house after Mallory got out of jail. I had stopped sleeping with Crystal because, she was pregnant (not mine) and she was getting pretty big. Leanna, however, was always good for a piece of ass, when she was out of pain pills, her main addiction. I kept some handy, just for such occasions.

Crystal being pregnant was a bit of a problem for me. I don't give dope to pregnant chic's, EVER! I don't even like to smoke around them, and Crystal knew it, but she would still beg me for dope every time she saw me. That, however, wasn't the main problem I had. My problem was, I knew that, if I didn't give Crystal dope, she would go someplace else and get some. Maybe even from John, who had finally figured out how to make a very low grade of Red P dope.

John used to keep a staph infection. It was normally pretty bad, and he wasn't the cleanest person you ever met to begin with. I knew, and I'm surprised nobody else thought of this, or cared, that John sat around squeezing those huge, puss filled knot's growing on his head and hands. That meant he had staph on his fingers while he was cooking and bagging up his dope. That shit spreads!

John used to give me dope, every time he came around me. It was a way of paying respects. I always threw the shit away, or gave it to someone I didn't like very much. I wasn't about to do any dope he had touched and

I was worried about Crystal catching something from it if she did any. So, when John was around, I would give her dope, even though I didn't like it.

Crystal was quite the hypocrite, when it came to her pregnant drug use. One of her friends, Vicky, was pregnant about the same time she was. Vicky was both a meth and pill addict. I used to use Vicky to buy pseudo pills for me, in exchange for money for morphine pills. I didn't feel too bad for giving her money for drugs, as long as I wasn't giving her the actual drugs.

Crystal often would cuss Vicky out, about all the horrible things Vicky was doing to her unborn child. For some reason, Crystal thought pills were harder on the baby than meth was. Anyway, one morning Vicky came by Mallory's begging for dope, pills, or anything to get high on. She was telling us that she was so sick; she had spent the entire night vomiting and shitting on herself. I told her I wasn't giving her shit but Crystal said she had some dope she would do with her, so they headed to the bathroom.

After they were in there for a little while, I heard a scream come from the bathroom. Crystal came running out, followed by Vicky, who was screaming, "I'm dying!! Please help me! I'm dying! Get my mommy! I'm blind! Help me!" I didn't know what to think but, before I had the chance to think about much, Vicky collapsed onto the floor.

I asked Crystal what had happened, as I rushed over to check to see if Vicky was dead or alive. I saw that Vicky was crying, so I knew she was still alive; for the time being anyway. Crystal told me that she had given Vicky a huge overdose of meth. She claimed she was afraid Vicky's baby was going to be born fucked up, from all the drugs, so she was trying to make Vicky have a miscarriage.

I told Mallory and Crystal to get the bitch up off the floor and into my Bronco. As they did that, I got my tank of ammonia out and put it in the closet. I told Mallory to make sure no one, including her, touched it or it would be her ass. Then, Crystal and I took off. We drove up the back side of Buffalo Mountain, in Johnson City. I found a secluded place to park, in an already secluded area, and pulled in.

Crystal asked me why we were just sitting there. I told her, we were waiting to see if Vicky dies. If the bitch died, we were going to have to bury the fucking body. She started to freak out then but I reminded her that it was her fault for overdosing Vicky in the first place. No need to start worrying about it after it's too late.

After a few hours, Vicky started coming out of it. We headed back to Mallory's but Vicky said she wanted to go to her cousin's house, so she could get a morphine pill. I took her, asking her along the way if she was alright. She said she thought so but she couldn't remember what had happened to her. COOL! We told her that Crystal found her passed out in Mallory's bathroom with a needle in her arm. That was a good enough story to keep us from being blamed, in case something happened to the baby later.

Chapter 53

I was out with a couple smurfs (smurfs are people who buy pseudo pills for meth cooks) when Mitch called my cell phone. He wanted to know if I was interested in doing a cook at his house that night. He said he had several boxes of pills I could get off of him to cook. I decided, I might as well go ahead and check the place out. I told him I would be by later that night.

When I pulled into Mitch's house, the first thing I noticed was that there was only one way in, or out, of where his house was located. There was only one other house on the road he lived on, and it was where you turn onto the road. That meant, there would be absolutely no random traffic. This was really good, for security reasons, as well as privacy.

Just as promised, there was a huge, red barn that sat about one hundred feet down the driveway from the house. The house was a tiny, one bedroom farm house with a small work shop/storage building beside it. Interstate 26 ran about 50 feet behind the house. That was kind of a down-side to the whole setup but, I could live with it.

I decided that the work shop would be the best place to do the cook. It didn't have power but it was close enough to the house to run extension cords to. Leaving Angelina, who had came with me, with Mary, Mitch's girlfriend, in the house, we set my lab up and got a lamp and fan set up as well. I told Mitch, he could stay in the building with me while I did the cook. That was more me still not trusting him than anything else. I wanted him where I could keep an eye on him.

Mitch was kind of irritating. He was always asking questions and getting in the way. I got to the point that I wanted him to just die or something. I asked him if he had a burn pile someplace. He said he did and I told him to go start a fire. I said the fire was to cover the ammonia smell, which was true, but mostly I just wanted him to get away from me before I went crazy. He spent the rest of the time I was cooking, burning the cook trash.

Once the cook was finished, we went back in the house. I found Angelina playing with one of three pit bull puppies Mitch was selling. I ended up buying the pup for $200, and giving it to Angelina as a Christmas present. We named it "Tweak".

I started cooking at Mitch's house quite often after that first night. By quite often, I mean I was cooking there at least four days a week. His place became my regular cook spot. It was also becoming my favorite place to hang out. Since very few people I knew, knew where Mitch lived, I didn't have to worry about people showing up to bother me. I did start to meet several of Mitch and Mary's friends there. It wasn't long before they were buying dope from me, or trading pills to me for dope.

The thing that I like most about new pill buyers is, they think they really know what they are doing. What I mean is, federal law states, a person can purchase nine grams of pseudoephedrine in a thirty day period. But, no more than 3.6 grams can be purchased in a 24 hour period.

Most new, even a lot of experienced, buyers incorrectly believe that the law means they can buy nine grams at the start of a new calendar month. Few even know about the law limiting their daily purchase amounts. I would get these new buyers to make a pill run like on the 30th of the month. I would send them out to buy me three boxes of pseudo; this is roughly seven to eight grams of pseudo. Then, a day or two later, it's a new calendar month so I would send them out again and they would believe they were within the law.

I got several people that I met at Mitch's to buy pills for me but, most of them bought pills for Mitch. He would just turn around and let me have them in exchange for finished product, so I ended up with them in the end anyway.

I took Mallory to Mitch's house once. We had been partying pretty heavily for a few days when Mallory noticed that her cell phone was missing. For about an hour, I had everyone looking for the phone. She always kept her phone on vibrate so it wasn't doing any good to call it but I tried anyway. I was hoping I would hear it buzzing somewhere. Finally, someone found it. Somehow, it had ended up in the toilet. It was sitting there in the bowl, vibrating as I called it. I don't know how it was still working.

During the time I was cooking at Mitch's house, I was doing a lot of running around. Mitch lived in Gray, Tenn. and I had to keep driving, from there, to Johnson City to sell dope. I also had to drive to Johnson

City and Elizabethton to buy cook supplies. I had a pretty good business starting up in Kingsport also. That meant I had to make a few trips over there every week to my buddy Chad's house.

Chad would let me cook whenever I wanted to. I would do a cook every now and then, if I needed dope right away to make a sale. Sometimes I would do a cook if I didn't want to drive all the way back to Mitch's just to do it. I didn't really like cooking at Chad's because his house was so close to his neighbors. John, however, was cooking regularly at Chad's. We would run into each other there from time to time.

One day, while I was watching John do a cook, he mentioned to me that he had seen his friend, Angel. Angel was also Chad's ex-girlfriend. I had been hearing a lot about Angel but I had yet to meet her myself. From what I understood, she was 18 years old, extremely wild, and half crazy. Best of all, I was told she was very sexy and loved meth cooks; my kind of girl. All the girls I knew who knew her always talked shit about her; that only made me believe that she had to be totally awesome.

I was at Mallory's asleep one morning when something woke me up. I looked around and saw a really pretty girl, sitting on the floor beside the bed, fixing her hair.

She said, "Hi."

I asked her, "Who the fuck are you?"

Well, it turned out to be Angel and the name fit her perfectly, she was an Angel.

I was happy to finally meet the girl I had heard so much about. We talked for a few seconds and I started wondering if she liked meth cooks enough to climb on in the bed with me. Before I got the chance to find out, I heard voices coming from the front yard. I asked Angel who else was there. She told me that John and Queeny were out in the yard with Mallory and Jessie.

I jumped out of bed and put my clothes on then ran outside. My tank of ammonia was in the back of my Bronco and I was not trusting John and Queeny out there around it. I carried it into the kitchen then covered it with a blanket. I normally kept it in the kitchen anyway.

While I was in the kitchen, Jessie came in and we got to talking. She was seeing Shawn at the time and I think she was complaining to me about him that day. I heard Johns truck leave, and when Mallory came inside, I asked her if Angel had left also. I didn't see her walk through the living room, which I had a clear view of, but apparently, she got by without me seeing her because Mallory said she was gone.

I was kind of disappointed that I didn't get to talk to her more before she left. She seemed really sweet and I wanted to try to hook up with her. Jessie knew me pretty well and she told me that Angel would be heading over to Marks house. I got in my truck and went to Marks myself.

I spent the entire day there, just hanging out and talking to Angel. Mark, I found out, was hooking up with her himself, so I had to be careful not to be too obvious about what I was saying to her. Even though I was a cook, I still didn't want to piss off another cook. It wasn't good business.

Around 2am that next morning, Chad and Shawn showed up at Marks. We were all hanging out in the garage when they got there. Shawn said they had been out four-wheeling and Chad's truck got stuck. They wanted to know if we would go help them get it out of the hole it was in. Why not we figured; what else did we have to do in the middle of the night?

Mark, Chad, and Angel all left in Marks truck. Shawn and I took my Bronco. The Bronco had been fixed since hitting the deer. The area we were going to was a pretty tricky place to get into. To make things worse, it had been raining, and there was a lot of mud where we would be going up the mountain. I decided it would probably be a good idea to let Shawn drive since he had gone into the area hundreds of time. Well, by the time he finally got us in there, my truck needed two new fenders and a door. I think he hit every tree in the woods.

We found Chad's truck in a hole that was approximately three feet deep, and full of water. We tried pulling the truck out, but it would not move. The front end was locked up and the wheels wouldn't turn so, after much trying, we gave up and went back to Marks. He would have to think of some other way to get his truck.

The night wasn't a total waste. I had sold my little .22 auto I used to carry around, to Leanna several days earlier. I was looking to replace it with something else and, while we were messing around with Chad's truck, I ended up buying Marks Colt 1911 .45 caliber pistol. I had been wanting one for quite a while so, when he offered to sell it to me, I jumped on it.

I finally made it back to Mallory's house. Luckily, I saw my tank sitting in the kitchen when I walked in the door. I had been worrying about leaving it there while I was gone so long. John, Kid, and Billy Jean were there when I got there, too. Billy Jean was asleep on the couch. Kid asked me if I wanted to sell any dope, which I did. We went into another room and I sold him an 8 ball.

It was almost day light out and I was pretty tired. I told everyone that they could hang out, if they wanted to, but Mallory and I were going to bed. After spending so much time around Angel, I was ready to screw something and Mallory was it. I woke up at about noon, to someone knocking on the bedroom door. Mallory got up to see who it was and Davy walked in with Winter. Always happy to see them, I got up and loaded up a foil. It was time to get high.

Jessie, Crystal, and John were there also, they came into the room to get high with us. Crystal had just gotten home from somewhere and had the urge to go someplace else. She suggested we all go to North Carolina to buy pseudo pills. We all agreed that she had a good idea, so we started planning how we were going to make the run. Suddenly, I had a really bad feeling about something.

I asked John where Kid and Billy Jean were. He said they had left right around sun up. I told Davy to go into the kitchen to see if my tank of ammonia was still there. He walked into the kitchen, then yelled back that the tank was there. That didn't do much for me to shake the feeling I was having. I told him to take the blanket off of the tank and bring it to me. He was quiet, then he appeared in the doorway, without the tank. Davy had a funny look on his face. When I looked at him, he just shook his head.

The tank was gone and I was pissed. I jumped out of bed and ran into the kitchen just to be sure Davy wasn't fucking with me. He wasn't. Someone had taken the tank, then they set a bag of garbage on the floor and covered it with the blanket, to make it appear that the tank was still there. Looking back, it was a pretty slick way to steal it, so I can't be too mad about it now.

I don't know for sure, but I'm going to assume for a moment that it's no fun to find one's self looking down the barrel of a loaded .45. Especially, if that .45 is being held by a really pissed off meth cook. The situation would be made even worse, I also assume, if that meth cook thinks you had something to do with $5000 worth of anhydrous ammonia being stolen from him. Well, that's the position Mallory suddenly found herself in.

I ran to the bedroom, grabbed my gun, and stuck it right between Mallory's eyes. Davy came to the room, saw what was going on and froze. John wasn't saying shit, and the girls were starting to cry, like girls do. Mallory, to her credit, was being very, very calm. She didn't move, and she was speaking very slowly and clearly as she tried convincing me that she had nothing to do with the tank being stolen. I didn't believe her.

Finally, John spoke up. He told me that Kid had gotten him to go into one of the other bedrooms to smoke some dope. Kid told him he didn't want Billy Jean to know he had bought the 8-ball, for whatever reason. John suggested that, maybe Kid was keeping him busy in the other room, while Billy Jean stole the tank. That, I decided, was a good possibility. I put my gun up and Mallory changed her underwear.

Chapter 54

While we were gone to North Carolina pill shopping, I called Mark to let him know I was going to need a new tank of ammonia. He said he would get it for me, but I would have to wait. He wasn't going to be home until sometime the next day. Since I didn't want to have to dig up my other tank, just to do one cook, I decided to make some home-made gas.

I took all of the pills we had bought that day and went to Angelina's. Everything I needed to make my home-made anhydrous was stored at her house. All I needed was some dry ice. I gave Angelina some cash, then sent her to the store to get me twenty pounds of ice. I stayed at the house to make a gas generator I would need to make the ammonia.

When Angelina got back, she handed me my cash back. She said she put the ice on her food stamp card. *That* is why I loved that girl. Anyone else would have just pocketed the money, but not her. She looked out for *me*. If it wasn't for me having that whole Lisa thing going on, I would have probably married Angelina. She was that awesome.

I put everything I would need into the Bronco. In the interest of saving time, I had Angelina drive me to Mitch's house while I sat in the back and started making the gas. I know the cops would have loved to have pulled us over with that shit going on in the back but we made it to our destination safely.

Mitch and I went out to the work shop to get the cook going. Not long after we started, we heard a vehicle coming down the driveway. Mitch said he wasn't expecting any company so, I told him to go see who it was and get rid of them. He left, and when he came back he said it was someone looking for me.

I walked out to the truck that was sitting in the driveway and saw that it was Kid. I got in the passenger side and the first thing I wanted to know was, where was my fucking tank of ammonia? He said that he didn't know but he was fairly sure Billy Jean had stolen it. According to Kid, Billy Jean was in a big hurry to get rid of him after they left Mallory's that morning. The more I thought about it, the more I was sure it had to be

Billy Jean who stole it. Kid didn't know how to cook but Billy Jean did. I let Kid off the hook, for the time being.

While we talked, Kid said he knew where we could get our hands on a big tank of ammonia, but we had to go get it right away. This was the whole reason for his coming to find me at Mitch's. I started asking him a few questions about the tank. It didn't take long for me to figure out where the thing was, and why we had to hurry if we were going to steal it. I told him to forget about it if he was thinking about stealing Marks tank while he wasn't home.

He really wanted to go get the tank and kept trying to talk me into it. Finally, I told him that I already own that tank. It was the one I was splitting with Mark and Will. Kid was quiet a few seconds, then he asked, "I just fucked up, didn't I?" I told him that everything was cool, as long as he didn't fuck with my tank.

After Kid left, I went back in to finish the cook. Neither of us ever mentioned it again. Something I didn't think about at the time, but bothered me later was, I don't know how he found me at Mitch's house that night. They didn't know each other, as far as I know. Maybe Mark really wasn't out of town and he sent Kid over to see if I would double cross him by stealing the tank from him. That sounds paranoid, I know, but Mark would do some shit like that.

As Angelina and I were getting ready to leave Mitch's, John pulled in. He had Angel with him. We talked for a few minutes then I told them to follow us to the house; Angelina's house. When we got there, John asked me if I knew of anywhere he could get some iodine. Apparently, all the local shops were out. Since it wasn't being produced anymore, they wouldn't be restocking. I made a couple calls and found him one pint. His cooking days were about to come to an end.

The next day, I took yet another propane tank to Mark's for him to fill for me. I just dropped the tank off with instructions for him to call me when it was filled. I took a small tank he had with me in case I decided to cook again before he got my tank ready. It began to snow that afternoon, so I went to Mitch's house to relax and take the day off. Something I rarely did.

Around 10 p.m. that night, I got a call from a very pissed off Mark. He said that Queeny had dropped off a small tank so that he could buy a gallon of ammonia. Occasionally, we would sell a little gas for $500 a gallon. Queeny was attempting to learn how to cook so, he needed gas. We were the only people he knew who had any for sale.

According to Mark, he told Queeny to come back in a few hours; his tank would be ready then. Sometime later on, Mark left, to go to the store, leaving the garage unlocked. When he returned, he discovered that, not only did Queeny take his tank, he also took my tank, as well as a tank Mark had just filled for himself. Mark wanted to kill Queeny, literally. I had to find him before Mark did.

I began calling everyone I could think of that might have some idea of where Queeny was at. Several hours of searching had turned up nothing. Finally, I got a call from someone saying that Queeny was at Mallory's house. That definitely was not a good place for him to be because I knew Mark would eventually go there.

I got to Mallory's just as Mark was getting out of his truck, gun in hand. He stormed through the front door with me right behind him. He asked Mallory where Queeny was. She said he was in the bathroom. Mark walked to the bathroom door, pointed the gun, kicked the door open, then fired six shots. Queeny was screaming, Mallory was screaming, and I was thinking to myself, "damn, now we are going to have to kill Mallory too, and I don't even know yet if she's really pregnant."

For a couple seconds, there was complete silence. Then, I heard Queeny say, "You made me piss all over myself." Mark busted up laughing at him. He had use blanks, just to scare the shit out of everyone. It certainly scared the piss out of Queeny. That is not the only time Mark has used that little prank. There was one night when he started to pull it on Mallory and it almost ended really badly. Looking back now, I have to wonder if it really was an accident.

Marks wife, Teri, was a lot like Lisa, in some ways. Mostly, she liked to disappear for days, even weeks at a time, to go screw around. In all fairness I should say that this was not always her fault. Many times, Mark would just kick her out, so he could move a little dope whore in for a while. Sometimes, he would try to keep the dope whore, even after Teri moved back home. That never worked out and it was exactly the reason Teri hated Mallory. He had tried that shit with them.

One evening, I had stopped by Marks, while Mallory and I were out. I had been in the house for a couple hours, completely forgetting that Mallory was outside in the truck, freezing her little ass off. Finally, she couldn't take the cold anymore so she blew the horn to remind me she was there. Mark asked who was in the truck and I told him. Teri jumped up to run outside to beat her ass. Mark grabbed her and got her to calm down. Teri hates Lisa just as much, but then, so do most of the women who know her.

So, Teri calms down and says she won't beat Mallory up, but she wants to scare the shit out of her. Teri tells Mark to give her the blank gun. The blank gun isn't actually a blank gun. It's a western style, .22 caliber revolver with a six inch barrel. Mark had two of them. One he kept blanks in, the other he kept real bullets in. You never know which is which.

Teri wanted to walk out to the truck, point the gun at Mallory's head, and start firing away. Without a doubt, Mallory would have shit her pants. Mark said he had an even better idea. He wanted me to run out the door, screaming bloody murder. He would run out behind me, shooting at me. I would pretend he killed me. It sounded like a great idea to me, and Mallory would have fallen for it because, people had been waiting for something to happen between Mark and me for a while.

Although Mark and I had never argued, or had any kind of problem for that matter, there had always been a tension between us. I can't really explain way. Shawn used to say, it was because I refused to basically bow to Marks will, like everyone else did. I, in Marks mind, had as much control over what he considered to be, *his* people, as he did. Shawn said that this made Mark uneasy around me.

Anyway, that was our plan. Given everybody's expectations of an impending conflict between us, it would have worked beautifully. I say, "Would have", because Teri wanted to be the one who terrorized Mallory. She grabbed the gun out of Marks hand, discharging it accidently as she did. Everyone in the room stared in silence at the little, round hole in the floor beside Marks foot. The hole left by what was supposed to be a blank. Mark freaked out that he had grabbed the wrong gun for the prank. Or, did he?

I have always wondered if that really was an accident. If we had gone through with what we had planned, I would have been shot for real. It was a perfect way to get rid of the competition, and since I was in on it, no one would ever suspect it was anything but what it would have appeared to be, an accident. That is how things went in my world. When you are awake for days and days at a time, you start thinking of ways to take out people you feel threatened by.

Back to Queeny. It turns out that he didn't actually steal the tanks. What had happened was, when Queeny got to Marks house, Mark wasn't there. Queeny see's the tanks sitting out, for anyone to come along and take, so he decides to hide them. Once they were hidden, and not knowing Mark will be back any minute, he left. We asked him where he hid them and he said the tanks were in the back of one of Marks trucks. The very truck Mark decided to use to hunt Queeny down. We went outside and sure enough, there they were. It's a damn good thing Mark didn't get pulled over that night.

Chapter 55

A day or two after getting the new tank of ammonia from Mark, I ended up hooking up with Angel. She was a fireball. Mean, tiny, and couldn't sit still, or shut up, for five minutes to save her life. Nothing scared this girl, and in truth, she did shit that scared the hell out of me sometimes.

I had her driving me up and down I-81 one evening, around 8 p.m. I was doing a small cook in the back of my Bronco. I wasn't really paying attention to where we were going, but I felt the truck slow down as she exited the interstate. Assuming she was just exiting so she could turn around and go the other way, I kept concentrating on what I was doing.

Angel drove for about half a mile, then she pulled the truck to the side of the road and stopped. This got my attention so I looked around to see what was going on. That's when I noticed we had just stopped in front of the state trooper's office. I flipped out on her, asking her, not too nicely, what the fuck she thought she was doing.

I believe my exact words were, "what the fuck are you doing? That's the goddamn state trooper's office."

She just looked at me and said, "I know, let's fuck."

Now, I've done a few stupid things in my life, but I was not about to fuck, on the side of the road, with a cook going on in the back of the truck. Especially, not in front of a fucking cop shop. No way in hell! Angel pretty much had her mind make up about this, and I hated to tell her no. I finally said I would let her give me a blow job, a very quick blow job. I just wanted to get the hell out of there.

Luckily, and I never thought I would call this lucky, my dick wouldn't cooperate, no matter how hard she tried. After a minute or so, she abandoned the idea and we got back on the road. That incident proved to me that Angel was a little too addicted to danger. But, I liked her even more for it. Unfortunately, I also learned that my pecker wouldn't work in dangerous situations. Well, not when cops are involved, anyway.

Hooking up with Angel was really good for me, in a way. The one thing it did, for sure, was make me want to step back from "the life" for a while. I wanted to spend more time with her than I spent running around, chasing money and pseudo pills. I also lost interest in the other girls, for the most part. There were a couple I had to keep sleeping with for awhile, but that was business.

I took Angel with me to Mitch's house, one night in mid-January, 2008. I had planned on staying there for a few days with her, while I did several large cooks, then we were talking about going out of town for a week or two. We didn't plan a destination, we just wanted to get away and spend some time together, without all the normal bullshit that seemed to follow us around.

The first night we were there, I did two, simultaneous cooks. One cook was with pills collected by Mitch and myself. The second cook was for Mary, Mitch's girlfriend. She had gotten her hands on a bunch of pills and asked me to cook them without Mitch knowing about it. I did as she asked, and Mitch never found out she had more dope than he did. It wasn't my business why she wanted me to do her cook; I just took my cut and forgot about it.

After I finished cooking, I left my lab set up in the shed. There was no sense in packing it all up when I was going to keep cooking out there. We partied until sometime the next afternoon, when I told Mitch that Angel and I were going to use his bedroom for a few hours. We screwed then slept until that night.

When I woke up, it was to my cell phone ringing. It was one of my regular customers, Ricky, who live only a few miles from where we were. I answered and Ricky told me that he was in need of some dope, right away, if I could bring it to him. I said I would be right over, then I woke Angel up and told her to get dressed.

When I walked into the living room, Mary and her friends, Larry and Linda, were there. I asked Mary where Mitch was and she said he was in the shed, with John, doing a cook. I ran out to the shed, to make sure they weren't trying to do a cold cook; especially with *my* gas. They weren't. John had gotten his hands on another pint of iodine and was doing a Red P cook. Probably his very last, he said, because there was absolutely no more iodine to be found in our area.

I told Mitch, I had to leave to take care of something at Rick's. I told him that I was leaving my tank in his shed, and for him to keep a close eye on it. He said it would be safe, so Angel and I headed over to Ricky's house. It was only a five or ten minute drive to Ricky's, and we had only been there a couple minutes, when my phone rang. It was Mary, so I hit the "ignore" button. I had no interest in talking to her.

My phone kept ringing and kept ringing, so finally, I answered it to tell Mary to stop calling. I didn't have time for her shit. As soon as I answered, Mary started babbling on about crazy shit.

"The house is on fire. John is on fire. The dogs are dead," - all kinds of weird stuff.

I told her, she needed to lay it down and get some sleep, then I hung up on her.

When my phone rang again a minute later, it was Mitch.

"No shit, the house really is on fire and John really is burnt up pretty badly. We're on our way to where you're at", he said and then hung up.

I looked at Angel and said, "They blew the fucking house up."

Now that right there is a perfect example of someone claiming a lab blew up when nobody said a damn thing about anything blowing up. But, hold on, it gets better.

Linda, Larry, Mitch, Mary, and John got to Ricky's house a few minutes later. The second they got there, I asked them what the hell happened. Mitch said, a half gallon jar of ether busted, then ignited from the kerosene heater in the shed. The flames ignited two more jars of ether that was sitting there, as well as Johns clothing that were soaked in ether. They got out, and the flames, from roughly a gallon and a half of burning ether, were so hot, they were melting the siding on the house. It wasn't actually "on fire", as they had claimed at first.

I told Mitch, he needed to get his ass back home and get a water hose on that fire before the cops, and fire department, showed up. Which would happen very soon. I wasn't thinking the water would put the fire out, I was thinking Mitch could make up a good story when the cops got there. Maybe, say a gas jug caught fire from the heater or something like that.

Anything, to keep the cops from investigating, which is exactly what would happen if they got there and no one was home.

Also, and this was my biggest concern, my tank of anhydrous would be found. When I mentioned this to Mitch, he went to the car and pulled the tank out of the back seat. He had run back into the burning building and retrieved it before the fire got too bad. He did get burned getting it but, the important thing then was, he got it.

Before Mitch could go back home, we heard sirens heading towards his place. Too late. I told Angel to get John into the Bronco, then I told everyone else to go to Angela's house and wait for me to get there. I got into the truck with Angel and John and we headed to Johnson City. I stopped along the way at a Walgreens to buy up a bunch of burn medications and bandages for John. I knew that the cops would soon have the pharmacies on the lookout for people buying this shit so, I had to get it while I could.

Once I got to Angelina's, and explained what happened to her, I had her call her friend, Ken. Ken was a, sometimes, customer of mine, through Angelina. He also worked for a Haz Mat company that did meth lab clean ups. I told Ken what happened and asked him to keep me informed as to what the cops found. John had dropped his wallet at the house, while rolling around to get the fire out. I told Ken, if he got the call to do the clean up, to find the wallet and return it to me. He said he would, but he never got the clean up call.

Larry and Linda went home. Since Angelina didn't really want the trouble of John being there, I took him and Angel to Chad's house. Mitch and Mary followed us there and Chad had no problem with us staying there for a while, even though he didn't know Mary and only knew Mitch through me and John. It was well known that Chad still had feelings for Angel, but luckily, he didn't have a problem seeing her with me. In fact, he even told her she was doing good to be with me, instead of some of the other dumbasses she usually gets with.

I had some pain pills (my Leanna supply) and I gave them to John. He was severally burned on his arms and chest. The fire had burned the shirt completely off his body. Hell, it even burned the shoe strings right out of his shoes. He was in bad shape, to say the least.

I knew mine and Angels little getaway wasn't going to happen now. Not anytime soon, anyway. We were going to have to babysit John until he got better, like it or not. He was like a brother to Angel, and Angel never turned her back on a friend. *Ever!* I mentioned that I needed to sell some dope but I didn't want to go back to Johnson City. John, since his cooking days were over now, offered to hook me up with his people in Falls Branch, Tennessee where he has a decent customer base established. He figured his friends would need a new hook up, and I was going to be it.

Chapter 56

I didn't know it then but, the fire at Mitch's house that night was the beginning of the end for me. It was a sign. From who, I don't know, but over the next eleven days or so, I would have many more signs telling me to stop what I was doing. I don't know how I didn't see them.

We went to Fall Branch around 2 a.m. that same night. Once we were there, we went to see a dude that John said could move a lot of dope for me. Over a three or four hour period, the dude sold about $1000 worth of product for me. That was not bad at all, for being in a really rural area, in the middle of the night. Especially considering, we never left the dudes basement.

We left right before day break to go back to Johnson City. Just a few miles from where we were, the Bronco began to overheat. I always kept a gallon of water in the truck, just in case, so I pulled into somebody's driveway to pour the water into the radiator. Unfortunately, the water was frozen so I placed the jug next to the engine block, hoping the heat would thaw it out.

After we sat there for maybe twenty minutes, Angel said she was freezing. She decided she was going to see if she could get some water from whoever lived in the house. I didn't want her beating on someone's door this early in the morning, but she didn't really care what I wanted. She wanted to get warm. After she knocked, a little old man answered. He was fully dressed, so I don't think we woke him. He probably got up when we first pulled into his drive. He gave Angel water, then he invited us all in to get warmed up. We thanked him, but declined his kind offer. We just needed water and then, we were gone.

Now that the truck was cooled off, we continued towards Johnson City. Unfortunately, it wasn't long before the engine began to overheat, yet again. I kept driving until the engine got hot enough to just die. Luckily, we were approaching a convenience store and I was able to coast in, and up to a gas pump. I suggested we all go in and eat, and warm up, while the truck cooled. They were cold and hungry so that's what we did.

Angel and John walked around the store for a few minutes, while I bought anti freeze and paid for some gas I would pump after we ate. We all went to the restaurant side of the store, placed our orders, then sat down to eat. Knowing that the Bronco needed time to cool off, we took our time.

Maybe fifteen minutes into our meal, John pulled the hood from his coat over his head. He started sliding down low in his chair saying, "Oh shit... oh shit... oh shit..." I looked out the window to see two police cars pulling in the parking lot. I told John to sit up and stop acting suspicious about something before he drew attention to us. At first, I figured the cops were there for coffee and donuts. After all, it was shift change for the sheriff's department. It didn't take long to find out, that wasn't the case. They were there for *us*.

There was one male, and one female officer. I continued to eat, as I watched them approach our table. I also saw a third officer pull into the parking lot, then enter the store. The female cop walked up to Angel, while the male cop stepped behind me. The female did the whole, good-morning-how-ya-doing routine as the third cop stepped in behind John. This definitely was not looking good and I was beginning to wonder if the old man had called the cops on us for some reason.

The female started questioning Angel about a hairbrush. Apparently, the store clerk thought she had stolen one, and he called the cops. Angel snapped off on the cop, she was mad that she was being accused of stealing. I don't blame her a bit. The female cop asked Angel to open her purse, but Angel told her to go fuck herself, she wasn't doing it. I thought, "Just open the fucking thing so these people will leave."

I tried telling the cop that Angel doesn't have to steal because she knows I will buy her anything she wants. It didn't matter, the cop wanted to see in that purse. Finally, the cop told her, if she didn't open the purse, we would all be arrested and she would see in the purse anyway. With absolute perfect timing, John and I both said, "OPEN IT!" Angel grabbed the purse and dumped it in the middle of the table. There was no brush.

The cop then asked Angel to walk over to the store area with her, to see if the supposedly stolen brush was still there. It was. As the cop stepped away with Angel, she turned and told the other cops to pat us down. I thought, "We're fucked". I knew John had an entire bag of syringes on him. Myself, I had at least an ounce of dope in my pocket, as well as a couple syringes. I don't mind telling you, I was scared.

I had my tank of ammonia in the back of my truck. My gun was in the door pocket. If we were arrested, they would find all of that shit, and we would go down for a long time. The cop behind me said something about letting him give me a quick check, "to make her happy", he said. I guess she out ranked him, and he saw that this was just a bullshit call to begin with.

Acting as offended as I possibly could, I stood up. As I did, I reached into my pocket and pulled out all the money I had made that night, and slammed it on the table. "Does it look like I need to steal?" I asked. The cop looked at the money and asked where I got it. I told him, I had been working at Exide for eight years so I had better have some money. Everyone in our area knows Exide is a very good-paying company.

The cop asked if knew a certain person, and by chance, I did. I began talking about the person like we were best friends. The cop ended up telling me to go ahead, sit down, and finish eating. John was standing across the table from me. He and the other cop were listening to our conversation. I could really see in John's eyes that he was calculating his chances of making it out the door, if he made a run for it. I'm glad he did not try, but for a second, I thought he really was going to.

The second the other cop grabbed a hold of John, to search him, John yelled out. The cop kind of jumped back, then asked John if he was alright. John answered by pulling his coat sleeve up, exposing his bandages. The cops seemed very concerned when they saw them. They asked what had happened to him and John said he was burned while working on the carburetor of my Bronco. He said he had gasoline on him, and when the truck backfired through the carborator, it set him on fire.

That story was the lamest bullshit I had ever heard, but they believe it. I was just hoping no one looked outside and noticed the "electronic fuel injection" sticker on the fender. They didn't, thankfully. The female walked back over with Angel and bid us a good day. We decided to get the hell out of there, quickly.

We walked out as the cops did, trying to make it seem like everything was cool. I put the gas that I had already paid for in the truck, as I waited for the last cop to leave. He was obviously waiting on us to leave first so, we did. I turned down the road one of the other cops had gone down, figuring we wouldn't seem suspicious if we were following another cop.

The road we were on was a very long, straight road. There were a lot of little hills so, every time you went up a hill, you could see a long ways ahead of, and behind, you. It was at the top of one of these hills that I noticed the first cop car. It was about a mile ahead of us, traveling slowly. The one that waited for us to leave, I also noticed, was coming up fast from behind. I told John and Angel that we were about to get boxed in, and pulled over.

John, knowing that area better than I, told me to take a left onto a road we were approaching, so I did. There was an old barn ahead of us, John told me to pull in behind it until the cop passed the road we had turned on to. Once the car passed, we continued on this back road until it brought us out at the store again. The Bronco was beginning to overheat again, but I wasn't about to stop at that store again.

I continued on towards Johnson City, traveling down state highway 81. I wasn't stopping for shit, unless the truck blew up, which I seriously hoped wouldn't happen. I was beginning to get extremely wigged out. By the time we got to Jonesborough, the engine was knocking loudly, due to it being so hot. One place you do not want to have car trouble is in downtown Jonesborough, Tennessee. The cops there live to harass people.

Wouldn't you know it, the Bronco engine finally quit on us right in front of the Jonesborough courthouse, at 8 a.m. I jumped out of the truck and pushed it out of the road, and into the courthouse parking lot. I was convince now that a cop was about to pull in behind us, and take us all to jail at any second. Any other time, that is exactly what would have happened. This, it seemed, was our lucky day. I just didn't know it yet.

While we sat there, waiting for the truck to cool off, I had the radio on. The top story on the news was the fire at Mitch's house, the night before. The news reporter said that police had notified local hospitals, and pharmacies, to be on the lookout for people with burns. I always wondered if the cops got that message right after we left that store, and that was why they were going to try to stop us.

I did have to laugh at one part of the news story. The reporter (and this is why people don't know as much as they think they do) said, "Witnesses to the explosion reported seeing several vehicles leaving the scene immediately after the blast." Okay, there was no "explosion", there was no "blast", there was a *fire*. That's all, just a fire.

I would be willing to bet, that if you asked around, in Gray, Tennessee, you would find maybe a thousand people, who would claim to have been driving down that tiny stretch of interstate, at the exact moment that shed burned down. Every one of them would claim to have seen the place got up like the fourth of July, but guess what, it never happened that way. It was simply a fire. That's all.

We sat in the courthouse parking lot, just long enough for the engine to cool enough so that it would start. Once it did, I drove it over to the Auto Zone, a couple of blocks away. When I parked, I got out of the truck and walked away from it. I was completely convinced the cops were watching it from somewhere and I didn't want to be in it. I sat on a bench, in front of a grocery store and Angel walked over, and sat with me. I told her that I just could not drive anymore. She understood and called her friend, Jimmy, to come get us, and take us to Marks.

When Jimmy got there, I had him pull in behind my truck. Once Angel and John were in, I grabbed the tank of ammonia and my gun, then I dove into the bed of Jimmy's truck with them. When we got to Mark's house, I ran into the garage. That's where I stayed, basically hiding from my own imagination, for the next several hours. John and Angel fell asleep in Jimmy's truck and Jimmy hung out with me, in the garage. Sometime later that day, Shawn showed up and I sent him to fix my truck, then bring it to me. I gave him $20 for a new thermostat, knowing that's what the thing needed to stop the overheating. I never did get the change back from that twenty.

That evening, John, Angel, and I went back to Chad's house. I was still really wigged out so Angel and I locked ourselves in a bedroom, then went to sleep. We should have never left that room. Things around us were about to get bad.

Wayne Huffman

Chapter 57

When Angel and I woke up about twenty-four hours had passed. We got up and took our showers, then ate before we got high so we could function. When you have an addiction like I had, like everyone around me had, you no longer get high to enjoy the feeling; you get high to be able to function.

Chad wasn't home when we got up. He had to go to court in Virginia, or maybe it was N. Carolina, and he wouldn't be back until the next day. John was asleep on the couch, probably in great pain, so I didn't wake him. Mitch and Mary were there so they sat around getting high with Angel and me.

Sometime around midnight, Angel and I went to Chad's bedroom to fuck, We were having us a good ole time when, about 3am, Angels best friend, Brittney, called my phone. I answered, thinking Angel would want to talk to her. They spoke for a minute then Angel handed me the phone, saying Britt wanted to ask me something. I got on the phone, and Britt asked if I would drive Angel over to her mom's trailer, to see her. Britt's mom was out of town, but the boyfriend, Benny, was there. From the noise in the background, I could tell that several other people were there, as well.

I told her, I really didn't want to go anywhere that late but she insisted it was important. Angel was shaking her head, to let me know she didn't want to go. I was just about to give Britt a final "no", when I heard a familiar voice in the background. I asked Britt if Queeny was there, and she said he was. I talked to Queeny for a few minutes, asking him if he had any pseudo pills I could get off of him, for a cook I was planning on doing later in the morning. He said he did have some for me so, I told him we would be right over.

Before we left, I smoked a foil with Mitch and Mary. The whole time, Angel was whining that she just wanted us to forget about going, and go back to bed. She said she had a bad feeling about going over but, I didn't care. I needed those pills so we were going, whether she liked it or not.

We got to the trailer around 5 a.m. Besides Britt, Benny, and Queeny, Angels ex-boyfriend, Adam, was there. Adam was also a friend of mine so, he wasn't upset about Angel being with me. Not that I really cared how he felt about it. Angel asked me for some dope so I gave her a gram to smoke with Britt and Adam, while I talked to Queeny. Benny was in his own little world as he surfed the internet.

Queeny had a cook going in the kitchen, and was in the process of gassing off another one. He showed me a glass dish that had several piles, of what appeared to be dope in it. The products of several cooks he had done throughout the night, he told me. I sampled the different piles, at his request, and none were really any good.

I asked Queeny, who had been teaching him to cook? He said he was just doing what he had seen other cooks do. Not always a good idea because, he might have seen someone do something that he shouldn't do, and that could cause a fire. So, basically, he was teaching himself, which I could respect. The problem I was having was, pills were no longer as cheap, or easy to get, as they were when I taught myself to cook. He was wasting a lot of pseudo, and money, every time he attempted a cook. I hated to see that.

I told Queeny to pack his lab up; I was going to show him how to do this the right way. I told him, we would go to Chad's and I would teach him in exchange for a few grams of finished product. He was happy to hear this, so he started taking his lab apart to pack it up. He had a lot of stuff to pack, too. Way more than any cook would ever need.

Angel walked into the kitchen, as I helped Queeny pack up. She asked if I cared if she ran to the store with Britt and Adam. She said they would only be gone for 15 minutes. I said, I didn't care but if she wasn't back before I left, I would come get her later. She understood, and then they left.

After they were gone, Benny got off of the computer, then started walking around, peeking out the windows. He began telling Queeny to hurry up and get his shit packed up. He said he didn't want the stuff in the house, now that it was turning daylight outside. We got everything out to Queeny's Jeep, and was standing there talking when Benny came outside. He walked over to us and apologized for wigging out on us. Then, he invited us back inside to cook.

Now, I didn't know this Benny dude very well, but I could tell he wasn't acting right. I told Queeny that something was up with him and we needed to get the hell out of there. Whether dude was up to something or not wasn't important, I wasn't starting a cook around someone who was acting all wishy-washy about the shit. He could freak out and want us to leave in the middle of the cook, when it wouldn't be exactly possible to do that. No, fuck that shit, I was leaving.

I told Queeny to follow me, then I got in my truck to leave. Angel wasn't back yet, so she would just have to hang out till I got back to get her. I drove to the end of the road in the trailer park. When I looked in my rearview mirror, I saw that not only was Queeny not following me, he was actually walking back inside the trailer. I decided I wasn't going to waste my time with him. If he didn't want to learn how to cook, then he could keep wasting his time and money. It wasn't my problem.

Since I didn't get any pills from Queeny before I left, I had to go on my own to do some shopping. I hit a few stores and bought what I could. I ended up at a hardware store, where I spent a couple hours looking around. That is very common tweaker behavior.

By the time I made it back to Chad's house, it was around 10 a.m. When I pulled into the driveway I saw that, not only had Chad made it home already, but Shawn was there also. I made this discovery not only because their trucks were there, but because they were both running towards me as fast as they could run. I rolled the window down, but kept the engine running, just in case I had to get out of there in a hurry.

When they got to my truck, Chad said, he thought I was in jail. When I asked, why would I be in jail, he told me a disturbing story. Apparently, I had narrowly escaped disaster, by a matter of minutes. Chad said he had received a call from Britt's mom, Donna. Donna said a neighbor had called her to inform her that her trailer was being raided by the cops. The neighbor also claimed that Britt's own trailer, directly across from Donnas', was also being raided.

This is what happened, as told to me by those that were there. The reason Queeny had gone back into the trailer, was to get a CD he had burned off of the internet. When he came back out, and saw that I had left him behind, he decided to go ahead and do another cook there. Queeny was carrying his stuff back in when Angel got back. Adam helped him carry his stuff to the kitchen.

Queeny got his lab set up, then started his cook. Benny suddenly said he had to go out to his truck for something. He was gone for quite a while when Angel decided to go get him to give her a ride to Chad's, so I wouldn't forget her later. Not that I ever would have. Angel tells everyone that she's leaving, then walks outside. As she steps out the door, she see's cops all over the place. Acting as normal as she can, Angel turns, drops her purse inside the door, says, "cops", then locks the door before closing it. She then walks over to Benny, who is having a conversation with some of the cops.

The cops were in the process of raiding Britt's trailer. No one in Donnas' trailer knew anything had been going on because all the curtains were pulled shut while Queeny cooked. Britt's boyfriend had already been arrested when the cops went in with a search warrant, finding dope, guns, and a pipe bomb.

When Angel approached the cops, one of them asked her, what her name was and where she was going. She, for some dumb reason, gives a fake name. She also said that she and Benny were on their way to visit friends. When asked, who else was in the trailer, she said, "nobody". They didn't believe her. I guess Britt's car sitting there kind of gave it away that Britt was there.

They handcuffed Angel and Benny, then took the two of them to the cop shop to wait while they got a search warrant for Donna's trailer. Inside the trailer, Queeny was putting jars in the kitchen cabinets, and hiding what he could, where he could. Britt was running around, freaking out, and Adam grabs a Bible then sits in the middle of the floor, reading it. Queeny yelled at him, "don't get religion on me now, I need help." Adam admits that this actually happened. He, of course, never moved until the cops took the Bible from him, so they could arrest him.

They got them with a lab and 128 grams of finished product. Queeny tried to take the blame but, they wouldn't let him. Everyone went to jail that day. The whole thing started because, Britt had sold a half gram of meth to a snitch. The cops came to arrest her for it, but she wasn't home. If her car hadn't been parked in her mom's driveway, they never would have gone in to look for her. If Queeny would have just tossed her ass out the door, or window, no one else would have went to jail that day, most likely.

After Chad told me about Donna calling, I told him and Shawn to go drive by the trailer park, to see if there really was a bust. They did, then called me to let me know that there were still cops everywhere. They said you couldn't even get into the trailer park for all the cop cars. Chad said he wasn't coming back home for a few days and I figured it would be a good idea to get out of there too, since so many people knew I was there.

Mary called Linda to come get her, then I took Mitch to one of his friends houses, and dropped his ass off. I went back to Angelina's to stay for a while, bringing John with me. When I got there, I had someone drive John and me to Mitch's house. John's truck was still there, and I wanted to get it, before the cops did. We got dropped off up the road from the house, and walked down. Hoping the cops were not watching, we jumped in the truck and hauled ass. We made it back to Angelina's with no problem.

Chapter 58

We stayed at Angelina's house for a night, then I wanted to go to Mallory's. She was still claiming to be pregnant, but I was beginning to doubt her story because it kept changing. She would tell some people she was pregnant, then tell others she wasn't. I didn't know what to believe, and had too much other shit to think about to have to worry about it.

After I was at Mallory's for a few hours, I got a text from Angelina, asking me to come back over. Alone. I figured she wanted to fuck, so I left John and went to see her. We spent some time in bed, then while we were laying there, Angelina started asking, what was I going to do about Mallory? I said I wasn't sure yet, which was the truth, and I told her of my suspicions that maybe Mallory was faking the whole thing.

Here is something that didn't seem strange at the moment, but would come back to me later on as being weird. Angelina suggested that I go out of town for a few weeks, to figure things out. She said, I should take off, alone, and not let anyone know where I'm at. I said, I would think about it then we started talking about the bust at the trailer. She told me things were happening just like they did to her friends in Georgia. Apparently, there had been a huge bust there, where almost everyone she knew went to jail. I never thought it strange that she didn't go to jail, if all her friends did.

I ended up back at Mallory's. I was about to leave to sell some dope when Scott showed up. He said he just stopped by to warm up. He was out of kerosene at his house so, he had no heat. I decided to help him out. I handed him a gram of dope and told him to go sell it. He was to give me $50 and he could keep the other $50 for kerosene, gas, food, or whatever.

The next day, I woke up and looked outside to see that my Bronco had been moved. I went into the living room to ask John if he had used it. He said, Mallory used it to go to Wal-Mart. This was a huge no-no. Nobody borrowed my vehicle, ever. I walked outside to check on things, my tank of ammonia was fucking gone.

Mallory was asleep in Crystal's room. I went in to ask her what she did with my tank, and she swore she hadn't seen it. She said that, had she known the tank was in the truck, she never would have borrowed it. That was possibly true because, she didn't even really like to ride with me when she knew the tank was in there. I decided to not worry about it. Hell, I had enough gas to last me a couple of years, if need be. It was my own fault for leaving the tank out there, and there was no telling who got it. A lot of people came in and out of the house all the time, anyone could have seen it and taken it. Leave it alone and move on, I figured.

I sent John, who had his own truck back, and a couple Smurfs to buy pseudo while I went to see Scott. When I got to Scott's, he was just getting in his car to leave. I walked up to him and told him I had come for the $50. He kind of fidgeted around a little, then he handed me $20. I asked if he was having trouble selling the gram, and he said he had sold it. $20 was just all he had for me.

Now, I try to be nice to people. I try to help people. I'm a fucking people-person, and while I don't normally give people cash to help them, I will give them dope like I did with Scott. That gives the person the chance to sell the dope to pay their bill, buy food, put gas in their car, or whatever their problem is at the time, it gives them the opportunity to help themselves.

Of course, the person can chose to do the dope to get high. In those cases, the person better not come ask me for more help, because I won't help them again. People, especially drug addicts, need to know what their priorities are. When Scott gave me $20 that meant he was stealing $30 from me to get high. Not the smartest thing for him to do. I told him, I would be back for my money, then I left.

On my way back to Mallory's house, I got a call from John. His trucks transmission had gone out and he was stuck at Wal-Mart. I picked John, and the Smurfs up, dropped the Smurfs off at their house, then John and I went to Davy's house to pick up a tank of ammonia I had stashed there. Once I had the tank, we went to Angelina's. That night, I decided to do a cook at her house. It was late, and her mom wasn't going to be home, having gone to Asheville, NC for the night. To me, it was too good a chance to pass up. Sometime during the cook, Mark called. He wanted me to come over to his house. I told him, I was in the middle of a cook, but he told me to bring it with me and finish it at his house. Sure, why not?

I told Angelina what I was going to do, and she asked to go with me. John wanted to stay there and sleep, so I said she could go. I was packing up a few jars and things I would need, while Angelina took some of her stuff out to the Bronco. The tank of ammonia I had was a small oxygen tank with a ball valve installed in it. I had it fit into a plastic box that once held a set of tire chains for a truck. That way, it could be carried without anyone seeing what was in the box.

I had the cook going in a one-gallon, plastic paint bucket so I put the lid on it for transportation. Angelina came back in for some more stuff (she never travels lightly) while I headed out to the truck with the cook and the lab. I walked through the carport, then stepped around the corner of the house, and found myself standing almost face to face with two cops.

I couldn't do anything. I had a duffle bag full of jars over one shoulder, the cook going in my hand, and a tank of anhydrous ammonia in my other hand. I was screwed. They noticed me almost immediately. I quickly turned to my right, where the garbage can was. Opening the top, I gently placed the cook inside as the cops approached me. One of them was even kind enough to shine his flashlight, so that I could see to put my "trash" into the can. Thank you, Johnson City Police.

Once I closed the lid on the garbage can, I stepped towards the cops. One of them asked me if the Bronco was mine. I said that it was. The cop then explained that they had been driving by when they saw the passenger door open. Thinking someone had broken into the vehicle, they stopped to check it out. I told him, my girl had just put some bags in there for a trip we were about to take. She must have left it open.

Angelina came cruising around the corner about that time. She almost screamed when she saw the cops standing there. I quickly began to bitch at her about leaving the car door open, so that she would know what was going on. She caught on quickly. After the cops left, we cancelled our little trip to Marks, and I finished the cook at the house. Yet another near miss I paid no attention to.

Chapter 59

Mitch called me one evening looking for some dope. I figured I could hook him up with a little and told him I would call when I got to Kingsport, so we could meet. He then told me he wanted a couple of ounces. A couple of ounces? This idiot didn't have a dime to his name so, where was he going to get almost $3,000 for a couple ounces of dope? The police, maybe? I decided against meeting up with him. He called and called but I didn't answer. Homey isn't stupid.

Carson called me the same night to ask if I wanted to do a cook at his place. He has a real nice piece of land on the side of a small, mountainous area. The place was mostly wooded and his mom's house sat at the bottom of the hill. I liked the place, and had actually done a cook in a camper Carson had there, so I said I would do it.

Angelina and John came with me as I met Carson at the cook spot. I did the cook but didn't gas off the dope while I was there. I didn't need the dope right then so, I decided to just leave it in the camp fuel until I did need it. I could just gas it off at that time. During the cook, I was still bitching about Scott pulling that bullshit with the $30. This seemed to piss Carson off, because Scott had stolen some car tires from him not long before this. He said he was sick of Scott's shit and he was going to make Scott sorry he ever stole from anyone.

The next night, Chad and Jessie came by Angelina's to see if I wanted to go to a party in Bulls Gap. I didn't, but they said there was going to be a lot of people there looking to buy dope. I finally decided to go and took John with us. Around 3 a.m. Angelina called to tell me she had just gotten a call saying Scott's house was on fire. John and I hauled ass back to town, and sure enough, Scott's trailer was burnt to the ground. So was his car, which was sitting next to the trailer. Scott himself was at his mom's house in North Carolina for a few days.

I knew I was going to be blamed for the fire, and I was, even though I was out of town. With witnesses! Now I don't know whether or not Carson was the one who burned the house down, but I do know I wasn't in town when it happened, and that's all that matters; to me anyway.

John and I went over to Carson's house a day or two later. Carson had called me, asking me to come over because he had something for me. When we pulled into the drive, he came outside carrying two duffle bags, which he handed to me when he got into the truck. I opened the bags to find them full of beakers, glass funnels, cold water condensers, and an assortment of other cool lab glassware. This is shit I had been wanting for a long time.

Carson worked at Milligan College in Johnson City as a cafeteria worker. At lunch time, he had began going to the science building, while everyone was gone to eat, and started stealing this stuff for me. I loved this stuff! We got to talking about doing a cook and he said he wanted to buy some pseudo for me. We made plans to hook up later that day then John and I left.

We went back to Angelina's house to pick her and one of her friends up. They were going pill shopping for me too. While we were out, Angel called. She was out of jail, had pills for me, wanted some dope, and needed fucked. We made plans for me to pick her up after I finished the cook. Our out of town trip was back on, Carson and Kim would be coming with us. I'm still not sure how I got talked into that.

I took Angelina home after we dumped off her friend. She asked me to come inside for a few minutes before John and I left to get Carson. As soon as I walked in, Angelina asked me to put off doing the cook. "Great", I thought, "now she's going to start with this jealous shit." I told her I was going to cook. End of discussion.

Angelina's mother is a very special lady. She is a former concert pianist, she now teaches piano, and she was born deaf. She is also very religious and says that God talks to her. When her mom tells you, God told her something will happen, you better believe it *will* happen - every single time.

As I was walking out the door, Angelina told me, her mother said I should not go to the places I normally go to. If I do, I'll go to jail. That was fine with me; I wasn't going anywhere I normally go to. I told her not to worry, gave her a kiss, then left. John and I picked Carson up and took him pill shopping.

Once we were done shopping, we stopped at Burger King for something to eat. While we ate, I got a text from Mallory, ask me where I was at?

She said she needed to see me right away, it was very important. To me, that's Mallory talk for, "I need some dope." Not wanting to fool with her, I texted back, saying I was busy and couldn't get away at the moment. She texted right back, "I've got your tank here. Come get it."

I asked by text, (I don't like talking on the phone), who was at her house? She said she was alone, so I told her to get dressed; I was on my way to pick her up. I figured I would pick the tank up and also take Mallory with me so I could screw her while the cook was going. It would be awhile before I'd get the chance to fuck her again so I decided to take advantage of the opportunity while I could.

I got to Mallory's and Billy Jean's Denali was parked in the driveway. I knew he was the motherfucker who stole my tank, now I had proof, since I had just caught him here with it. I was pissed at him anyway because, the same night my second tank was stolen, someone stole my 1911, and I had been hearing that he had been going around trying to sell one. Dirty bastard!!

I slammed the truck in park and was getting out to beat the hell out of him when John and Carson grabbed me to keep me from getting out. They knew, and convinced me that, it would be a bad idea to start shit with a lab in the truck so, I got back in and we left without the tank or Mallory. Immediately, I got a text from Mallory saying, Billy Jean was only there to give my tank back and apologize. I didn't really give a fuck what he wanted to do.

We stopped at a store to get gas and something to drink. While I was putting the gas in the truck, Billy Jean pulled up next to me. He started saying he was sorry for stealing my tank and all that bullshit. I told him that I really didn't have anything to say to him at the moment. Before he left again, he asked if I was going back to Mallory's. I said I was.

Carson and John didn't want me to go back to Mallory's. But, I didn't want Mallory to "lose" my tank again before morning so I overruled them and headed to her house. Just as I was about to pull into Mallory's driveway, I had a strange feeling that something wasn't right. I drove past her house, turning up a side street, where I turned around then stopped at the stop sign. I sat there, looking towards her house, trying to figure out what had me spooked.

I told John and Carson how I was feeling. They wanted me to get out of there and I was inclined to agree with them for once. As I was about to pull out from the stop sign, Vicky came running out of the house that sat on that particular corner. She lived there with her grandmother. She waved for me to stop so, I did. Vicky came up to my window and said she needed to speak to Carson about his girlfriend, Kim. Kim was also Vicky's aunt. He got out of the truck and they stood in the street, a few feet away talking. Suddenly, three vehicles came around the corner at a high rate of speed. They were coming straight at us.

When Vicky saw them, she took off running towards her house. A couple dudes jumped out of the cars and grabbed her, then wrestling her to the ground in her yard. My mental state was not all that great at the moment, as I tried to figure out what was going on and which way I should go. Before I figured out anything, someone was standing next to my truck, with a gun to my head.

At that moment, all I could think about was that scene from the movie "Good Fellas", where Henry Hill says something like, "If it was a hit, I wouldn't have heard a thing." Nothing was making much sense to me. There were people running around with guns, Vicky was screaming and crying, and John was in the back seat cussing.

"Turn the vehicle off," ordered the guy attached to the gun pointed at my head.

I did as I was told then I was ordered to get out of the truck. I did that too. When I got out, I still didn't know what was going on. Everything was happening way too fast for my mind to keep up. I asked the dude, who had ordered me out of the truck, who the fuck he was? "Johnson City Investigators", he said. We were so screwed!

Chapter 60

I guess I should have listened to Angelina that night. Or, maybe I should have listened to John and Carson. Or, my own gut, when I felt something wasn't right. But, I didn't.

The cops claimed they were there to arrest Vicky that night. She did have warrants out for her arrest. The cops had been trying to find her for several months. All of this I knew to be true. What I never understood was, why didn't the bitch go to jail that night, if they really were there for her?

The DTF and the DEA were called in, when the cops found the lab in the back of the Bronco and the glassware Carson had given me earlier. As they searched my truck my cell phone kept going off, so one of the DTF agents took the phone. He looked through the text messages that were coming in, from Mallory, who was standing in her doorway watching what was going on. Mallory was well known to them. After they found the text about her having my tank, and the new ones saying she was hiding the tank in her closet, they paid her a little visit. They found the tank but, oddly enough, she wasn't arrested that night either.

Since Carson wasn't in the truck when the cops pulled up, he wasn't arrested. John and I, however, were arrested for multiple meth related charges. This was January 30, 2008, the day before my 39th birthday. All of those charges would eventually be dismissed because Vicky wasn't in my vehicle. The arrest affidavit stated, the cops pulled me over in order to serve Vicky's arrest warrant on her, so, since she wasn't in the truck, the cops had no right to harass me, detain me, or search my vehicle.

While in jail on these charges, I was finally charged with violation of probation. I got, basically, time served on the smaller charges I accumulated since my return from Alabama, but I had to serve the 3 years of my probation time from the older charges.

In May, 2008, I was indicted, along with 48 other people, by the federal government. There were a multitude of charges, with different people getting different charges but everyone was charged with conspiracy to manufacture and/or distribute meth. I was personally charged with conspiracy to manufacture 500 grams, or more, of meth, and conspiracy to distribute 500 grams, or more, of meth.

The feds began arresting everyone on July 01, 2008, but it would be over 6 months before they had everyone in custody. Queeny, Adam, and Angel were all arrested at Angelina's house. We found out later, Angelina was working with the feds. She admitted this to me in a letter I received from her, while I was in jail. Lisa was arrested in January 2009, while on The Hill. There were approximately 13 people arrested that night.

One of the people arrested on The Hill, the night Lisa was arrested, was Shawn. What nobody knew was, Shawn had been picked up several months earlier by the feds. They kept him locked up for a few days then turned him loose. He was working for them then, but nobody on the street was aware of it. By the time everything was said and done, everyone got federal prison time, except for Shawn and Angelina.

Something that really pissed me off about the whole thing was how everyone turned on everyone else. There were very few people who stuck together. If you asked someone, who told on who? That person would give you a list of snitches. The problem was, the person would have nothing to base their claim on.

I don't know who told what on who, but, I do know this; Everyone, except the people who were arrested in the bust with Angel and Queeny (who were all charged with 128 grams of meth), was charged with "conspiracy to manufacture 500 grams, or more, of meth". Some were charged with other things as well, but everyone was at least charged with the manufacture conspiracy.

A 500g conspiracy carries a *mandatory* minimum sentence of 10 years. That means, you have to get a 10 year sentence, *no matter what*! There is no, "the judge liked me", "I had a good attorney", or "I got lucky". NO! Not in the federal system. It simply does not work like that. Anyone who got less than 10 years on our case had to have cooperated with the feds.

It doesn't really matter now, who did what. I don't care. I got 15 years out of it, and I was charged as one of four leaders of the "loosely organized criminal enterprise". Will, Mark, and another dude were the other 3 "leaders". Lisa got 8-1/2 years, John got 6-1/2. Mallory got 63 months, Crystal got 72 months, same as Scott. Mitch got 7 years, Kid got

10 years. Mark, who was the only other person to get as much time as me, got 15 years, and Will got 10 years. The fourth "leader" got 7 years.

Angel got out in 2010. Carson got out in November 2011. Sam got out in April of 2012. Queeny got 10 years also, same as Davy. Billy Jean got 168 months; he is currently serving his time in Beaumont, Texas. I'm not sure how much time the rest of my co-conspirators got. Not everyone got busted. The twins didn't, thankfully. And several other people I knew never got indicted.

I found out later, from Kid, that it definitely was Billy Jean who stole, not only my tank of gas, but my 1911 as well. I knew it, but it was nice to find out for sure. Kid also told me that it was Billy Jean who set me up the night I got busted. I always felt like it was a setup. He had Mallory get me to come over for the tank, so the cops could use the story about being there to arrest Vicky to bust me. She was in on it as well.

The whole reason Billy Jean set me up, according to Kid, was because he wanted to hook up with Mallory and was trying to get me out of the way. Hell, I would have given the bitch to him, if he would have asked. I also heard he was mad because I had pulled my gun on her. Oh well.

Angel and I communicated regularly while she was locked up, then stopped when she got out. I hope she is off having babies and staying clean. Lisa writes me every now and then. She said Tina was in a bad motorcycle accident and can't walk now, due to her knee being destroyed. That isn't the only bad news Lisa has gotten since being locked up. Her father died, her sister Katy died, and FJ, and FJ's youngest daughter were both killed in a car accident.

Joy is doing great, working and attending high school. Levi was taken by his father and still lives with him today. I'm told the family rarely gets to see him anymore.

The life of a meth cook definitely is not what I would have expected it to be. I know sometimes it seems that I was always broke, or near being broke, but I really made a lot of money. I just happened to spend a lot more. Money didn't really mean much to me like you would think it would. I cooked meth because I loved cooking meth.

I lost a lot too. Everything I had actually, and that happened more than once. I lost my marriage, friendships, and the respect of some people who were important to me. My son hates me, but that has a lot to do with his mother poisoning his mind. One thing I don't do is sit around whining about all the bad things that happened to me while I was on dope. I'm not a "survivor", or any of that other, "I survived the nightmare of addiction", N.A. crap people use to feel sorry for themselves. It was anything but a nightmare.

I still have all of my teeth, so that's a good thing. The reason I have them is because I had enough sense to brush my teeth after smoking meth. Seriously people, smoking meth is not automatically going to give you "meth mouth". Brush the residue off after smoking and you won't have a problem. If you eat chocolate a lot and never brush your teeth, guess what? Your teeth will start to rot eventually. It's the same thing.

Meth didn't kill me, and I'm also not going to start claiming, "Going to jail saved my life", either, because people don't die from meth. Really, look it up on the internet. Even in the drug education classes I have taken, meth isn't ever mentioned in the list of drugs that will kill you. Sure, you can get ridiculous and start saying, "use enough of it and you will die", but you can use enough aspirin to kill you too.

I don't look 20 years older than I actually am. Everyone has seen the propaganda pictures where the person did meth from a couple years, now they look really old. The government is even doing commercials on TV against cigarettes with the same stuff. Well, that shit rarely happens either. If you pay attention, you will see that you are being shown pictures of maybe 10 people, that's about it. There are more photo's out there of people who got permanently screwed up off of bad make-up than there are of people messed up, permanently, from meth.

Do I regret that I ever got involved with meth? I got 15 fucking years in prison, what the hell do you think? Okay, maybe that's not exactly the truth. If you ask most incarcerated meth cooks, and they are honest with you, I think they will answer that question similar like this.

I regret that I hurt some of the people I did, mostly my son, Damian. I regret losing my home, cars, my long time job at Exide. I definitely regret this incarceration. On the other hand, if it would not have been for my involvement with meth, I might never have went back to Alabama and reconnected with my family there.

My nephew, Timothy, who lived with me in Alabama was a long-time drug user when I moved down there. After my arrest on these federal drug charges, he stopped doing drugs, got his GED, and joined the Army. I don't care what anyone else thinks, to me that alone was worth coming to jail, and everything else that happened. Timmy also married and they had a little girl so he got to be a father. Unfortunately, Timothy died in January, 2012 from a drug overdose. Sadly, he couldn't stay clean.

I don't associate with my sister, at all. She, in case you didn't notice, was never named in this book. I wouldn't give her the privilege of using her name. After Timothy, her own son, died, she was mad that she wasn't getting his Army life insurance. She called the military and tried to convince them he had committed suicide, just so Timothy's wife couldn't get the money. It didn't work but that was still some sorry ass shit.

Any former meth user, who is being honest with you, will tell you that they had a lot of fun on meth. How can you regret having fun? I didn't like the way my marriage to Elvira turned out, that doesn't mean I regret ever being married to her. We had a lot of good times. I just regret how it ended. I feel the same way about meth. I had some fucked up things happen to me while dealing and using that drug, but I had a lot of fun as well. I guess, the only thing I can honestly say I regret about my life in the meth world is the consequences. The pleasure was worth the pain, but not the price.

About the Author

Wayne Huffman has lived every level of meth addiction, from casual user to one of four 'alleged' leaders of a methamphetamine manufacturing and distribution organization that included over 250 known members and spanned several states.

Wayne began his career as a meth cook in east Tennessee where he has made his home for the last 23 years.